Twayne's Themes in Right-Wing Politics and Ideology Series
Roger Eatwell, General Editor

The Nature of the Right

The Nature of the Right
American and European Politics and Political Thought since 1789

Edited by
Roger Eatwell and Noël O'Sullivan

Twayne Publishers · Boston
A Division of G.K. Hall & Co.

First published 1989 in Great Britain by
Pinter Publishers Ltd.
25 Floral Street, Covent Garden, London.

Published 1990 in the United States and Canada by
Twayne Publishers, a division of G.K. Hall & Co.,
70 Lincoln Street, Boston, Massachusetts.

Twayne's Themes in Right-Wing Politics and Ideology Series, no.1

10 9 8 7 6 5 4 3 2 1

ISBN 0-8057-9550-2
ISBN 0-8057-9551-0 (pbk.)

Library of Congress Cataloging-in Publication Data

The Nature of the right : American and European politics and political thought since 1789/edited
    by Roger Eatwell and Noël O'Sullivan.
        p. cm. — (Twayne's themes in right-wing politics and ideology series : no. 1)
        ISBN 0–8057–9550–2. — ISBN 0–8057–9551–0 (pbk.)
        1. Conservatism — United States — History. 2. Conservatism — Europe — History. 3.
United States — Politics and government. 4. Europe — Politics and government. 5.
Comparative government. 6. Right and left (Political science) I. Eatwell, Roger. II. O'Sullivan,
Noël. III. Series.
JA84.USN28   1990
320.5'2'0973 — dc20   89–27363
                                                                                        CIP

Contents

Abbreviations

BBC	British Broadcasting Corporation
EC	European Community
GRECE	Groupement de Recherche et d'Etudes pour la Civilisation Européenne
IMF	International Monetary Fund
MP	Member of Parliament
NATO	North Atlantic Treaty Organisation
NPD	Nationaldemokratische Partei Deutschlands
NSDAP	Nationalsozialistische Deutsche Arbeierpartei
PAC	Political Action Committee
SPD	Sozialdemokratische Partei Deutschlands
SS	Schutzstaffeln
TUC	Trades Union Congress

Preface

This book began with a suggestion from Roger Eatwell to Noël O'Sullivan that they should cooperate to produce a book that would map out the nature of the right. The idea seemed simple enough, but subsequent discussions illustrated why there is a complete lack of works which approach this topic in a systematic way. Problems centre around the fact that the concept of 'the right' is extremely elusive, a point which would be hard to infer from the uncritical use of the term by many commentators. In particular, Marxists have tended to see 'the right' simply as a short-hand for defences of capitalism and private property; and social scientists, heavily influenced by the 'end of ideology' debate and the behavioural approach, have tended to downplay the ideological side of the nature of the right. These problems have been compounded by the fractionalization of academic knowledge: the tendency towards ever-greater specialism. If the right is to be given a meaning outside a narrow national–time context, it must be approached on a broad front. Part I of this book, therefore tries to break free from traditional academic categories, such as political theory, or sociology. And Part II involves the work of five experts, whose collective focus transcends time and national barriers.

Part I of this book is in effect a long introduction, discussing the various problems which have emerged in terms of approaching the concept of 'the right'. As such, we felt it unnecessary to include a separate Introduction, especially as such chapters often do little more than repeat what comes later. The overall structure of the book is clear, and sub-headings have been used to help quickly elucidate the drift of each chapter. The chapters in Part II were written to a general outline devised at the outset by the editors. Each contributor was approached because of his expertise in a field which we felt helped to illustrate an important style of right-wing thought. Contributors were then left to interpret the topic in their own way; no attempt was made to 'fit' the contributors' views exactly to those of the editors. Indeed, over some issues there are significant differences of emphasis, even interpretation, between the editors and contributors. However, one of the points which this book seeks to underline is that the nature of the right has many facets, and is a topic which attracts very different interpretations — not least among self-styled members of the right!

We hope that readers will find that Part I offers a clear rationale for our approach. The informed reader-in-a-hurry could skip the contemporary scene-setting Chapter 1 without losing the drift of the argument, though this chapter seeks to include some material which should interest even the specialist. Part II offers a more substantial discussion of some of the central questions raised by right-wing philosophies. These latter chapters largely follow chronologically, but it is not vital to read them in this order. Each stands as a self-contained essay on an aspect of the right.

Both editors benefited greatly from their discussions whilst devising this structure, though inevitably differences of interpretation and focus remained. To the extent that there is an individual responsibility for the final product, Noël O'Sullivan stressed the need to appreciate the many varieties of right-wing thought, whereas Roger Eatwell argued for an approach which was not simply a collection of political theory essays grouped loosely around a theme.

We were pleased to have attracted so well-qualified a set of contributors to help us fulfil our task, and would like to thank them for responding, in the main, to suggestions for alterations in their chapters. We have also been helped by colleagues, and others who have discussed ideas, or looked at all or parts of the draft. In particular, we should like to thank (in alphabetical order) George Eatwell, Judith Eatwell, Paul Gottfried, Jolyon Howorth, Elizabeth Meehan and Brian Neve. Finally, but by no means least, we should like to thank Dr Iain Stevenson, the Editorial Director of Pinter Publishers, for his encouragement and patience while waiting for the manuscript.

R. E. and N. O'S. July 1989

PART I
Approaching the Right

1 Right or Rights?
The Rise of the 'New Right'

Roger Eatwell, University of Bath

During the twentieth century the language of 'left' and 'right' has become central to political debate. The terminology is more common in some countries than others, and in the United States the terms 'liberalism' and 'conservatism' have often been used as synonyms. However, as Donald Stokes, a leading American political scientist, has noted:

> The use of spatial ideas...is a universal phenomenon of modern politics. Such ideas are the common coin of political journalists and have extraordinary influence in the thought of political activists. Especially widespread is the conception of a liberal-conservative dimension on which parties maneuver for the support of a public that is itself distributed from left to right. [Stokes, 1963, p.368]

During the 1980s the terms have become, if anything, even more commonplace. The nature of the 'new right', and the failure of the left, especially Marxism, have been major sources of discussion (e.g. Girvin, 1988; Green, 1987; Hoover and Plant, 1989; King, 1987). In the picturesque words of *Newsweek* on 2 January 1989, 'The symbol of our times is a statue of Karl Marx lying shattered in the marketplace'.

Predictably, there are countless books on aspects of right-wing politics in individual countries. Other works have sought to examine facets of the right that have transcended national boundaries. However, there has been a notable scarcity of works which have tried to produce a more comprehensive analysis of the problems involved in defining the nature of the right. This seems a particularly surprising omission in view of the importance of the right-wing tradition in liberal democracies during the two hundred years since the French Revolution, an event marking a key point in the development of the modern right. A key reason for this gap are the problems posed by attempting to produce a coherent map of what constitutes right-wing thought. As Eugen Weber notes in the introduction to a major book on the history of the European right, 'The more we have inspected the image of the Right, the less sure we have become of what it is' (Rogger and Weber, 1965, p.5). In particular, it seems difficult to find a common linking strand in what is normally considered right-wing thought. Indeed, significant differences, even contradictions, appear to exist! Moreover, members of the right can at times display as much energy when engaged in internecine strife, as when combating the left. For example, the bitter splits in contemporary American conservatism could be characterized by adapting an old Democrat adage: what is the difference between a conservative and a cannibal?; answer, cannibals only devour their enemies! (On these splits see Gottfried and Fleming, 1988).

These difficulties in conceptualizing the right emerge clearly by considering the electoral and, especially, the ideological renaissance of the right which has occurred since the 1960s — developments which underline the importance of understanding the nature of the right.

The Crisis on the Left

'A spectre is haunting Europe — the spectre of Communism.' With these words Karl Marx and Friedrich Engels began *The Communist Manifesto,* first published in 1848. During the 1980s, in both Europe and the United States the spectre seems less a haunting fear, more a fading ghost. In electoral, and especially in ideological terms, the right has been in the ascendant.

The first major Marxist party to emerge in the nineteenth century was the German SPD. By 1959 it had dropped all claims to being radical; from 1966 until the early 1980s it was never out of office, but in the 1980s it lost two general elections in a row. During the 1960s John F. Kennedy and Lyndon Johnson won the Presidency fighting on liberal programmes; yet in the 1980s Ronald Reagan and George Bush were to launch telling attacks on the left-wing views of their Democratic opponents; 'Do we want this country to go that far left?', was Bush's barb to Dukakis in their first televised debate.

In 1960s Britain, leading political scientists wrote of the Labour party becoming the natural governing party; since 1974 Labour has lost three general elections in a row. Among the major democracies, only France has seen the left gain notable electoral success in the 1980s, and here much of the answer lies in the left's movement away from radical concerns. In 1988 '*Mitterrandolâtrie*' rather than *Jacquerie* swept the country. A similar pattern of consensual (even right-wing), and personal themes has been a major factor in other left election victories in the 1980s, notably in Spain and Sweden.

The success and failure of these parties can in some ways be explained by relative economic performance, which has become an increasingly important determinant of voting. However, left-wing parties also seem caught in a sociological crisis. For almost a century Marxists have debated why a revolutionary mass working class has failed to emerge. Many still adhere to the Micawberish principle that something, usually an economic crisis, will turn up. Unfortunately for Marxist historicism, economic downturns have benefited the right as much as the left. As a result, some have sought to develop a more sophisticated view. Their conclusions often have similarities with those of many moderate socialists, who have sought to understand the failure of what the leading British Fabian theorist, Sidney Webb, once called 'the inevitability of gradualness'.

One major conclusion holds that the left has been undermined by what sociologists, with their characteristic love of ugly jargon, call 'embourgeoisification'. 'The New Dealers have been replaced by the car dealers' was the intellectual Democrats' self-flattering joke in 1950s America. Thirty years on many blue-collar former Democrats owned two cars, and voted Republican. Some Marxists talk of the key change from 'Fordist' to 'Post-Fordist' forms of production. This analysis holds that the basis of Western economic activity has moved away from alienating large-scale factory production. In its place has emerged a flexible, service-based economy, where class lines are more complex. In October 1988 the British Communist Party's theoretical journal, *Marxism Today*, even came to the sensational (for Marxists) conclusion that class could no longer provide the basis for effective political action.

Many on the left hold that overt, or more usually covert, racism has further helped right-wing parties. For example, Jesse Jackson has claimed that when some Americans talk of the threat from the left, they really mean blacks. Certainly a fear of black political activism seems to have helped Bush in the 1988 Presidential election. The victory of David Duke, a former Ku-Klux-Klan leader, in the 1989 Louisiana legislature election served as a dramatic confirmation that racist credentials were far from a handicap in some areas.

These arguments have often been reinforced by the claim that the mass media have been key factors in helping the right. If class has declined as a determinant of political allegiance, clearly the ways in which issues, and especially personalities, are portrayed is crucial. In the United States many right-wingers believe that a liberal establishment dominates the media (remember Vietnam!). In reality most of the media is owned by an increasingly small number of companies, and Reagan enjoyed remarkably favourable coverage. The same pattern is true of much of Europe. Media magnates have therefore become central to left-wing demonology. This 'hegemonic' media argument has been especially popular on the left because it implies that the problem is one of perception rather than reality, a conclusion which has helped divert attention from the more fundamental crisis in left-wing ideology.

Ideological problems on the left are hardly unique to the 1980s. In the immediate post-1945 era, revelations concerning the horrors of Stalinism proved particularly traumatic for the radical left throughout the West. Among the more moderate left, Stalinism reinforced arguments for the mixed market as an aspect of a system of checks and balances. Stalinism further reinforced the hand of those on the moderate left who had been influenced by the New Deal in the United States, or the post-war full employment, welfare state in Britain (and earlier in Sweden). These were seen as offering the practical proof of what John Maynard Keynes had argued in his *General Theory of Employment, Interest and Money,* first published in 1936. Namely, a stable and prosperous economy could be secured through macro and micro government economic policy. The ensuing economic growth could provide the tax revenue to fund an expansion of the welfare state.

These, and other, arguments proved highly controversial within the left, but they led to a flowering of left-wing thought more than self-doubt. Out of the ashes of Western gramophone-communism emerged a 1960s 'new left'. In some ways its themes, such as ecology and gender, exerted an important corrective to the increasing economic-technocracy of much moderate left-wing thought. However, new left thought was often based on a romantic opposition to developments in industrial society rather than a clear vision of an alternative. New left issues also tended to appeal to small sections of the educated middle class, rather than a mass audience. Yet, they involved dangers for established left-wing parties, especially as the new concerns often spawned single-issue groups outside the party system. Within the moderate left there was less intellectual ferment, and even signs of the beginning of self-doubt, especially in Europe. However, ideological debates involved incrementalism more than a total change of focus. In particular, the major discussions centred on the exact degree and nature of state intervention, rather than on what was to replace the state

By the late 1980s many on the left had come to accept that they faced an ideological crisis. For example, the British Labour Party's journal *New Socialist* in May–June 1988 was devoted to 'Learning to Live with Markets' (a development opposed by Labour's radical left). The British socialist intellectual, R. H. Tawney, once noted that Labour programmes would nationalize several industries in one sentence, and abolish fox-hunting in the next. He was pointing to the fact that Labour programmes involved vague policies (what exactly is public ownership?) and priorities (a gradualist party needs to have a view of the order in which industries should be nationalized, or which welfare policies should have priority). In spite of this vagueness, before the 1980s the general direction was clear: that the extension of the state would help most citizens, a form of paternalism captured by the 1940s catchphrase 'the man from the Ministry knows best'. By the 1980s socialists were less clear about the role of the state, and there had been a revival of views which focus on smaller units.

In the United States, Democrats have debated whether it is possible to win a Presidential election on a liberal platform. Can the divided Democrats even agree on a programme which does not either reflect, or try to hide, its 'rainbow coalition'? The 1988 campaign document was one of the shortest and vaguest platforms for years. Would it have been better for Dukakis to have stressed his liberal credentials from the outset, rather than just at the end of a campaign he was clearly losing? This has been linked to debates inside the Democrats about the decline of the old Democratic coalition which had been forged in the 1930s, and the demographic shift which further weakens the New Deal base. In West Germany, too, there has been considerable debate within the SPD about its future. Does the party need to adopt more green issues? Can it promise further expansion in welfare given the increasing problems of funding the present system, notably the ever-rising health budget and the cost of an ageing population?

The New Right's Key Ideas

To some extent these debates on the left are pragmatic responses to the electoral successes of right-wing parties. More fundamentally, they reflect the failure of left-wing policies, especially in the economic sphere. Even the Soviet Union and China seem to have moved in a 'capitalist' direction under Mikhail Gorbachev and Deng Xiaoping. However, it is important to stress that an aspect of the crisis on the left stems from a powerful revival of right-wing intellectual thought. This can be seen most clearly in the proliferation of 'think-tanks' during the 1970s and 1980s (though the oldest pre-date this period). Among the best known in the United States are the American Enterprise Institute (though this has also published work by non-right-wingers), the Heritage Foundation and the Hoover Institute. In Britain the leading groups include the Adam Smith Institute, the Centre for Policy Studies, and the Institute of Economic Affairs. Such organizations mark a notable change of focus from earlier business lobby groups, such as Aims of Industry in Britain. The business groups tended to have a narrow conception of their interests, for example campaigning against nationalization or regulation, or lobbying for and against specific laws. The new groups are part of an attempt to destroy socialism intellectually.

Many commentators on this new right have argued that it encompasses two main strands: individualist – *laissez-faire*, and authoritarian–traditionalist. A fourfold division would produce more fruitful insights. (Whether some aspects are truly new, or equally right-wing is another matter.)

Firstly, there is a small, but intellectually assertive, *libertarian* strand, which believes in the minimal state. Secondly, there is a *laissez-faire* strand, which is more concerned with reversing the 'ratchet effect', whereby in the post-war world the state continued to grow, regardless of the political complexion of the government. This group accepts some form of state activity within the economic and social realms. A positive role for the state is also accepted by the third strand: namely, the *traditionalist* wing. This strand is worried by the individualist aspects of the previous strands. It especially seeks to stress the continued importance of institutions such as religion and the family. Fourthly, there is what might be termed the *mythical* wing, which is more specifically concerned with securing support for the right, especially through ideas such as the nation and race, or eulogizing the 'will of the people'.

There is no rigid division between these categories. Some views, especially anti-communism, tend to cut across groups; and the more moderate members of the second and third tend to share the important concept of 'balance' between authority and freedom. Nor is it argued that all new-righters can be neatly fitted into four groups. For example, the American 'neo-conservatives' are mainly converts from the left, such as Daniel Bell and Irving Kristol (e.g., Bell, 1976; Kristol, 1978). They have some similarities with the moderate *laissez-faire* wing of the new right, but are more sympathetic to welfare provision activity. They also tend to focus on an alleged loss of authority, which is usually a concern of the traditionalists. There also tends to be a continuum of opinion within each category. Thus there are differences of opinion even within the relatively small group of American neo-conservative intellectuals. Moreover, it is possible to point to other types of contemporary right-winger, for example what could be termed the American 'Genghiscon': the critically-unthinking, super-patriotic, anti-communist.

However, it is possible to proliferate typologies until almost every small group or tendency becomes a movement. This makes succinct analysis effectively impossible. It is also important to stress that the focus of this chapter (and the book as a whole) is ideas rather than personality. As such, the book can also largely ignore the question of right-wing government outputs, and the claim that these often tend to remain pragmatic, even ideologically inconsistent. The argument here is that the intellectual new right, especially in terms of domestic policy, can usefully be grouped around the four strands: libertarian; *laissez-faire;* traditionalist; and mythical.

Arguably the most influential academic libertarian attack on the growth of state power has come from the American Robert Nozick, especially in a critique of his colleague John Rawls (Nozick, 1974). Rawls asked his readers to imagine that they were in a state of nature, and able to choose what sort of society they lived in — but not their position within this society. Thus someone who chose present-day America would have to accept the risk of being 'reborn' black, a member of a Hispanic gang, or a welfare-claiming white. Rawls uses this argument to claim that reasonable people should choose a system which limited extremes of wealth. Nozick counters that such arguments are typical of the end-state concerns, usually focusing on equality, which characterize left-wing thought. For Nozick, such philosophies justify coercion in seeking to achieve the end of greater equality. In the unlikely event that a high degree of equality could be achieved in a modern society, further state interference with individual freedom would be necessary to maintain this distribution; in Nozick's words, the socialist society would have to forbid capitalist acts between consenting adults. Nozick therefore claims that the central concern should be process rather than end states — namely, whether a particular income/wealth distribution has been acquired without coercion. If it has, there is no moral basis for redistributing property against the owner's wishes. The state's role therefore encompasses little more than setting the rules.

Nozick's individualism is central to the libertarian and *laissez-faire* new right. Thus the British academic Stephen Davies has argued that six broad themes are central to the new right, of which: 'The most fundamental is individualism' (Davies, 1985, p.21). This view sees the individual as the primary unit of society, and rejects all claims made by collectivist ideologies (of both right and left) which stress groups, such as class or the nation. As such it is highly anti-statist, and holds that freedom can only be legitimately restricted where it can be shown to involve direct harm to others.

This has been accompanied by a major philosophical attack on the language of welfare 'rights': the right to social security, the right to work and so on. Indeed, some claim that the moral basis of the new right 'is the idea of natural rights' (Graham and Clarke, 1986, p.77). These arguments come in various forms, but often centre around the concepts of negative liberty (freedom from legal restraint) and positive liberty (what individuals can actually do). Civil or political rights (free speech, universal suffrage, and so on) can be met without excessive state cost, and are necessary in a civilized society. On the other hand, social, or entitlement, rights (such as a 'decent' standard of benefit for the unemployed) are potentially open ended, and could therefore undermine the economic viability of a state. Some extreme libertarians have used these arguments to reinforce their belief in the minimal state.

However, for others the attack on the concept of social/entitlement rights is linked more to a concept of duty: those genuinely in need should be provided for, but they must do something in return. This concept of rights related to duty is central to much of the thought of the traditionalist right. A real-world example of this is the 'workfare' system in parts of the United States, where those claiming benefit are expected to perform work. Others, often in the *laissez-faire* new right, are not averse to helping the weak, but want the task provided by private companies rather than state bureaucracies. The American journal *The Public Interest*, founded by Irving Kristol and Daniel Bell in the 1960s, has been a particularly notable source of such attacks on the Big Government welfare state, and its underlying philosophy. Nevertheless, many of its members do not share the view, common to much of the American right, that the 1980s budget deficits require massive cuts in state welfare expenditure. Indeed, two leading members have even argued that the solution to what is seen as a problem rather than a crisis involves substantial tax increases (White and Wildavsky, 1989).

Another influential attack on the growth of the state has come from *laissez-faire* economists. Friedrich Hayek's book *The Road to Serfdom* (1944) was published largely unnoticed, as were many of his works until the 1970s (see especially Hayek, 1960; Hayek, 1973-9; and Hayek, 1988). Today his thought is central to an understanding of the philosophy of the right. For example, David Stockman, one of Reagan's Budget Directors, spoke of wielding the sword 'forged in the free market smithy of F. A. Hayek'. Hayek's work involves a notable attack on middle-way economics and politics, reviving the idea that the centre was a confused fudge rather than an honourable compromise. His critique of planning has been especially influential. For Hayek, the market was not based on the old naïve assumptions of perfect competition. Nor were market outcomes necessarily seen in terms of the old Protestant work ethic: a reward for virtue. Rather the market was viewed as a discovery mechanism, complete with uncertainty and shocks. Hayek argued that it was ludicrous to think that any form of planning could efficiently encompass the literally millions of decisions which take place every day about price, colour, etc. Any attempt to do so would not only produce economic inefficiency; it would also bring Big Brother — the bureaucratic, authoritarian state. However, it is important to stress that Hayek's views are not libertarian, or at the more extreme end of the *laissez-faire* continuum. For example, he developed an important distinction between the provision of a generous, but limited welfare net, and more extensive schemes in which welfare was seen as part of a quest for greater equality. The former were acceptable in a civilized society, whereas the latter again led to Big Brother, and inefficiency.

Hayek may have been the first major figure to take up the sword in the *laissez-faire* revival, but Milton Friedman has a claim to being as important a warrior in the cause. Indeed, in many ways he is a more unqualified defender of the market. Within the field of economic theory Friedman is most associated with monetarism, the view that strict control of the money supply is the key to controlling inflation, and thus to ensuring economic growth. Such views became popular against the background of 1970s stagflation. So too did his belief in the need to curb the powers of unions, his view that unemployment was in part the result of unions pricing labour out of the market (e.g., Friedman, 1962; Friedman and Schwartz, 1963; and Friedman and Friedman, 1985).

His market-oriented views were especially influential among a disparate group of American new-righters. For example, the so-called 'supply siders' advocated the need to stimulate production by cutting taxes and encouraging individual enterprise (e.g., Wanniski, 1979). They also served as an inspiration to those who argued the need to privatize and de-regulate. This group claimed that state-provided services were almost always more expensive in terms of production costs than privately provided ones, while raising capital for them 'crowded out' the private market. There was also an increasing perception, especially in Europe, of the public sector as a bastion of trade-union power. More generally, government was seen as 'overloaded'. It had taken on too many roles which it could not carry out efficiently. This 'creeping socialism' had raised popular expectations, not all of which could be fulfilled; the result was a loss of faith in government institutions.

Among the growing legion of *laissez-faire* disciples are others who have been influenced more by public choice theory, with its assumptions of rational actors operating maximizing principles. This has been based mainly on the works of American economists, such as Jim Buchanan, William Niskanen, or Gordon Tullock (e.g., Buchanan, 1975; Niskanen, 1971; Tullock, 1970). Public choice theory tends to view major political parties as 'vote maximizers', seeking to win elections by promising more welfare and state services; attempting to fulfil these promises requires ever higher taxes. The resulting analyses have similarities with Marxist critiques of social democracy's 'fiscal crisis of the state', whereby the needs of the capitalist profit-driven market limit the amount of welfare which can be provided. Seeking to move beyond this undermines the economy through too high levels of taxation, or state interference. Public choice theory has also challenged the success of the welfare state in terms of its providing substantial benefits to the weakest. It sees statist provisions as tending to encourage bureaucratic power, based on the monopolization of information. This is accompanied by the rise of the middle class, or producer pressure groups. In Europe especially, such trends have furthered a tendency towards corporatist structures, where business and unions as well as the bureaucracy gain undue power.

The attack on extensive welfare provision has come from sociological, as well as economic, perspectives. Many on the right have alleged that welfare produces a 'dependency-culture', where people find it difficult to break free from state-funded relative poverty (e.g., Murray, 1984). Critics of the libertarian and *laissez-faire* new right claim that it is unconcerned with the weak. Such new-righters would counter by arguing that the left's tendency to point the blame at the system rather than the individual has been counter-productive, that it is better to judge policies by results than caring rhetoric. Thus it is could be argued that American blacks, after a generation of equal rights legislation, have done little to redress white 'superiority' in relative income and wealth terms. Indeed, some even argue that blacks have become more hostile to 'white' society. A belief in the endemic nature of white racism leads to a sense of helplessness; in extreme form it even leads to a form of conspiracy theory which holds that white (sometimes Jewish) society has spread drugs and Aids among the black population.

The growth of the drug problem in the United States and fears of Aids have also influenced part of the right, especially its traditionalist and mythical wings. Decadence has become a key word, in the way it was for many earlier fascists. Drugs and Aids are seen as part of a permissiveness and tolerance, which, it is argued, have allowed subversives to undermine social stability. For example, radical curriculum reform in schools has often been aimed more at social engineering than improving educational standards (or improving the status of teachers, an important producer group). The idea of a 'new class', a left-wing elite bent on social engineering of this type, has been a central idea of many American neo-conservatives. Although the definition of this new class is somewhat vague, the concept has found a ready echo among many on the right. The claim that the moral authority of religion has declined in the face of secular attacks has also been a common one, most vociferously from the Moral Majority in the United States (e.g., Falwell, 1980). The result, according to many on the right, has often been the growth of a statist collectivism at the institutional level, countered by anomic individualism at the level of political culture.

The idea of culture, both in its artistic and political sense, has been central to much recent thinking on the right. In France the Nouvelle Droite, and especially its key theorist Alain de Benoist, have highlighted the implications for social organization of recent psychological and scientific literature in various books, and magazines such as *Nouvelle Ecole* (the most interesting book is Benoist, 1977). E. O. Wilson, the leading Harvard socio-biologist, and others have been enlisted to demonstrate that financial and social inequalities are inevitable, and to prove that a deeply-rooted common culture is a necessary basis of a stable society. De Benoist, and especially some of the leaders of the French Front National, have also been interested in the manipulative function of ideas centring on race and community — traits which have leds to accusations of fascist sympathies.

In Britain, the academic polymath Roger Scruton and many in the Salisbury Group have been less interested in these scientific developments, but have shared a belief in the continuing importance to social unity of concepts such as authority, religion, tradition, nation (or Europe) and even race (e.g., Scruton, 1980). *The Salisbury Review* (founded in 1982, and named after a former Conservative leader) has been especially important in disseminating such views among intellectuals. Its main focus of attack is the left, again often in the cultural more than the economic spheres. Thus the magazine has taken a particular interest in topics such as attacks on 'multi-cultural' education, or the politics of literature (e.g., Cronin, 1989). However, there have also been barbs for those on the right who focus excessively on individualism and freedom, an emphasis which is seen as highly dangerous to social stability.

The emphasis on prosperity in market economics rhetoric could also be dangerous in the event of a recession, or the growth of a major under-class even in a 'healthy' capitalism. Early capitalism had a strong element of moral legitimation in the form of the Protestant work ethic, where hard work was rewarded by profit, where charity was virtuous. The casino-capitalism of the late twentieth century, exemplified by its well-publicized yuppy money traders and insider-dealers, seems less defensible ('greed is good' served as the motto of one 1980s Wall Street raider). The new legitimating myth of *laissez-faire* economics is the 'big-cake' argument: 'a rising tide lifts all boats'. Capitalism may be inegalitarian, but it maximizes Gross Domestic Product, and in absolute terms even the poor are better off through the 'trickle-down effect'.

A major problem for this view is that capitalism retains a secondary legitimating economic myth which harks back to the Protestant ethic: this is the myth of fair reward. Inequalities seem easier to accept if they can be related to hard work, or talent, than if they stem from, say, insider-dealing. This problem has been compounded by the growth of the tertiary economy. Early entrepreneurs tended to produce something of clear value in material terms: pots, pans, cars and so on. The Protestant ethic is more sceptical of the merits of parts of the service economy: do we really need poodle parlours, or two face-lifts before forty years of age?

Political myth is an elusive concept for social scientists; how is it defined, how can the existence of such myths be proved? Nevertheless, it is interesting to note that some of the points in the previous paragraph clearly are part of contemporary popular culture. For example, the 1987 American film *Wall Street* focused on the chicanery of the insider-dealer, and the corrupting influence of greed that totally lacked social responsibility. 'Create, instead of living off the buying and selling of others,' a working-class father tells his yuppy son. The film also highlights a problem for the *political* myth of capitalism: namely, the view that the market is the guarantor of freedom. The recent move towards the market, accompanied by an erratic political liberalization in communist countries may have strengthened this myth. On the other hand, the myth seems hard to square with the growth of multi-national corporations, with fact that the livelihoods of thousands, even millions, can be traded by corporate raiders. Insider-dealer Michael Douglas in *Wall Street* tells his young disciple-in-dollars, 'Now you're not naive enough to think we live in a democracy, are you buddy? It's the free market!'

For many on the right, this would be an example of how culture has been infected by a left-wing new class. Nevertheless, the late 1980s rhetoric of British Conservatism, with its renewed emphasis on themes such as religion, serves as a good example that some on the right are aware of the need for a more moral dimension for a system which has become rooted deeply in hedonism and self-interest (though the concept of a potential crisis has advantages for those on the right who seek to strengthen the state). George Bush's 'caring' rhetoric during 1989 reflects a similar concern (though part of the change compared to Reagan reflects Bush's more patrician version of conservatism). The growth of ecological rhetoric among right-wing parties reflects a similar consideration, though it would be wrong to see an interest in the countryside as new. There has always been a strand in right-wing thought that was suspicious of urban society and stressed an affinity with nature.

The Ascendancy of the New Right?

The problems just discussed indicate the need not to overstate the ascendancy of the contemporary right. In ideological terms, major questions remain about its central tenets. For example, the celebration of markets and the minimal state ignores the fact that some of the most successful post-1945 economic growth records can be found in countries where the state has taken a significant role in guiding the economy, such as Japan. It could even be argued that Reagan's supposed supply side economic miracle of the 1980s owed more to luck (falling real oil prices), or military Keynesianism. And the latter helped produce a massive budget deficit, which could bring ruin in the 1990s. Nozick's arguments, whilst influential, have many critics. Even on the right many point to the fact that a case can be made for more than a minimal state. His arguments gloss over key philosophical questions, such as how an original distribution of income and wealth was arrived at, or what constitutes coercing and harming others. The point about coercion is especially important to free marketeers, who argue that freedom is only diminished by intentional actions, and markets do not produce intended outcomes. Left-wing economists have argued that giant corporations can manipulate demand, and philosophers have revealed the hidden assumptions in studies of power which fail to consider corporate and social influences.

More generally, new right economic theory tends to be stronger on grand theory than on detailed case studies. Public choice theory illustrates the dangers of assuming that bureaucrats are necessarily public spirited, but survey studies show that many actually are. Socialists may have become increasingly interested in markets, but this does not mean that there are not examples of market failure. The planned privatization (in Britain) and de-regulation (in the United States) of electricity can offer clear cases of sweeping economic analyses having led to the neglect of more technical issues. For example, what are the implications in terms of the reliability of the transmission grid in the United States of an influx of small, independent producers, which lack a utility's legal obligation to provide uninterrupted service? (IEE, *Spectrum*, May 1989). On the other hand, the electricity industry also provides an example of how the market can be more 'democratic' than state provision. Public opposition to nuclear power plants has been a major factor in preventing new nuclear construction in the United States (another factor has been high capital costs). State-owned European electricity industries have paid far less attention to such opposition.

Part of the new right has little interest in such 'details'. Thus for libertarians and the more extreme *laissez-faire* supporters, virtually all aspects of state activity are seen as bad. New right critics of the state would argue that government almost invariably makes problems worse rather than better. For example, some refuse to see the post-1929 Great Depression as an example of market failure, preferring to stress government actions such as reduction in the money supply, or the raising of taxes and tariffs. Such analysis is rejected by most economists, who do not see these factors as prime causes of the depression, though they may have had a marginal effect after the initial market failure. And even many within the new right are antagonistic towards the more extreme forms of market argument.

It is difficult not to see part of the appeal of the libertarian and *laissez-faire* new right as stemming from their rational universality at a time of intellectual confusion and doubt. David Caute has argued that the fellow-travelling with communism phenomenon of the 1930s was a 'postcript to the Enlightenment' (Caute, 1973). The Enlightenment had led intellectuals to believe that society could be improved by the actions of rational man. However, by the early twentieth century this belief had been undermined by psychological theories stressing the unconscious and irrational, by horrifying world war, renewed economic depression and a loss of faith in parliamentary democracy. The great Russian Revelation of the 1930s was the discovery of planning, and the naïve belief that the Soviet Union had solved the basic problems of social organization. The fellow travellers entered a world of millenarian fantasy, eulogizing the 'humanity' of Stalinist Russia. Some fellow travellers were deceived, but others deceived themselves: they sought a universal, rationalist panacea. Economic reconstruction, measured in quantifiable Gross Domestic Product, took precedence over more subtle arguments about balance and constitutional rights. It is hard not to see an element of this in the 1970s and 1980s fashion for libertarian and *laissez-faire* views. In many ways, the new right has been an intellectual phenomenon rather than a popular one, just as fellow travelling was a feature of part of the educated middle class more than the workers.

New-right intellectuals have undoubtedly influenced governments, but in analysing their success it is important not to confuse political rhetoric with policy. Reagan's early 'Make My Day' foreign policy rhetoric was followed by a remarkable *détente* in East-West relations, much to the anger of right-wingers for whom the Soviet Union remained the 'Evil Empire'. Reagan's domestic right-wing rhetoric was not matched by serious policy initiatives in many social-policy areas, though his appointees to the Supreme Court helped lead to a series of conservative decisions in 1989 on issues such as equal rights and abortion. In Britain, Thatcher has undoubtedly presided over radical administrations since 1979, especially the massive privatization programme. However, aspects of this were pragmatic as much as ideological; privatization raised revenue to fund tax cuts, and reduced the public sector borrowing requirement. Moreover, studies of policy-making in both the United States and Britain have shown the continuing importance of the bureaucracy, inertia, crisis-management or simply 'buying' votes (e.g., see Thompson, 1986).

In electoral terms, the ascendancy of the right is even less well founded. Morris Fiorina has argued that there is no strong or even consistent evidence that Americans have made a right turn (Fiorina, 1988). Certainly Bush's comfortable victory produced no coat-tail ripple in elections for Congress and state legislatures. In Britain, polls show that in many areas there is significant opposition to Conservative policies, and in the 1989 European

Parliament elections the Conservatives trailed well behind Labour. Ivor Crewe has argued forcefully that the electorate 'is hardly suffused with Thatcherite values on either the economic or the moral plane' (Crewe, 1988, p.41). Among some, notably working class youth, there are high levels of alienation ('May I slash my wrists tonight, on this fine Conservative night' runs the chilling refrain of a mid-1980s song from the left-wing British pop group, The Style Council). The Conservatives have won sweeping parliamentary majorities based on only just over forty per cent of the popular vote. Division between the Labour and centre parties has been a vital factor in allowing the Conservatives to monopolize national office.

The electoral fortunes of the right on continental Europe also illustrate the importance of considering the whole party system, and specific national factors. Nevertheless, the right has made a remarkable come-back from the 1960s. Opinion poll evidence suggesting that the contemporary electorate has not changed its views dramatically should be treated with caution. Polls on complex issues have a tendency to favour the status quo. Moreover there has been a strong tendency to measure the sociological success of the right in terms of its individualist-market philosophy. Thatcherism may lack support in some areas of welfare policy, or new privatization, but it is strongly supported on general themes such as firm leadership, defence, law and order, nationalism and populist anti-bureaucratic/intellectual attacks. A similar point could be made about America, where a desire to restore national glory after the humiliations of Vietnam and the hostages taken in Tehran was arguably a more important factor in Reagan's victory than a whole library of free-market literature.

Modern voting involves a strong element of economic instrumentalism, which could be disastrous for the governing right in the event of an economic downturn. Nevertheless, there remain more subterranean myths which favour the right (whereas there has been a decline in the appeal of left-wing myths, notably the equation of the left with a progressive 'movement', and the right with economic depression). For example, the impact of race in Britain in the late 1970s almost certainly helped the Conservatives more than commentators such as Crewe concede (Eatwell, 1989); and the French Front National provides a particularly good example of the potential for racist politics. Polls do not always reflect the importance of such issues, but it is important to remember the behavioural psychologists' 'say–do–think' maxim: people's poll answers do not necessarily reflect their actions or thoughts.

In terms of policy, it is important not to make a false division between pragmatism and ideology. The Nazis in some ways pursued a pragmatic policy towards the Jews before the Second World War (Jews were even allowed to leave Germany until early 1940), but this does not prove that anti-semitism was not a central Nazi ideological concern. The fact that the outputs of the Reagan and Thatcher administrations have been influenced by bureaucratic pressures, the power of producer groups, or electoral concerns, may be important in terms of policy analysis. However, in terms of ideological analysis, such pressures could be seen as confirming the right's case, rather than as evidence against a right-wing intellectual renaissance.

Indeed, the self-confidence of the post-1945 left has given way to a self-assured new right. This is not to argue that there has been a mass conversion of the intelligentsia; in Europe especially, many academics have been critical of new-right doctrines. However, the forcefulness of the right's critiques have encouraged self-doubt on the left, which is apparent in its lack of a clear agenda. From the 1930s until the 1960s left-wing intellectuals helped set the political agenda among elites. During the 1980s right-wing ideas have become more the focus of debate. Thus Gerald Cohen, the Professor of Social and Political Theory at Oxford University has written: 'I was raised in a Marxist home and I was bored by academic political philosophy until I read Nozick, who roused me from my dogmatic socialist slumber' (Cohen, 1986, p.9).

It could be argued that for much of the twentieth century in liberal democracies the left thought and the right governed. Now the right both governs and thinks (though those who govern are rarely the thinkers).

References

Bell, D., 1976. *The Cultural Contradictions of Capitalism*, Heinemann, London.
Benoist, A. de, 1977. *Vu de droite*, Copernic, Paris.
Buchanan, J. M., 1975. *The Limits of Liberty*, Chicago University Press, Chicago.
Caute, D., 1973. *The Fellow Travellers*, Weidenfeld and Nicolson, London.
Cohen, G., 1986. The ideas of Robert Nozick, in N. Deakin (ed.), *The New Right*, Runnymede Trust, London.
Crewe, I., 1988. Has the electorate become Thatcherite?, in R. Skidelsky (ed.), *Thatcherism*, Chatto and Windus, London.
Cronin, R., 1989. The politics of literature, *Salisbury Review*, Vol. 7, No.3.
Davies, S., 1985. The spectre haunting the left, in A. Seldon (ed.), *The New Right Enlightenment*, Economic and Literary Books, Sevenoaks.
Eatwell, R., 1989. Fascism and political racism in post-war Britain, in K. Lunn and A. Kushner (eds), *Traditions of Intolerance*, Manchester University Press, Manchester.
Falwell, J., 1980. *Listen, America!*, Doubleday and Company, New York.
Fiorina, M. P., 1988. The Reagan years: turning to the right or groping toward the middle?, in B. Cooper *et al.* (eds.), *The Resurgence of Conservatism in Anglo-American Democracies*, Duke University Press, Durham, NC.
Friedman, M., 1962. *Capitalism and Freedom*, University of Chicago Press, Chicago.
_____ and Schwartz, A. J., 1963. *A Monetary History of the United States*, Princeton University Press, Princeton.
_____ and Friedman, R., 1985. *The Tyranny of the Status Quo*, Penguin, Harmondsworth.
Girvin, B., (ed.) 1988. *The Transformation of Contemporary Conservatism*, Sage, London.
Gottfried, P. and Fleming, T., 1988. *The Conservative Movement*, Twayne, Boston.
Graham, D. and Clarke, P., 1986. *The New Enlightenment*, Macmillan, London.
Green, D., 1987. *The New Right*, Wheatsheaf, Brighton.
Hayek, F. A., 1960. *The Constitution of Liberty*, Routledge and Kegan Paul, London.
_____ 1973-9. *Law, Legislation and Liberty*, 3 Vols., Routledge and Kegan Paul, London.
_____ 1988. *The Fatal Conceit: The Errors of Socialism*, Routledge and Kegan Paul, London.

Hoover, K. and Plant, R., 1989. *Conservative Capitalism in Britain and the United States*, Routledge, London.

King, D., 1987. *The New Right*, Macmillan, London.

Kristol, I., 1978. *Two Cheers for Capitalism*, Basic Books, New York.

Murray, C., 1984. *Losing Ground*, Basic Books, New York.

Niskanen, W. A., 1971. *Bureaucracy and Representative Government*, Aldine Atherton, New York.

Nozick, R., 1974. *Anarchy, State and Utopia*, Blackwell, London.

Rogger, H. and Weber, E. (eds), 1965. *The European Right*, Weidenfeld and Nicolson, London.

Scruton, R., 1980. *The Meaning of Conservatism*, Penguin Books, Harmondsworth.

Stokes, D, 1963. Spatial models of party competition, *American Political Science Review*, Vol. 57, No.2.

Thompson, G., 1986. *The Conservatives' Economic Policy*, Croom Helm, London.

Tullock, G., 1970. *Private Wants, Public Means*, Basic Books, New York.

Wanniski, J., 1979. *The Way the World Works*, Basic Books, New York.

White, E. and Wildavsky, A., 1989. How to fix the deficit — really, *The Public Interest*, No. 94.

2 Conceptualizing the Right: Marxism's Central Errors

Roger Eatwell, University of Bath

The discussion in the previous chapter uses the terms 'left' and 'right' (or 'liberal' and 'conservative') in a way that corresponds with the style typical of the more informed political journalist, or activist, among whom Donald Stokes notes that such spatial language is almost universal (Stokes, 1963, p.368). However, the more thoughtful reader may already be pondering the question: is it possible to produce a general typology of the nature of liberal and conservative, or left and right?

The terms 'liberal' and 'conservative' pose particular problems. There are some in the United States, especially on the right, who hold that the term 'liberal' is deliberately misused to refer to many in Congress and the media, who really should be termed 'left' (*Mother Jones*, January 1988). Recently, some have been unhappy with the generic term 'conservatism', partly because of the bitter splits between conservatives. The problem is compounded by the fact that some countries have political parties which bear these names, but whose ideologies do not always correspond with popular American usage. For example, an important strand in British Conservatism is antipathetic to the individualistic, anti-statist philosophy of mainstream historic American conservatism. There is also a potential confusion in Europe over the use of the term 'liberal', which is frequently used in relation to *laissez-faire* economics. However, European usage can encompass the terminology of liberal policies on abortion, or the death penalty. Many Americans would agree with the latter usage, but would probably see *laissez-faire* economics as conservative (or in an extreme minimal state form, libertarian, though this term is not in common usage, and could be confused with libertarian in the sense of lacking moral standards in, say, sexual matters). The use of a liberal–conservative spectrum also seems less appropriate to countries with more important political extremes than American politics, where fascism, communism and other radical ideologies have never taken root substantially. There seems something strange about seeing extreme liberal and extreme conservative as polar opposites. Having liberal and libertarian as opposites seems even more bizarre.

This points to a more fundamental problem, which also afflicts a left–right spectrum. Are Democrats in the United States, or the Socialists in France, moderate left-wingers, whereas communists are extreme ones? It could be argued that there is no fundamental similarity. Communism is based on a rejection of capitalism, pluralism and democratic constitutionalism. Yet all these values are accepted by the vast majority of even the most radical Democrats in the United States, and probably most Socialists in France. If Hayek's emphasis on individual freedoms and *laissez-faire* economics are right-wing, how can one also include within the right-wing camp social authoritarians, such as the Moral Majority in the United States? Do they not want to restrict individual freedoms, such as the right to abortion? All generalizations can have exceptions without invalidating them, but can an argument involve a logical contradiction? Can the right encompass both those who preach libertarianism and those who support a form of authoritarianism? (Or can the left encompass both those who support a major extension of the state, and those bitterly opposed to the encroachments of Big Brother?)

The right clearly can in the sense that there have been individuals, lobby groups and parties that have been commonly termed right-wing, but which nevertheless exhibit these diverse traits (this is true both between and within groups and parties). However, this does not resolve the fundamental problem of whether it is possible to produce an acceptable general typology. There are countless examples of the ways in which political terms (of both left and right) can be used in a confused, even contradictory fashion. The manner in which the term 'fascism(t)' has been abused serves well to illustrate the point. Recently in the United States, the black separatist Louis Farrakhan has been portrayed as fascist because of his anti-semitism, though his views on other issues diverge significantly from classic fascism. The novelist Ishmael Reed has claimed that the inner-city drug gangs are brutal crack fascists; here the term seems to have little more than a pejorative connotation. Such terminology has little relevance to the construction of an academic model of fascism, unless the point is simply to show that the term has been used in a myriad of inconsistent ways.

The problem concerning inconsistencies between and within right-wing ideologies could be analysed within three broad frameworks. One approach would not see the term 'right' as referring to an ideology in the sense of attempting to delineate a coherent set of values regarding the organization of political and social life (for a discussion of the problems involved in providing a more elaborate definition of ideology see Hamilton, 1987). Rather the term 'right' is simply a spatial reference point, which links various styles of thought that have emerged as responses to the left. As such, there is no requirement for consistency between right-wing (or left-wing) ideologies, though they could be examined for potential internal inconsistencies (for example, why do most free marketeers not adopt an extreme libertarian position, where even defence is privatized?). A second approach would involve an attempt to produce an essentialist definition. This would admit that differences exist between various right-wing ideologies over specific issues, but it would hold that there remains a common core which allows the term 'right' to be more than a spatial reference point. Given the large number of right-wing ideologies, it is unlikely that every one could be neatly fitted into an essentialist definition. Nevertheless, it might be possible to find a core which had significant heuristic value. A third approach is an essentialist one which stems from

Marxist analysis. This sees right-wing ideologies as simply a mask for capitalist interests, as a defence of private property.

Marxism and the Right

The Marxist approach, therefore, provides the necessary starting point to a discussion of the right, especially as it has been influential even among non-Marxists. In its classic form, Marxism involves a conflict/coercion model of society, in which the problem of consent is underplayed. It involves a reductionism, where ideology is seen as 'superstructural', and the state as an instrument of the ruling class. If this is correct, then a study of the right is little more than an exercise in analysing how different ideas have been used to reinforce the 'false consciousness' of the masses, and thus defend the capitalist system. Howard Williams (1988, p.118) sums up neatly both the appeal and implications of this Marxist analysis when he writes:

> The Marxian account provides probably the most powerful tool for placing in perspective an ideological tradition. By attempting to trace a political doctrine to what are regarded as its economic roots, the focus is valuably taken away from the realm of ideas to a sphere which undoubtedly has an important influence upon the growth and development of society.

Marxists would argue that the quest for logical consistency in an ideological model is misguided. For example, they often claim that German National Socialism's early rhetoric was radical, even left-wing, but this was followed by a reactionary regime phase. The point being made is that fascism's public (ideological) statements were largely for propaganda purposes. The reality (on which it should be judged) involved the propping up of a collapsing capitalism, and the destruction of working-class organizations. Thus all ideas must be viewed essentially within the context of class relationships.

Marxism rejects the Platonic view, which highly influenced Christianity, that there can be objective truth. Instead, it adopts a dialectical view of society and its development, which involves a criticism of the formal logic analysis of propositions as static. Thus capitalism is riddled with contradictions, but it is these very contradictions which give it identity, and provide the motor for change. Within capitalist society there is a major contradiction between the interests of the bourgeoisie in its pursuit of profit maximization, and that of the proletariat in its quest for emancipation from both poverty and alienation. Ideology serves the role of resolving this contradiction, by producing 'false consciousness', a failure to perceive the reality of capitalist dominance.

This argument about ideology can be seen more clearly by considering the claim of the British academic Andrew Gamble that the best short description of Thatcherism is 'free economy/strong state' (e.g., Gamble, 1988). There are some on the right who would accept this characterization of Thatcherism. Many within the Conservative party have been worried about the growth of the state, notably in the area of limiting local autonomy. Others have pointed more fundamentally to the lack of a clear constitutional aspect of

Thatcherism, a particular problem in a country such as Britain, which lacks a clearly codified constitution (e.g., Boyle, 1988). However, such arguments on the right have been conducted largely within the context of the need for pragmatism, or 'statecraft', to be exercised within a more clearly thought-out framework of the nature of limited politics. For Marxist academics the apparent contradiction between individualism and authoritarianism in Thatcherism is explained in terms of the needs of the capitalist system (e.g., Fine and Harris, 1987). British capitalism in the 1970s entered a period of crisis, characterized by declining profits, and rising unemployment. It was necessary to provide greater freedom for the market, but at the same time impose more social control to counter the effects of the ensuing inequalities. Thus tax cuts were matched by a greater emphasis on law and order to 'police' the poor, and attacks on trade-union rights to control the working class.

For Marxists, people do not perceive these contradictions because they are held in a state of false consciousness. This refers to the way in which the values of the dominant class become the socially dominant values. This process begins within the family and at school. Propaganda here is to be found not only in the teaching of history and politics, which obviously tend to be a celebration of the nation's own values. Even arithmetic books are often full of examples involving capitalist concepts such as profit and rent. In later life, false consciousness is maintained through the media and other institutions. Magazines such as *Readers' Digest* preach the virtues of self-improvement, and portray a world lurking with danger. Glossy television programmes, such as *Dallas* or *Dynasty*, portray aspirational life-styles, where the injunction to 'have a nice day' countenances making millions of dollars. In Britain the Conservative-supporting 'newspaper', *The Sun*, greeted income tax cuts in the 1988 budget with the jubilatory headline, 'Lotsa Lovely Lolly'; a quarter of the electorate read this newspaper.

This analysis raises some interesting points, but it is important to stress that there are a series of problems for the Marxist view of ideology. Firstly, even if it is fair to characterize 1980s Thatcherism as 'free economy/strong state', does this necessarily involve a contradiction? A strong state could be necessary in the short term to correct imperfections in the market, for example by reducing excessive trade-union power. And does the passing of new laws forcing trade unions to hold ballots before striking *necessarily* involve a reduction in democracy? More seriously, the reduction of ideologies to class relations is far from a scientific exercise. In the 1970s there were Marxists who argued that growing economic problems would require an increase in state control over markets, investment, etc. Marxist critiques of the 1970s corporatist literature tended to focus on its failure to stress class interests, rather than a rejection of the literature's central claim that the role of the state was extending significantly in the economic sphere. Indeed, a classic Marxist analysis of fascism sees it as the dictatorship of capital when faced with a terminal crisis. Thus Marxists are capable of arguing both that capitalism in crisis can bring dictatorship, and that it can lead to a revival of free market principles (admittedly tempered by an increase in state control in other areas). These arguments could be refined by claiming that the fascist response was only necessary in an 'extreme' crisis, but the key concept is vague, and the reasoning ultimately tautologous (an 'extreme' crisis is one where fascism appears!).

Other problems for the Marxist analysis of ideology emerge by continuing to examine Gamble's characterization of Thatcherism within the context of a discussion about human nature. Many on the right would hold that 'free economy/strong state' is a philosophy perfectly consistent with their interpretation of human nature. Putting it simply, man is seen as aggressive, and in need of authority. On such a view, there seems no contradiction in holding that incentives are necessary in the economic sphere, but a firm framework of order is necessary in the social sphere. There would be a problem if free-market or authoritarian views were taken to extremes, but the idea of balance has long been central to much moderate right-wing thought.

Secondly, Marxists have a problem with the counter-factual statement in relation to socialization. They have to argue that social values would be very different *'if not for'* socialization, but such a view is little more than an assertion. Many on the right would argue that the institutions and values of society, far from being imposed, were the summation of a long process of development, which reflected fundamental traits about human nature and social organization. It is possible to find societies whose organization and values differ significantly from Western democracies, but these are invariably more backward in terms of economic wealth. Sometimes they are small communities, cut off from the mainstream of historical development. Thus anthropological studies of 'Edenist' communities tell us little about social organization in societies that have been shaped by the major social forces of aggressive and competitive behaviour, including foreign conquest.

The problems posed by Marxism's 'economism', that is its tendency to reduce everything to the needs of 'capitalism', can also be seen by considering non-economic issues, such as women's rights or abortion. These are normally seen by Marxists (and many others) as left-wing. The argument holds that capitalism in crisis needs to push women back into the home, hence the attack on their 'rights'. However, it is hard to agree with such an analysis, especially as it can produce bizarre conclusions. For example, there have been times, notably the Second World War, when 'capitalist' countries were short of labour and women were encouraged to move out of the home; was this development therefore right-wing? Or what if a 'capitalist' country, which was experiencing long-term unemployment, felt it might be helped by a cut in the birth rate. Would pro-abortion views in such a case be seen as right-wing? Moreover, the pro-abortion argument stresses the right of one individual above that of others. Yet extreme individualist arguments are often seen by Marxists as right-wing (admittedly a misleading claim, as there is right-wing collectivism). The point is not simply one about rights for the foetus; it is also the claim that the pregnant mother's will overrides that of the father, of family, of others who might wish to adopt children, of society's possible 'need' for a higher birthrate. Is it left-wing to support the termination of female foetuses in Third World countries, where male babies are valued more highly? Viewing abortion as a left-wing issue may have a relevance if the point is simply one concerned with the *perception* of issues, but the argument is much more complex if the focus becomes *philosophical* (this point is developed in more detail in Chapter 3).

Even many Marxists have come to reject a crude economism, where ideology is viewed as purely 'superstructural'. Followers of Antonio Gramsci, a founder member of the Italian Communist Party, in particular have taken an interest in ideology as a major factor in producing 'hegemony in civil society'. Gramsci rejected economic determinism of the crude type, and focused on the ethico-political realm, a term derived from the idealist Italian philosopher, Croce. Gramsci's emphasis was on culture, both as a means of domination and liberation. This led to a belief that the left needed to gain hegemony in civil society. In other words it was important to establish a counterculture before the revolution; otherwise the left would be plagued with the problem of dictatorship, so clearly illustrated by Stalinism.

A notable contemporary British disciple is the academic Stuart Hall. He argues, 'The hope of every ideology is to naturalize itself out of History into Nature, and thus to become invisible, to operate unconsciously' (Hall, 1988, p.8). In other words, political ideas can be a major factor in shaping the consciousness of a society, a point which Hall (1988, p.3) uses to attack many on the left when he claims:

> political analysis on the left seems pitifully thin, and ideological analysis is, if anything, in a worse state...This is...because the left...tends to hold a very reductionist conception of politics and ideology where, 'in the last instance' (whenever that is), both are determined by, and so can be 'read off' against, some (often ill-defined) notion of 'economic' or 'class' determination.

Hall continues by arguing that 'the underlying social, economic and cultural forces which are bringing the era of "organized capitalism" to a close...have decomposed and fragmented class as a unified political force, fracturing any so-called automatic linkages between economics and politics' (Hall, 1988, p.281). He sees Thatcherism as a form of 'authoritarian populism', which has been notably successful in attracting working-class support.

This position reflects an important drift in Marxist thinking, though it could be argued that the emphasis on culture hides a new form of totalitarianism rather than acceptance of pluralism. Moreover, the currency of terms such as 'Post-Fordism', 'conjunctures', or 'periodizations' reflects that economism is far from dead (see also Jessop *et al*, 1988). Nor is the tendency towards a banal or pretentious argot, the language of a pedantocracy. Is 'Post-Fordism' anything more than what sociologists for over twenty years have called 'post-industrialism'? The claim that class is less and less relevant to political loyalties can be found in countless academic works (e.g., Inglehart, 1977). And what, exactly, is a 'conjuncture'?

The term 'authoritarian populism' in relation to Thatcher poses more specific problems, though one which again reinforces the point about imprecise terminology. Britain lacks the frontier tradition of the United States, and the resonance of the partly-related appeal to 'the people'. Hall is therefore presumably pointing more to the 'every man a king' glosses on market philosophy, and Thatcher's humble (albeit middle-class) origins. However, the term seems to confuse as much as enlighten. The American left has sometimes sought to inherit the populist tradition, for example the post-1960s emphasis on local community action. Is the term 'authoritarian populism' a paradox, in which populism is seen as normally 'democratic'? Or is populism seen in the way that Daniel Bell and others have viewed much twentieth-century American populism; namely in terms of the authoritarianism of Huey Long, or McCarthy (Bell, 1964)? There also seems a confusion between 'populism' in its classic ideological sense, with 'popular'. Classic populism focused on a celebration of the simple, agrarian life, or the referendum as a political device — hardly features of Thatcherism.

The centrality of the concept of a Thatcherite, or Reaganite, drive for hegemony also seems problematic. It more than hints at a form of conspiracy theory, or at least the existence of a unified power-elite, possessing a clear 'project' (another example of such terminology can be found in Gunn, 1989, pp. 29, 38, etc.). The hard evidence seems to produce a more complex picture. The Reagan Presidency can be used to illustrate this point.

Reagan's many business friends, the links between spoils such as ambassadorships, or the rise in America of business-funded PACs could be seen as the public face of this subterranean power. Certainly they raise interesting points about the influences on politicians. Yet it is hard to believe that Reagan, personally, came to office with a carefully defined 'project', or that he subsequently worked assiduously to a well-laid plan. This seems to leave two broad possibilities: either his administrations were more pragmatic than the term 'project' would imply, or an economic, or bureaucratic, elite manipulated affairs. Neither fit the picture painted by the leading new right economist and Presidential economic adviser, William Niskanen, who depicts a President uninterested by intellectual debate, and surrounded by divided advisers (Niskanen, 1988). Other evidence confirms the divisions among Reagan's advisers, and the legion of new right theorists and others who prayed for a revolution on the right. There were also some notable changes in right-wing views which do not fit neatly into Marxist theories. In the late 1980s, for example, the Heritage Foundation proposed a vastly-expanded health-care system for the poor! A case could be made that the experience of government influenced some on the right wing, at least as much as the right wing influenced government outputs.

Such problems have led Marxism into an abstract retreat. Unable to prove a clear link between the state and capitalist interests, theorists such as Ralph Miliband and Nicos Poulantzas have entered a jargon-ridden world of debates about the state as 'autonomous' (and various other argot terms). Thus some Marxists argue that there is no direct link between capitalism and the state, but nevertheless the state operates in the interest of capitalism. Miliband, a leading British Marxist, has accused Poulantzas of 'structuralist abstractionism', in which an abstract theoretical approach seeks to explain one example in terms of another abstract concept; the process is therefore circular. Marxism as science has been forced to retreat into Marxism as theology.

This discussion of Marxism and ideology is not meant to imply that there is no relationship between ideas and society. Indeed, the brief discussion in the previous chapter of the contemporary ascendancy of the right indicated that there is a complex symbiotic relationship. Any complete discussion of the nature of the right over the last two hundred years would therefore need to pay careful attention to questions of social change and institutions as well as political thought. However, it would be impossible in one volume to do full justice to the nuances of this relationship. This book therefore concentrates primarily on the political thought of the right, largely separated from sociological concerns. The main reason for this focus was stated at the outset of the first chapter: namely, there is a lack of any systematic academic literature which tries to analyse in one volume the main strands of right-wing thought. To this can now be added the argument that debates about the nature of the right seem especially pertinent after a decade which has witnessed a significant ascendancy of right-wing ideas — even to the point where many Marxists now take them seriously in their own right.

This recent growth of interest in ideologies is not confined simply to some Marxists. As the American academic Gar Alperowitz notes (in Hoover and Plant, 1989, p.ix):

> an important lesson of the decade [the 1980s] is that ideology on its own plays a powerful role in politics — an idea which had far less currency only a few years ago, especially in the United States.

The reasons for this change are far less important to the problems of conceptualizing the right than the discussions surrounding Marxism. Nevertheless, they raise several points of relevance to understanding the right. They also underline the fact that it has not only been Marxism that has been guilty of downplaying ideology.

One central problem concerns the very use of the terms 'ideology' and 'right'. The term 'ideology' was coined during the French Revolution as a term referring to the scientific study of ideas, but it quickly acquired a pejorative content, in particular denoting extreme, or impractical thought. In the twentieth century, some have sought to restrict its use to totalitarian systems, where there is an officially prescribed doctrine on all major aspects of economic, political and social life. This reflects the fact that the definition of an ideology is highly contested, a situation which has encouraged semantic rather than substantial discussion of the term.

A particular problem in discussing right-wing ideologies stems from the fact that in some countries, for example America and France, the term right (or conservative) has often had a negative connotation (in the United States, the left has also been a highly pejorative term). The American conservative academic Peter Viereck noted in the 1960s that conservative 'is among the most unpopular words in the American vocabulary' (Viereck, 1962, p.20). R. A. Schoenberger has written of America that 'Right-wing organizations, by whatever definition employed, were few and their memberships limited, ephemeral, or secret' (Schoenberger, 1969, p.3). Clearly, 'right-wing' is being equated with extremism. In France immediately before the Second World War, such was the the strength of left-wing rhetoric, that the most right-wing party in the Senate ran under the label of Gauche Républicaine! During the 1950s the Gaullists and Poujadists objected strongly to being placed on the right of the National Assembly's Chamber (Williams, 1964, p.8).

Other problems relating to understanding the role of ideology, especially the right, stem from the nature of the academic discipline of politics. Political theory has tended to focus more on the study of 'great' texts, or abstract concepts, than on 'isms'. Thus the French academic Raoul Girardet (1970, p.78) has written:

> How would a course on the concept of the right be organized?...The question doesn't bother me. I teach the history of political ideas. Such history ignores this approach. Was Machiavelli left or right wing? And Voltaire, and Rousseau, and de Tocqueville and Proudhon? Applying such labels has no interest.

In political science, the twentieth century behaviourist and positivist revolutions have stressed approaches such as the survey method, or quantification. Public administration has often focused on the role of the bureaucracy, though before public choice theory the emphasis was mainly on civil servants as rational, pragmatic actors, who mitigated the worst excesses of dogma. Within political sociology, especially in America, an influential debate during the 1950s and 1960s concerned the so-called 'End of Ideology' (see especially Bell, 1960). This held that radical ideologies, such as communism and fascism, would disappear in an increasingly affluent Western world. In their place would emerge a technocratic politics (for example, debates between Keynesians and monetarists), involving incremental decisions (say, the exact rate of marginal taxation), rather than grand moral visions. 'Democracy' was essentially the institutionalization of competition between political and lobby group elites. Against such a background, most electors were seen as taking little interest in politics, voting mainly in terms of 'economic instrumentalism' — in other words, in response to the success of the government's economic policies. The remnants of radical political activity were channelled mainly into single issue groups, such as opposition to the Vietnam war or feminism, which to some extent cut across ideological boundaries.

The implication of such an approach was that ideology was largely irrelevant. How to conceptualize the right, therefore, seemed a minor order problem. Often ideology was viewed as a means of explaining something else, rather than as important in its own right. For example, in psychological studies of conservatism and fascism, there was usually no serious attempt to refine these concepts. The point was more to illustrate arguments about personality, and other psychological issues. Or in sociology, followers of Durkheim tended to see ideologies mainly as clues to social structure and social solidarity. Such views are still common among many academics, and it is important to reiterate that stressing the revival of interest in ideology is not meant to signify a belief that contemporary voters have a clear view of policy, or necessarily support the revival of free-market philosophy. Nor is it meant to deny the importance of pragmatism, crisis management or the continuing influence of bureaucracies and pressure groups. Nevertheless, there has been a broad growth of awareness that ideology, especially the marketing of political ideas, could be more important than had been assumed.

The Right as a Set of 'Isms'?

Arguing the need for a book on the nature of right-wing ideas, considered in their own light, does not resolve the problem of whether the right can be seen in qualified-essentialist terms, or whether it is better to see it more in terms of a series of responses to the left, as varieties of styles of thought. So, how to proceed? Clearly, it would be impossible in a single book to do justice to all aspects of the right, in every country over the last two hundred years. Even excluding questions relating to whether the terms 'left' and 'right' can be applied outside Western liberal democracies, the number of potential case studies seems endless. In view of the preceding discussion, it might be thought that the best way to proceed was by considering political 'isms'. The vast majority of politically aware people would accept that Marxism, communism and socialism are left-wing ideologies, though there have been bitter debates within the left about its true nature (for example, when the Communist International in 1928 declared its 'social fascist' phase: the claim that parliamentary socialist parties were 'fascist' because they were helping to prop up a failing capitalism by not preaching revolutionary politics!). Why not analyse the nature of the right within the context of the main 'isms' which have been mentioned in the previous sections: namely, conservatism, liberalism, populism and fascism?

It seems difficult to deny that conservatism is a right-wing ideology, but it is important to remember that the term can have very different connotations in both Europe and the United States. In the past, many Americans would identify a conservative with someone like Goldwater, who (in domestic politics) opposes the strong state, and has a highly individualistic view of political life. Today, it is more difficult to generalize, as the term conservative can encompass many positions in the United States. The classic conservative tradition in Britain and Germany has encompassed leaders such as Benjamin Disraeli or Otto von Bismarck, who saw politics in collectivist terms, and were responsible for significant extensions in state activity (the fact that some historians have seen these policies as pragmatic, or attempts to defuse socialism, does not invalidate the point about different traditions). However, in neither country has there been a uniform conservative tradition; a hundred flowers (and some weeds) have bloomed.

Within the British Conservative party during the 1980s there has been a debate centring on what is the 'true' Conservative tradition. The argument has its uses in terms of party infighting; in particular, it has been used to attack Thatcherism's preference for liberal market solutions over 'One Nation' politics. From the point of political theory, it seems more sensible to conclude that conservatism (with both a small 'c' and large 'C'), encompasses more than one right-wing form of thought, especially as other self-styled 'conservatives' have even stressed collectivism linked to mass activism, and a rejection of liberal democracy (O'Sullivan, 1976)! Nevertheless, there are enough common strands in different forms of conservative thought (for example, the idea of balance or ordered liberty) to make it a viable candidate for inclusion in a typology of the right.

Liberalism (in its classic, non-American, sense) poses far more problems in terms of classification as a right-wing ideology. Marxists see its individualistic and *laissez-faire* prescriptions as inherently right-wing, but historically liberalism was a challenge to what are usually thought of as right-wing views: hierarchy, tradition, religion, privilege and so on (for a good history see Ruggiero, 1927). Moreover, liberalism is not a fully integrated ideology: for example, in the late nineteenth century it could encompass both the traditional emphasis on individualism and *laissez-faire*, and the 'New Liberalism', which encompassed a positive rather than negative view of liberty. There is a sense in which the statist implications of positive liberty can be seen within traditional liberal concerns: they could help the individual become independent, more self-reliant. Thus those, such as the British political theorist Rodney Barker, who argue that freedom is therefore 'redefined in terms of its ends' (Barker, 1978, p.14) offer a potentially misleading perspective. It might help here to distinguish between the state as *liberator* (which could encompass individualistic approaches), and the state as *nanny* (which has more collectivist assumptions). Nevertheless, this development in liberalism undermines any simple division between individualism and collectivism.

Philosophically, liberalism also has much in common with many left-wing ideologies, for example its rationalism and universalism. Similarly, its emphasis on toleration, often linked to arguments about natural rights, hardly corresponds with much right-wing thought. Its central emphasis on liberty also seems to fit strangely with the more tempered view of liberty found in conservatism, let alone more extreme right-wing ideologies. Some, especially Marxists and fascists, have challenged liberalism's conception of liberty, claiming that it is a mask for capitalist manipulation, and a source of alienation in its emphasis on the pursuit of economic wealth at the expense of a true human community (the *Gesellschaft* rather than the *Gemeinschaft*). Such arguments have many objections. The British academic Kenneth Minogue puts a central argument clearly when he notes that the last two hundred years in Western liberal democracies have seen not only a vast increase in living standards (and thus positive liberty), but also an extension of civil and political rights (Minogue, 1985, p.221). At the same time, many left-wing regimes have failed to fulfil the economic aspirations of their populations, and abused civil and political rights. In such circumstances, there seems something strange about calling liberalism right-wing, unless it is a perverse way of rehabilitating the right!

The claim that 'liberal' economics is inherently right-wing is also debatable. Neo-classical economics, which has dominated Western academic teaching, claims to be 'positive' in the sense that it is a value-free form of study (e.g., Lipsey, 1963). Whilst it could be argued that such economics contains value-laden definitions (notably the concept of economic demand defined as demand backed by the ability to pay), it is possible to see a large part of economics as inherently neither left- nor right-wing. For example, although the implications of public choice theory have been picked up by many on the right, even some left-wingers have argued that it must be taken seriously. Buchanan seems to have been attracted to public choice theory through ideological persuasion, but for others the fascination stems more from the professional economists' concern with the rational analysis of behaviour (see Buchanan, 1986). Economists are not forced to believe that the film-star Bo Derek's husband married her simply for the money! Rational, utility-maximizing assumptions are simply necessary for model building (even some mathematical economists find no difficulty in agreeing, with Dudley Moore, that Bo Derek rates 11 out of 10).

Populism also cannot simply be seen as a right-wing ideology. Historically, the classic populist movements celebrated an agrarian/small town *Gemeinschaft*, where virtue resided in the common people, united by a deeply shared culture (Canovan, 1981). They disliked organized politics, stressing individualism. Thus in Frank Capra's populist films of the 1930s, *Mr Deeds Goes to Town*, and *Mr. Smith Goes to Washington*, Gary Cooper and James Stewart are forced to sort out the evils inflicted by urban bureaucrats, businessmen and politicians. They also tended to be ethnocentric, even racist, as can be seen in the major post-Second World War manifestation of populism, the Poujadist movement in France. The 1980s witnessed a revival of the term 'populism', especially in connection with aspects of the politics of Ronald Reagan and Margaret Thatcher. The imagery was of young Margaret, the grocer's daughter from small-town Grantham, learning at the knee of her public-spirited father. The horse-riding President reminded Americans of their frontier past, rekindling myths of community and nation-building. However, a series of objections can be made to using the 'populist right' as a major typology. A semantic argument would focus on the fact that populism was 'primitivist', and not a true ideology: certainly, it failed to produce any extensive body of political theory. More substantially, many commentators have pointed out that populism had elements of both the left and the right. The former would include calls for government intervention in the economy in late nineteenth-century America, or 'agrarian socialism', based on communes, in Russia. The latter side of populism would include its strong defence of private property in America, or its tendency towards ethnocentrism.

Including a chapter specifically on fascism would also be problematic. Fascism has traditionally been seen as an extreme right-wing movement, especially by the left (such branding helps to divert attention from similarities with the left). In terms of its brief governing practice, or most minor post-war manifestations, this argument could be defended. However, in terms of generic ideology the argument is more complex. Noël O'Sullivan has shown that fascism's philosophical roots were far from purely right-wing, and recent commentators such as Zeev Sternhell and D. S. Lewis, focusing on political debate in France and Britain respectively, have concluded that fascism is better seen as a doctrine of the 'revolutionary' or 'authoritarian' centre (O'Sullivan, 1983; Sternhell, 1983; Lewis, 1987). S. M. Lipset, adopting a more sociological approach to the spectrum, has similarly concluded that fascism should be seen as 'extremism of the centre' (Lipset, 1960). Renzo De Felice, stressing the differences between Italian Fascism and German National Socialism (for example over race), has even concluded that the former had its origins on the left, whereas the latter was rooted more deeply on the right (De Felice, 1977)! Others have seen fascism as a form of 'developmental dictatorship', a type of regime which can emerge at a particular stage in economic growth, especially during the political and social upheavals of industrialization (e.g., Gregor, 1969). On this view, some countries which have styled themselves as 'socialist', even 'communist', might be better termed 'fascist'.

Fascism poses many problems for political theory, not least the lack of 'great texts'. This problem becomes less serious if attention moves away from Hitler and Mussolini towards more interesting thinkers, such as Brasillach, Drieu La Rochelle, Feder, Gentile, De Man, or the Strassers. However, there were significant differences between these theorists; for example, some were romantics, whereas others adopted a more technocratic, even scientific approach (in economic matters as well as racial ones). As a result, a strong case could be made that it is impossible to produce a generic model of fascism.

To the extent that fascism had a common core of theory, it involved an attack on the idea of limited politics as truly democratic and meaningful. It championed a revolutionary cult of the will, which aimed at mobilizing the masses, and keeping them in a condition of permanent revolution. Fascism sought the destruction of the rule of law, in order to replace it with a personal concept of leadership. Such views attracted support from both the left and right of the political spectrum. The turn of the twentieth century saw a crisis for the right in the sense of having to face the emergence of universal franchise. How were the masses to be diverted from red revolution? In Europe especially, where the First World War had been so traumatic yet revealing an event, the answer for some was radical nationalism. A parallel crisis on the left stemmed, paradoxically, from the failure of a mass revolutionary working class to emerge. This led some, notably former revolutionary syndicalists, to an interest in political myths, and again ultimately to nationalism. In a sense, fascism synthesized the left and right, especially in the economic sphere, with its emphasis on state control of a private market.

These points are not meant to reject the view that fascism in practice was far less radical than it appeared in its pre-regime phase, especially in its early days (fascism in both Germany and Italy developed more conservative traits even before coming to power). However, this is a question of history rather than political theory. A Marxist would argue that this approach fails to see ideology's role as a creator of false consciousness: fascism is a right-wing ideology precisely because fascist regimes stabilized a failing capitalist system. Such an argument glosses over the historical point that detailed studies have shown that fascist relations with business were complex, and that business tended to have little influence outside its direct sphere of expertise (Hayes, 1987; Sarti, 1971). At this point, the more theological Marxist views of the 'autonomous' (or substitute several other pieces of Marxist argot) state reappear...

Such arguments are ultimately beyond empirical discusssion, but they clearly encompass a simplistic conception of the right, which revolves essentially around support for the capitalist system as the key to the left–right spectrum. This simplistic view of the right remains strong even in recent Marxist thought which has been influenced by Gramsci, and which sees ideology as having an important role of its own. For example, Hall has written that 'restoring the free-market principle to its former ascendancy is once again the fulcrum of politics, the key dividing line between right and left' (Hall, 1988, p.225). These arguments clearly point to the need to continue by taking a more careful look at how the terms 'left' and 'right' emerged, and especially by analysing how the left–right spectrum has been used.

References

Barker, R., 1978. *Political Ideas in Modern Britain*, Methuen and Co., London.
Bell, D., 1960. *The End of Ideology*, The Free Press, Glencoe.
_____ (ed.), 1964. *The Radical Right*, Doubleday, New York.
Boyle, N., 1988. Understanding Thatcherism, *New Blackfriars*, July/August.
Buchanan, J. M., 1986. *Liberty, Market and State*, Wheatsheaf, Brighton.
Canovan, M., 1981. *Populism*, Junction Books, London.
De Felice, R, 1977. *Interpretations of Fascism*, Harvard University Press, Cambridge, Mass.
Fine, B. and Harris, L., 1987. Ideology and markets, in R. Miliband *et al.* (eds), *The Socialist Register, 1987*, Merlin Press, London.
Gamble, A., 1988. *The Free Economy and the Strong State*, Macmillan, London.
Girardet, R., 1970. *La droite*, in J.-P. Apparu, *La droite aujourd'hui*, Albin Michel, Paris.
Gregor, A. J., 1969. *The Ideology of Fascism*, The Free Press, Glencoe.
Gunn, S., 1989. *Revolution of the Right*, Pluto Press, London.
Hall, S., 1988. *The Hard Road to Renewal*, Verso, London.
Hamilton, M. B., 1987. The elements of the concept of ideology, *Political Studies*, Vol. 35, No. 1.
Hayes, P., 1987. *Industry and Ideology*, Cambridge University Press, Cambridge.
Hoover, K. and Plant, R., 1989. *Conservative Capitalism in Britain and the United States*, Routledge, London.
Inglehart, R., 1977. *The Silent Revolution*, Princeton University Press, Princeton.
Jessop, B. *et al.*, 1988. *Thatcherism*, Polity, Cambridge.
Lewis, D. S., 1987. *Illusions of Grandeur*, Manchester University Press, Manchester.
Lipset, S. M., 1960. *Political Man*, Heinemann, London.
Lipsey, R. G., 1963. *Positive Economics*, Weidenfeld and Nicolson, London.
Minogue, K., 1985. *Alien Powers*, Weidenfeld and Nicolson, London.
Niskanen, W. A., 1988. *Reagonomics*, Oxford University Press, New York.
O'Sullivan, N., 1976. *Conservatism*, Dent, London.
_____ 1983. *Fascism*, Dent, London.
Ruggiero, G. de, 1927. *The History of European Liberalism*, Humphrey Milford, London.
Sarti, R., 1971. *Fascism and the Industrial Leadership in Italy, 1919-1940*, University of California Press, Berkeley.
Schoenberger, R. A. (ed.), 1969. *The American Right Wing*, Holt, Rinehart and Winston, New York.
Sternhell, Z., 1983. *Ni droite, ni gauche*, Editions du Seuil, Paris.
Stokes, D, 1963. Spatial models of party competition, *American Political Science Review*, Vol. 57, No. 2.
Viereck, P., 1962. *Conservatism Revisited*, Collier Books, New York.
Williams, H., 1988. *Concepts of Ideology*, Wheatsheaf Books, Brighton.
Williams, P. M., 1964. *Crisis and Compromise*, Longmans, London.

3 The Rise of 'Left–Right' Terminology: The Confusions of Social Science

Roger Eatwell, University of Bath

The first use of the terms 'left' and 'right' in the context of a specific political situation stems from revolutionary France in 1789. Subsequently, especially during the twentieth century, the terminology of 'left' and 'right' has become a universal aspect of political debate. It transcends national boundaries, offering a form of political Esperanto. However, whilst there may be few who speak Esperanto, it is still a language with formal meanings and rules. The language of left and right has emerged with no agreed forms. There are no textbooks which can be consulted to resolve problems, which is hardly surprising as major differences exist between the interpretations of Marxists, liberals and others.

As a result, most authors have found it difficult to offer precise definitions, or have not even tried. Thus the Canadian psychologist, J. A. Laponce, writes in one of only a handful of books which has sought specifically to deal with the question of using the terms 'left' and 'right': 'At no point in the following chapters do I impose my own definition, my own perception, my own 'vision' of what is left and of what is right' (Laponce, 1981, p.9). Many writers adopt an implicit definition, or seek more to assert what the left, or right are not, rather than argue systematically what the parameters of left and right are. For example, the British political scientist, Nigel Ashford (1985, p.33), has described himself as a neo-liberal Conservative, but objects strongly to being called right-wing. He adds:

> I am not a Conservative of the Right. To me, the Right is associated with hostility to social minorities, the enforcement of popular morality by the state, capital punishment, racism, support for South Africa, and xenophobic nationalism.

What exactly links these examples of right-wing politics is not made clear. The answer cannot simply be common usage, for many would see Ashford's neo-liberal commitment to individualism and *laissez-faire* economics as inherently right-wing. It could also be argued that some of his right-wing traits, most notably capital punishment, can be found in some left-wing regimes. Even xenophobic nationalism has at times featured in communist countries, especially in the Soviet Union during the Second World War, or China during the Cultural Revolution (and more generally if popular rather than official attitudes are considered).

It is not surprising, therefore, that some academics have sought to dispense with the terms 'left' and 'right' altogether. As far back as the 1950s, the American academic Edward Shils was writing of: 'The obsolete belief that all political, social and economic philosophies can be classified on the Right–Left continuum' (Shils, 1954, p.28). Over thirty years later the new right theorist, David Green, wrote: 'anyone approaching these ideas for the first time will almost certainly find it helpful to abandon altogether the habit of thinking about political philosophies as if they can be ranged along a straight line from left to right' (Green, 1987, p.2). Leonard Schapiro (1972, p.84) has even argued in his classic study of totalitarianism that:

> There are probably no two terms in the language of politics which are more imprecise and subjective in the meanings which are attached to them than 'left' and 'right', and which are more misleading in their common usage...there is no illumination to be derived from the misleading 'Left–Right' classification.

There are clearly major problems involved in using the terms 'left' and 'right' in a generic way, applying to all countries, at all times since the French Revolution. However, many of the difficulties can largely be resolved if the problem is considered within four approaches: by seeing left and right in an historical context; by considering various social science discussions; by considering whether it is possible to produce an essentialist philosophical model; and, finally, by seeing the right mainly in terms of styles of thought which have emerged as responses to challenges from the left.

The Historical Origins of 'Left' and 'Right'

France offers the necessary starting point for a historical analysis, because the terms 'right' and 'left' have their origins in revolutionary France. In 1789 a seating pattern emerged in the new National Assembly in which most of the nobility and clergy could be seen to take up positions on the right, whereas the Third Estate, which demanded a constitution and limitation of the King's power, occupied the left. This may have reflected a tendency in Christian culture to identify the right with God, with authority and tradition. More likely, it stemmed from accident, for in the Estates General before the revolution, the seating arrangements had no ideological significance (for a provocative account of revolutionary France see Schama, 1989).

Whatever the reasons for the initial physical split, the terminology of 'left' and 'right' quickly became commonplace in France. Its meaning revolved around three sets of issues: political, economic and social. It is impossible to draw a neat dividing line between these categories, and it is important to remember that one of the reasons for the appeal of the left–right spectrum is its ability to operate both as a duality and a continuum. In other words, on some issues there were shades of opinion rather than polar opposition. Nevertheless, conceiving the original split between left and right in terms of political, economic and social issues offers a helpful starting point.

In terms of political issues, the immediate post-1789 right tended to be associated with defence of the absolute monarch, whereas the left sought a representative body elected by universal and equal suffrage. It also tended to be republican rather than royalist. In economic terms, the right defended feudal relations, and government monopolies. The left tended more to defend the free market, though it could accept government regulation was necessary to protect the poor. In the social sphere, the right defended the role of the Catholic church, and more generally of authority and tradition. The extreme left tended more to be secular, even atheistic, and elevated reason and self-expression above mysticism and duty.

One problem which emerged for this left–right characterization by the late nineteenth century was that several distinct groups and movements had emerged which were considered to be right-wing. Ren Rémond has distinguished three very different elements in the French right-wing tradition: the Legitimists, or those who defended authority stemming from traditional groups; the Orleanists, or those who accepted parliamentary democracy and the idea of limited change within a liberal society represented by the emerging middle class; and the Bonapartists, or those who sought a more charismatic appeal, often appealing to lower social classes, and who were therefore not hostile to universal suffrage (Rémond, 1966). It is possible to criticize this (highly influential) triple schema, but it serves to illustrate the point about the emergence of significantly different strands within the right.

In some ways, Rémond's threefold distinction reflects a class distinction within the right. The Legitimists represented the interests of the old aristocracy and church. The Orleanists were more the new middle class, with its emphasis on liberal freedoms and constitutional rule. The Bonapartists were a more complex mixture of a threatened peasantry and an emerging working class. Behind this class division, lay important ideological distinctions. Orleanism was essentially rationalist in that it stressed individual self-interest and economic motivation. The Legitimist and Bonapartist traditions had important irrational elements in them. French philosophers like de Maistre held that the Enlightenment was premised on a central error. For them, society could not survive if it were based on concepts of contract, equality and questioning; stable social systems involved an acceptance of hierarchies and unquestioning obedience based on religious duty. The Legitimists held that the monarchy and church were vital to provide a point of reference. The Bonapartist tradition rejected a simple equation of working-class self-interest with that of the left. This tradition saw man as a political animal motivated by myths, by individuals of vision, an insight which some have seen as proto-fascist.

Further problems for the left–right spectrum emerged in the late nineteenth century, especially if the focus moves from France to Europe as a whole, or America. One difficulty concerns the tendency for the central divisions between left and right to differ between countries. In France, for example, religion remained a key factor, whereas elsewhere a more class-based polarization often emerged. The 'accident' of the Dreyfus Affair in the 1890s was an especially important factor in holding back class differences; French politics polarized around a non-economic issue. A second problem stems from the fact that the language of 'left' and 'right' was adopted more quickly in some countries than others. For example, although common in France and Germany, it was much rarer in America and Britain (thus the language of left and right is more common among historians of the first two countries than among the latter two). Different seating patterns in assemblies, and a tendency towards less overt, polarized, ideological debate are important factors explaining this difference. In America, this was compounded by the irrelevance, or low salience, of many of the issues which were central to European political development, notably the break with feudalism, and clericalism. The inherent Lockean individualism of America's development and the tendency for ethnicity and 'Americanism' to undermine class politics were also crucial factors.

In Europe the rise of class issues reflected the fact that the left was increasingly associated with socialist ideas, which involved some notable changes from the early left. For example, *laissez-faire* ideas in the late eighteenth century were radical in the sense that they threatened the existing order. By the turn of the twentieth century *laissez-faire* ideas were more accepted (especially in America and Britain). Power had moved decisively away from the landed aristocracy to a business class in many countries. At the same time, *laissez-faire* politics had become more socially conservative. They now tended to defend the interests of rising business elites against those of the peasantry and working class (and the remaining landed aristocracy). At the same time, there was an increasing tendency (heavily influenced by Marxism) to operate a reductionist view of the right, seeing it as any form of ideology which defended capitalist (or pre-capitalist) relations.

There were also important developments concerning socialism and the state. In the late eighteenth century the right had defended the strong state. By the turn of the twentieth century it was the left which was increasingly becoming fascinated by the possibilities of the strong state, though there were left-wing ideologies which rejected this development, notably anarchism and syndicalism. The focus was moving from constitutions and political institutions, or the general framework of economic life, towards socio-economic ends. Thus socialist defenders of the strong state saw it as necessary in the pursuit of prized goals, notably economic equality.

One problem with the growing socialist identity with the strong state was how to adapt this view to the earlier left-wing belief in universal suffrage. The dilemma was especially acute for the more radical socialists, as it was clear that the masses in Europe were still largely tied to religion, the existing institutions and nationalism. This led to a significant split within the left. One major group, typified by the Fabians in Britain or the Bernstein 'revisionists' within the German Social Democrats, held that it was possible to move gradually towards socialism. There would thus be an evolution (Darwinian metaphors were powerful on the left as well as the right) of public opinion in the direction of 'progress'. However, other groups on the radical left, most notably Lenin and the Bolsheviks, held that even after the revolution some form of interim regime would be necessary whilst 'false consciousness' was eradicated. Lenin did not reject universal suffrage on principle, as the old right had done, and Marx had talked of the 'withering away of the state' under communism.

Nevertheless, the Soviet Union in practice marked the reincarnation of many former right-wing principles in the guise of the left!

There was also an increasing equation from the late nineteenth century of the left with internationalism, and to a lesser extent pacifism. During the 1790s the left in France had been the staunchest advocates of revolutionary wars; the left also wished to continue the war with Germany after the humiliations of 1870. On the other hand, there had been an element of internationalism in the Catholicism of the right, and inter-linkages between royal dynasties. During the nineteenth century Marx in particular preached the cause of internationalism, of a working class united across boundaries by capitalist exploitation. Prior to the First World War, many socialists had advocated an international general strike of the working class in the event of war. Right-wing capitalist and nationalist elites were thus to be frustrated in their designs. However, when the call to the colours came, nationalism proved a far more powerful myth than international brotherhood.

During the early twentieth century the concept of mythology became increasingly central to activist political thought. In part, this reflected a growing psychological dimension, a challenge to many of the ideas central to the Enlightenment. Freud's theory of the irrational was a powerful counter to the rationalism of the left. Le Bon's classic work on the crowd as the amorphous, easily swayed mass, pointed to the potential of mass movements based on the appeal of propaganda, rather than Marx's laws of history. The French theorist, Sorel, in particular developed the idea of man motivated by (unfalsifiable) myths (Jennings, 1984). Sorel is an especially important theorist in terms of the left–right spectrum, for both Lenin and Mussolini acknowledged their debt to him! In Lenin's case, his thought reinforced the commitment to elite, revolutionary politics, seeing the masses as too easily swayed in conflicting directions. On the other hand, Mussolini during the First World War came to see nationalism as the great myth which could sway the masses, and provide the basis for national development (Gregor, 1979). Thus fascism, which is conventionally seen as right-wing, began with a view that politics could be founded on mass activism, a view which previously had tended to be seen as left-wing.

If communism posed problems for the left–right spectrum, fascism proved even more troublesome. This was not simply a question of its activism, and belief that the individual and nation could transcend deleterious influences such as as social division, or religion, by a 'Triumph of the Will' (to use the title of Leni Riefenstahl's classic film of the 1934 Nuremberg rally). The problem can be seen even more clearly by considering fascism's economic policies. In spite of the differences between the various forms of fascism, there was a general acceptance of private property as the basis of society, but such ownership was always to be subject to the ultimate needs of the nation rather than the individual. Fascist governments, therefore tended to be highly interventionist, adopting policies which could be seen as proto-Keynesian, or anticipating much of what was to be found in post-1945 social democratic thought. Indeed, commentators such as Zeev Sternhell have used this type of argument to see fascism as a political doctrine of the 'revolutionary centre' — revolutionary in the sense that parliamentary democracy was rejected, but centrist in its attempt to find a middle way between capitalism and communism (Sternhell, 1983).

The Social Science Development of 'Left–Right' Terminology

The totalitarian model of communism and fascism, developed especially by American social scientists in the 1950s, seems to pose further problems for the creation of a generic left–right spectrum. The model held that there were fundamental similarities rather than polar opposition between Nazi Germany and Stalinist Russia. However, it is possible to criticize this approach (which was heavily influenced by the Cold War) on several grounds. Two seem especially important in this context. Firstly, there were notable differences between the systems, for example attitudes to private property, nationalism and race. Secondly, the totalitarian model confuses means with ends; both forms of regime had secret police and extensive propaganda networks, but the Nazi goal of the *Volksgemeinschaft* differed significantly from 'socialism in one country', let alone Marxism viewed as a doctrine of egalitarian world revolution!

The totalitarian model serves as a particularly useful introduction to social science approaches to the terms 'left' and 'right', because it illustrates a central point about the social science literature. Stalinist Russia and Nazi Germany could be seen as ideological regimes *par excellence*. However, the totalitarian models pay little attention to ideology *per se*. Thus the classic Brzezinski and Friedrich six-point model is essentially a heuristic outline of a *regime* rather than an ideology (Friedrich and Brzezinski, 1956). This tendency to pay little or no serious attention to the content of ideology is characteristic of all social science approaches to the left–right spectrum. This in turn has helped encourage a neglect of the terms 'left' and 'right' at the ideological level.

The point can be seen clearly by considering the classic political sociology approach to the left–right spectrum, which focuses on class allegiance or interests. The most influential formulation of this approach has come from S. M. Lipset (1960, p.129), who has argued that:

> If we look at the supporters of the three major positions in most democratic countries, we find a fairly logical relationship between ideology and social base. The Socialist left derives its strength from manual workers and the poorer rural strata; the conservative right is backed by the rather well-to-do elements...and those segments of the less privileged groups who have remained involved in traditionalist institutions, particularly the Church. The democratic centre is backed by the middle classes, especially small businessmen, white-collar workers, and the anticlerical sections of the professional classes.

However, there are major problems for this formulation. In terms of interests, it is far from clear that the working class (if it is possible to talk in such sweeping terms) gains from left-wing politics. Even at the level of simple sociological support, this approach has problems.

These can be seen by first considering Britain, where class has been an important factor in voting behaviour, but where there have been significant

'deviant' minorities. In particular, on average one-third of the working class
has voted Conservative ever since the franchise was extended in the nineteenth
century; recently, Conservative working-class voting has even been growing.
In America there have always been strong regional patterns of voting which
tended to cut across class lines, especially in the post-reconstruction south.
Moreover, in the 1980s the Republicans have made important further inroads
into the blue-collar vote. In France until recently, attitudes to the church have
often been more important factors than class. In the 1950s the communists
gained some of their best results in the peasant, anti-clerical, departments of
Corrèze and Creuse. In the 1980s the Front National gained, if anything,
more votes from the working class than the middle class.

Fascism poses a particular problem for Lipset; he sees it as a movement of
the 'extremist centre', holding that at times of economic crisis the middle
classes can turn to extremism. This glosses over the evidence that nationalism
had a strong appeal among sections of the working class, and the fact that there
are still major arguments about the class-chronological basis of fascism (e.g.,
Larsen *et al.*, 1980). Moreover, a simple sociological view of the left–right
spectrum ignores more subtle questions about the rise and fall of parties. For
example, there is evidence that the neo-Nazi German NPD in the late 1960s
attracted many votes from 'pressured' sections of the middle class; but during
the more serious economic crisis after 1973 the NPD attracted only minimal
support; and its revival in the 1989 Hesse elections cannot simply be analysed
in terms of a 'pressured' centre. A class-reductionist approach to the left–right
spectrum therefore not only plays down ideology, but is often historically
inaccurate, and has problems explaining dynamic change.

This simple class-reductionist model has become increasingly untenable in
view of the evidence emerging from the growth in academic opinion polling
that has taken place since the 1950s. In terms of the left–right spectrum, this
literature has investigated three main questions: (a) do people place
themselves on a left–right spectrum? (b) What do they understand by these
terms? And (c), to what extent can voting be considered within such
ideological terms?

Butler and Stokes in their study of the 1960s British electorate found only
a quarter of respondents placed themselves on a left–right spectrum (Butler
and Stokes, 1969, p.250). By 1985 82 per cent of British voters were willing to
locate themselves on a spectrum, in part a reflection of the growing use of such
terms among journalists and politicians (Heald and Wybrow, 1986, p.21).
However, most voters seem unable to offer any serious analytical definition
of the terms. For example, when Butler and Stokes (1969, p.259) interviewed
a Sheffield lubricating engineer they were given the following explanation of
the left-right continuum:

> Well, when I was in the Army you had to put your right foot forward, but in
> fighting you lead with your left. So I always think that the Tories are the right
> party for me and that the Labour Party are fighters. I know that this isn't right
> really, but I can't explain it properly, and it does for me.

Not surprisingly, they deduced that ideology was rarely a major factor influencing voting behaviour, arguing the socialization, especially the family and class, were more important factors. More recent studies have shown that candidate personality, and especially issues have become increasingly important, but these cannot necessarily be analysed in clear ideological terms (for a rare example of the argument that ideology can be important see Scarbrough, 1984). Self-assessment on the left–right scale poses particular problems in terms of ideological analysis. One major problem is that respondents who do not understand the terms may place themselves in the centre, feeling it is the 'safest' answer. Another problem can be seen by considering the British people who in the 1980s have self-identified as 'far right' (over 5 per cent). Does this mean that they saw themselves as fascists, racists, libertarians or what? Was the self-ascription of 'far right' a reflection of seriously-held beliefs, or simply a reflection of alienation from conventional politics?

These studies replicate the conclusions of, and illustrate the problems with, much American political sociology. For example, Campbell's classic study argued that the concepts of left and right provided a useful abstraction for elites, but claimed that most voters were influenced more by socialization than ideology: 'We have suggested that the types of attitude structure presumed in ideological accounts of political behaviour are not very prevalent in the American electorate' (Campbell *et al.*, 1960, p.215). Writing shortly afterwards, Converse found that less than a fifth of Americans understood the 'liberal-conservative' dichotomy (Converse, 1964). Like Butler and Stokes in Britain, Converse also found that people's views appeared to change frequently, and could be internally contradictory.

In France there has historically been a greater recognition of, and self-identification on the left–right scale, with 90 per cent in the 1960s placing themselves on the spectrum (Deutsch *et al.*, 1966, pp.13–14). This may have been a reflection of the centrality of such terminology to the French political tradition, though the transitory nature of many French parties may also have encouraged spatial rather than partisan identification. On the other hand, Italians seem to perceive politics in terms of 'system' and 'anti-system' parties as much as left and right (Sani, 1976). Thus the communists could be placed close to the fascists as both are outside the government. Banfield, in his study of 'amoral familism' notes how the local organizer of a southern Italian monarchists party joined the communists when he was not paid for some months, rejoining the monarchists when subsequently paid (Banfield, 1971).

These surveys provide interesting information about the extent to which the terms 'left' and 'right' (or 'liberal' and 'conservative') have an objective sociological reality, but they do nothing to resolve the definition of the terms 'left' and 'right' in philosophical terms (for example, why is fascism usually rated as 'extreme right'?). There are also serious methodological problems relating to these surveys. This is not simply a question of the basic problems which afflict opinion polling. There is also the question of dynamic interpretation. For example, the classic Nie *et al.* study of America argues that in the 1950s there was little relation between 'liberal' and 'conservative' positions over domestic and foreign issues, but by the 1960s there was a growing congruence (Nie *et al.*, 1976, p.130). This could reflect the emergence of an ideologically more sophisticated electorate, one in which policy rather than socialization was becoming the major influence. But who is to say what is a logical set of views? Such a view assumes, for example, that a supporter of welfare will support black civil rights, but there is no necessary connection. Gallup for many years has asked Americans to self-identify on a 'liberal–conservative' scale; this has shown a decline in the percentage of liberals. However, this could simply show that the meaning of the word has changed; in the early 1940s 'liberal' was associated with the recovery of the New Deal; by the 1960s it had links with drugs, permissiveness, even lack of patriotism.

This point about the changing meaning of key terms is highlighted by the 'post-industrial' literature, an approach which also further undermines the simple class-reductionist position. For example, Inglehart sees the working class as a bastion of contemporary conservativism in the sense that it's still mainly tied to the pursuit of material goals (Inglehart, 1977). The radical groups in society are seen as the highly educated, often public or service sector workers, who are committed to 'post-material' values (and who form the archetypal ecology activists). This approach pays more serious attention to ideology in the sense that it argues there is a split between new and old left–right issues. Inglehart and Rabier (1986, p.479), using Eurobarometer self-assessment surveys of the left–right spectrum, show that best predictors of whether someone is 'left-' or 'right'-wing are the 'New Politics' issues:

> For Western publics, the crucial issues that distinguish most decisively between Left and Right no longer are the old familiar issues of class conflict, but New Politics issues concerning the quality of life, the role of women, and the implications of recent technological developments concerning the environment and the nature of modern warfare.

The 'old' and 'new' left–right axes do not necessarily correspond; in particular, the old socialist parties have not been very interested in ecological issues (though the rise of ecology parties has forced them to respond).

The post-industrial argument is an interesting one, but it has a series of flaws. Its basic approach confuses structural change with necessary value change. In particular, the move to a tertiary, service based economy is perfectly compatible with profit maximization, managerial hierarchies, etc. For example, does the growth of the banking sector, or the provision of fast-food outlets, really herald the onset of 'post-industrial' society in any meaningful sense? In terms of the left–right spectrum, the post-industrial debate highlights interesting points about how perceptions of the spectrum, and in particular how issues change. However, the relationship between these factors is complex, and some argue that self-placement on a left–right spectrum still affords the best predictor of voting (van Deth and Geurts, 1989). The most serious problem from the point of view of this book stems from the fact that as the approach is sociological, there is no attempt to consider why a particular set of issues is seen as left- rather than right-wing. For example, historically ecology issues have often featured on the right. The left often admired industrial society (if not its organization and income distribution) as the producer of an abundance of goods, which could solve the problem of poverty. The defence of rural, small-town life or criticism of the ravages of individualist-capitalist society, tended to be conservative, or reactionary responses in the nineteenth century. It is true that in the 1970s and 1980s ecology movements attracted disillusioned left-wingers, but they also include others of very different persuasion, as can be seen in West Germany by the split between the 'Red Greens' and 'Green Greens' (and neo-fascist attempts to enter green movements). So why is ecology seen as a left-wing issue? Or why is abortion seen as left-wing? (see the discussion in Chapter 2).

This tendency to ignore philosophical questions is very strong in the psychological literature relevant to the left–right spectrum. The point applies especially to the classic Berkeley team study of the 'Fascism Scale' (Adorno *et al.*, 1950). This approach was heavily influenced by Freud and was a study of personality rather than ideology (hence the approach is often known as 'the authoritarian personality'). For example, the 'F' scale sought to measure traits such as a tendency to be superstitious, or to be excessively concerned with sexual activities! Such traits may feature in 'pop' psychology analyses of Hitler, but they find little or no place in the more sophisticated analyses of fascist ideology (e.g., Lane and Rupp, 1978; O'Sullivan, 1983, etc.).

The 'F' scale has been criticized by many psychologists. In the main these have concerned methodological issues, relating to questionnaire design, etc. (for example, the charge that the scale tested acquiescence as much as authoritarianism). Predictably, this has meant that subsequent work has been obsessed with questions of methodology. Wilson, for example, produced a 'balanced' fifty-point single or double word test of 'conservatism', which simply required 'Yes' or '?' or 'No' answers, thus avoiding charges of leading phraseology, or one-directional questioning (Wilson, 1973, p.52). However, the test itself is open to methodological objection. A median score is obtained by someone with no opinion on any issue (and who answers honestly as a 'don't know'). Opposition to immigration, or strip-tease shows, is seen as conservative, though libertarians tend to support both. And so on. The point about immigration/strip-tease reflects the fact that the focus is again psychology rather than ideology, let alone party politics. Nevertheless, this does not negate the charge that the term 'conservatism' is used in an ideologically confused manner. Thus 'conservatism' is defined as a 'sense of resistance to change and the tendency to prefer safe, traditional and conventional institutions and behaviour' (Wilson, 1973, p.5). Yet on the following page Wilson claims that 'In the US the Ku Klux Klan and the John Birch Society are widely recognised as conservative organisations, as are the National Front, the Gideons and Monday Club in Britain'. Associating groups such as the Ku-Klux-Klan, or National Front, with 'conventional institutions and behaviour' seems nothing short of bizarre! It is clear that Wilson, like many psychologists, is especially concerned with deviant behaviour, but his approach does not sufficiently distinguish between different types of conservative or right-wing thought.

Eysenck, in a famous study undertaken in the 1950s, put forward an argument which placed psychological arguments within the spatial framework implied by the left–right continuum. He argued that political behaviour could be conceptualized in two dimensions: radicalism versus conservatism, which basically corresponded to left and right; and tender-minded versus tough-mindedness, which corresponded more to psychological concepts of introversion and extroversion (Eysenck, 1954). He argued that the best indicators of the radicalism and conservatism poles were, on the one hand, support for internationalism and the abolition of private property, and on the other, support for harsh punishments, and hostility to public ownership. This approach has been heavily criticized by psychologists on various grounds: in particular, there have been accusations of distortion and suppression of evidence, and doubts about whether the tender–tough minded axis is helpful. However, others have used the basic approach to argue that many of the problems surrounding the left–right spectrum can be resolved by employing an x and a y axis, rather than a single linear approach.

This raises the general question of the helpfulness of graphical representations of left and right. Some surveys have asked respondents to place parties, and more rarely ideologies, on the spectrum. In Britain this typically produces the results shown in Figure 1. This clearly provides important information in terms of perceptions, but in terms of ideological analysis it has little relevance. For such a spectrum to have ideological meaning it is necessary to know what factor is being measured across the scale.

Communism   Socialism   Liberalism   Conservatism   Fascism

Figure 1

The most common approach in Anglo-American social science stems from the work of Anthony Downs, who sees the key to the left–right spectrum as the level of government intervention in the economy (Downs, 1957, esp. p.116). A multi-country survey by by the British academic Ian Budge (Budge *et al.*, 1987, pp.394–5) similarly holds:

> the meaning of 'Left–Right' is definite and reasonably constant throughout the analyses. Principally it refers to classic economic policy conflicts — government regulation of the economy through direct controls or takeover...as opposed to free enterprise, individual freedom, incentives, and economic orthodoxy.

This works at the simple level of distinguishing most Conservative and Republican representatives as more right-wing than those of Labour or the Democrats. However, in broader ideological terms it has a series of major problems. For example, fascism ceases to be an extreme right-wing ideology on this approach. This corresponds with some recent historical interpretations, and it may be the problem can be resolved simply by moving fascism nearer the centre (e.g., Lewis, 1987; Sternhell, 1983). But this ignores further problems. If government intervention is the key, then libertarians are the most extreme right-wingers; this neither corresponds to common usage, nor to what have historically been seen as key elements on the right (the more collectivist themes of traditionalism, authoritarianism, etc.). There is also something strange about conceiving fascism as more centrist, when it totally rejects the liberal democratic system which is accepted by what are normally seen as centrist parties/ideologies.

This has encouraged the view that the key to the left–right spectrum in spatial terms may lie in using an *x* and a *y* axis. Such representations allow more than one philosophical principle (including non-economic ones) to be measured, and has been defended by Laponce (1981, p.8) in the following terms:

> The horizontal left/right classification, born from a revolution that sought to deny the very notion of verticality, became a mirror where up and down became reflected...Indeed, the omnipresence of the vertical in our political perceptions is such that we can make it a law of politics that we are unable to explain sociopolitical phenomena without recourse to the up and down dimension.

Eysenck has advocated using an authoritarian–democratic versus a radical–conservative set of axes (Eysenck, 1954, p.110f.). Brittan suggests that three sets are particularly helpful: (a) radicalism–orthodoxy versus egalitarianism–elitism; (b) liberalism–authoritarianism versus egalitarianism–elitism; and (c) liberalism–authoritarianism versus radicalism–orthodoxy (Brittan, 1968, pp.88–9); Figure 2 is adapted from this approach. It is not necessary to draw up all the variations to see the strengths and weaknesses of this approach. The main strength is that it underlines that there are significant differences between ideologies such as conservatism and fascism. However, there are a variety of major objections.

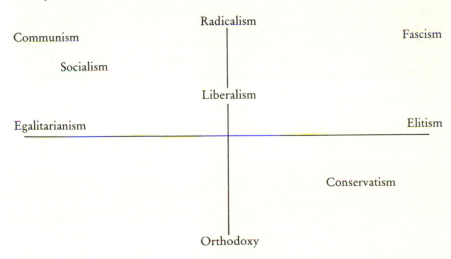

Figure 2

Firstly, when dealing with ideologies it is important to ask how the 'ideal type' is conceived. Should communism be seen as highly egalitarian, and favouring the withering away of the state, in the way which many Western Marxists view their ideal? Or should a model be based more on Soviet experience, noting new elites and state power? Is fascism a racist ideology? It is important to remember that its Italian variant had no significant indigenous racist aspect. Similarly, common defining terms such as 'leader-principle', and 'nationalism' have to be understood in different lights in the Italian and German fascist context. Even more common Western ideologies such as conservatism and liberalism pose problems. Is a liberal ideal-type definition to concentrate solely on ideas of individualism and *laissez-faire*, or should it try to encompass the important concept of 'positive liberty' developed by Green, Hobhouse and others? And the splits between contemporary American conservatives illustrate the problems with this ideal type: is the conservative a social authoritarian, an individualist libertarian — or what?

A second problem stems from the fact that the x axis is clearly the dominant one. This point can be seen by revolving the above diagram through 90 degrees in an anti-clockwise fashion. Communism and socialism stay on the left, but fascism moves from the right to the left! In mathematical terms the (graphical) relationship remains unchanged, but as the point is to produce a spectrum which corresponds as closely as possible to common usage, the egalitarianism–elitism scale is clearly the key. This would not matter if there were no problems in constructing this (or alternative) scales. However, the key terms used by Eysenck and Brittan (and others) tend to be vague and open to very different interpretations, or not to be true opposites. For example, does not egalitarianism and elitism confuse economic, social and political factors? Fascism was elitist in the political sense, especially its advocacy of the leader principle. However, there was a strong element of economic and social egalitarianism in fascism: it supported welfare programmes, public works, and was hostile to conspicuous consumption.

Some have argued that the key to the spectrum in spatial terms is to conceive it in terms of a closed, or nearly closed circle (e.g., Rossiter, 1962, p.11); this is represented in Figure 3. This approach has much to do with totalitarianism.

Communism   Fascism

Figure 3

Thus, spatially, communism and fascism could be close together in one direction, but far apart in another. This is an improvement on the totalitarian model in the sense that it recognizes major differences. However, there are serious objections to using the circle model. Firstly (as with x and y axis models), it does not correspond to common usage; people in surveys, if they perceive the spectrum, tend to see it in straight unilinear terms. This would not matter in terms of ideological analysis if the circle model provided a clear picture of the similarities and differences between communism and fascism, or more generally between left and right. In practice, the circle model is nothing more than a simple mental picture; what could be measured around the circumference is undefined. If an attempt were made to offer scales in terms of principles such as 'egalitarianism', elitism' — or whatever — a similar problem would emerge to the one which afflicted the x and y axis model. Namely, these are complex terms, and need more substantial discussion.

A three-dimensional model could conceive left and right in terms of a hot air balloon (a metaphor which should appeal to those who do not see ideology as a very important political factor). The balloon model can also be conceived as having two states: inflated and deflated. Inflated represents the 'high' politics of ideological debate, with clearly defined position; deflated reflects the jumble of popular attitudes. However, before social scientists with a bent for spatial representation become too excited, it is important to reject the model by reiterating the recurring problem with social science approaches: namely, their failure to take ideology seriously, and especially the tendency to ignore, or have a simplistic view of the key terms which might be used to distinguish between left and right.

References

Adorno, T.W. *et al.*, 1950. *The Authoritarian Personality*, Harper and Row, New York.

Ashford, N., 1985. The bankruptcy of collectivism, in A. Seldon (ed.), *The New Right Englightenment*, Economic and Literary Books, Sevenoaks.

Banfield, E., 1971. Amoral familism in southern Italy, in M. Dogan and R. Rose (eds), *European Politics*, Macmillan, London.

Brittan, S., 1968. *Left and Right: the Bogus Dilemma*, Weidenfeld and Nicolson, London.

Budge, I. *et al.*, 1987. *Ideology, Strategy and Party Change: Spatial Analyses of Post-war Programmes in Nineteen Democracies*, Cambridge University Press, Cambridge.

Butler, D., and Stokes, D., 1969. *Political Change in Britain*, Macmillan, London.

Campbell, A. *et al.*, 1960. *The American Voter*, John Wiley and Sons, New York.

Converse, P., 1964. The nature of belief systems in politics in D. E. Apter (ed.), *Ideology and Discontent*, Free Press, Glencoe.

Deth, J.W. van and Geurts, A. T. M., 1989. Value orientation, left–right placement and voting, *European Journal of Political Research*, Vol. 17, No. 1.

Deutsch, E. *et al.*, 1966. *Les familles politiques aujourd'hui en France*, Les Editions de Minuit, Paris.

Downs, A., 1957. *An Economic Theory of Democracy*, Harper and Row, New York.

Eysenck, H., 1954. *The Psychology of Politics*, Routledge, Kegan Paul, London.

Friedrich, C. J. and Brzezinski, Z. K., 1956. *Totalitarian Dictatorship and Autocracy*, Harvard University Press, Cambridge, Mass.

Green, D., 1987. *The New Right*, Wheatsheaf, Brighton.

Gregor, A. J., 1979. *Italian Fascism and Development Dictatorship*, Princeton University Press, Princeton.

Heald, G., and Wybrow, R. J., 1986. *The Gallup Survey of Britain*, Croom Helm, London.

Inglehart, R., 1977. *The Silent Revolution*, Princeton University Press, Princeton.

Inglehart, R. and Rabier, J. R., 1986. Political realignment in advanced industrial society, *Government and Opposition*, Vol. 21, No. 4.

Jennings, J. R., 1984. *Georges Sorel*, Macmillan, London.

Lane, B. and Rupp, L. (eds), 1978. *Nazi Ideology before 1933*, Manchester University Press, Manchester.

Laponce, J. A., 1981. *Left and Right: the Topography of Political Perception*, University of Toronto Press, Toronto.

Larsen, S. *et al.*, 1980. *Who Were the Fascists?*, Universitetsforlaget, Bergen.

Lewis, D. S., 1987. *Illusions of Grandeur*, Manchester University Press, Manchester.

Lipset, S. M., 1960. *Political Man*, Heinemann, London.

Nie, N. H. *et al.*, 1976. *The Changing American Voter*, Harvard University Press, Cambridge, Mass.

O'Sullivan, N., 1983. *Fascism*, Dent, London.

Rémond, R., 1966. *The Right Wing in France*, University of Pennsylvania Press, Philadelphia.

Rossiter, C., 1962. *Conservatism in America*, Vintage Books, New York.

Sani, G., 1976. Mass constraints on political realignments: perceptions of anti-system parties in Italy, *British Journal of Political Science*, Vol. 6, No. 1.

Scarbrough, E., 1984. *Political Ideology and Voting*, Clarendon Press, Oxford.

Schama, S., 1989. *Citizens: A Chronicle of the French Revolution*, Knopf, New York.

Schapiro, L., 1972. *Totalitarianism*, Macmillan, London.

Shils, E., 1954, Authoritarianism: 'Right' and 'Left', in R. Christie and M. Jahoda (eds), *The Authoritarian Personality*, Free Press, Glencoe.

Sternhell, Z., 1983. *Ni droite, ni gauche*, Editions du Seuil, Paris.

Wilson, G., 1973. *The Psychology of Conservatism*, Academic Press, London.

4 The Nature of the Right, 1: Is There an 'Essentialist' Philosophical Core?

Roger Eatwell, University of Bath.

Some academics have tried to create a definition of the right by offering a list of key philosophical principles. William Pickles gives the following definition of left and right (Pickles, 1964, p.382):

Left
(a) a belief in a greater rather than lesser degree of educability of the human race
(b) greater faith in the power of institutions to influence human conduct
(c) the recognition of many social rights and social needs

Right
(a) the acceptance of the importance of established authority in controlling irrational individuals
(b) the acceptance of only evolved institutions

(c) an emphasis on individual rather than social rights and needs except where they relate to bodies like the church or state

Roger Scruton, a key member of the British new right, gives the following definition of the right (Scruton, 1982, p.408):

(i)   conservative and perhaps authoritarian doctrines concerning the nature of civil society, with emphasis on custom, tradition and allegiance as social bonds;
(ii)   doctrines of political obligation framed in terms of obedience, legitimacy and piety rather than contract, consent and justice;
(iii)   reluctance to countenance too great a divorce between law and morality — i.e. between enactments of the state, and the sentiments of society, hence a resistance to liberalizing reforms in the law;
(iv)   cultural conservatism;
(v)   respect for the hereditary principle and prescriptive rights;
(vi)   belief in private property, not as a natural right, but as an indispensable part of the condition of society;
(vii)   belief in elementary freedoms, and in the irreplaceable value of the individual as against the collective;
(viii) belief in free enterprise and a capitalist economy, as the only mode of production compatible with human freedom, and suited to the temporary nature of human aspirations;

(ix)   varying degrees of belief in human imperfectibility and original sin.

These definitions pose a variety of problems. Firstly, they tend to gloss over the fact that some of the key terms are vague. What are 'elementary freedoms'? Freedom of speech or religion? The freedom not to be taxed heavily? Or the freedom not to starve? Other aspects seem contradictory. Is there not a tension between a commitment to authority and tradition, and a belief in individualism and the free market? The concept of 'balance' may help resolve the problem for some right-wing ideologies, but there have been ideologies, which are normally seen as right-wing, that do not stress, or even reject, the concept of balance. Finally, do lists such as Pickles's and Scruton's clearly distinguish major ideologies as left or right? Thus fascism might be thought to be on the left in terms of (c) 'the recognition of many social rights and social needs', since it was concerned with group rights over individual rights. Libertarian or *laissez-faire* new-righters would also appear to be on the left in terms of (a) 'a belief in a greater rather than lesser degree of educability of the human race'. In particular, new righters of this type accept neo-classical economic theory's view of rational economic man. The claim that the right believes in the 'value of the individual as against the collective' also seem problematic. Even if fascism is excluded, there remain right-wing ideologies which stress the collective, especially traditionalist appeals based on the community of church or nation. On the other hand, some on the left have argued that the individual can only truly be fulfilled under socialism (e.g., Lukes, 1973).

Towards an 'Essentialist' Definition?

These arguments point to a need highlighted in the previous chapter. Namely, the principles which have commonly been used as keys to the left–right spectrum must be seen as ambiguous and often contested concepts. Each could warrant chapters or books in their own right, but it is possible to illustrate briefly the main problems relating to them by grouping approaches under seven broad headings. Such a list is not meant to imply that there are no other relevant concepts, or that there is always a neat division between those discussed. However, the approach serves to illustrate the philosophical difficulties in seeking a key word, or essentialist, definition of the right.

(Note: the focus is on the left–right spectrum, not more general philosophical questions, for example how egalitarianism or elitism might be *justified*.)

Change.

It is tempting to think that the left–right dilemma can be solved in terms of attitudes to change. The left at the time of the French Revolution wanted a change from the *ancien régime*; socialists and communists subsequently wanted a change from the capitalist system. Thus the French political scientist

Maurice Duverger has written: 'Right and Left are thus defined by their aims: to preserve the existing order, or to replace it' (Duverger, 1966, p.142). The American political scientists Lipset and Raab have argued: 'It is the axis of preservatism which most essentially and invariably distinguishes "Left Wing" from "Right Wing"' (Lipset and Raab, 1971, p.20). The point is put somewhat differently by the Canadian psychologist J. A. Laponce (1981, p.5):

> The polarity of left and right has more to do with hierarchies, including the divine one, than it has to do with capitalism and communism: to rebel against or question the god, the prince, the chairman is of the left; to support them is of the right.

Using this distinction, *laissez-faire* ideas would have to be seen as left-wing in late eighteenth-century France, but right-wing in the late twentieth century. Fascism would also need to be classed as left-wing in the sense that it totally rejected liberal democracy, and brutally suppressed it where it came to power. The Labour party in Britain fought the 1979 general election on a policy of minimal change; it would therefore have to be termed right-wing. On the other hand, Margaret Thatcher's radical promises to break with the post-war consensus would have made the Conservatives left-wing. And how would someone advocating market-oriented change in the Soviet Union be viewed: as left-wing?

A Marxist might argue that fascism, or Thatcherism, were right-wing because they did not involve any real change from the capitalist system; indeed, they propped up a failing capitalism! The Soviet example would present no problem in the sense that such an advocate of market economics would be seen as a right-wing defender of 'reaction'. The *laissez-faire* problem might be resolved by claiming that the terms 'left' and 'right' only have meaning in post-feudal societies. However, such an analysis makes capitalism, or property the key to the left–right spectrum rather than change: and this involves a series of fundamental errors.

Capitalism/Private Property

The defence of capitalism and private property have competed with change as one of the most popular concepts used to analyze the left–right spectrum (see Chapter 2 for a more detailed discussion of Marxism and the right, and Chapter 3 for a discussion of the problems involved in using intervention in the economy, a common approach among social scientists). At first sight, there seems to be something in the assertion that the left opposes private property as the basis of society, whereas the right supports it.

It is important to stress at the outset that support for capitalism is not the same as support for private property. And opposition to private property does not mean that property relations can be ignored; it is hard to imagine anything other than the most primitive society lacking rules as to the use of property (what if someone else wants your bed tonight?) There is a general tendency, not only among Marxists, to use the term 'capitalist' in an extremely vague way. This involves confusing attitudes to property, profit maximization, and aspects of social structure (especially the relationship between who benefits from the structure and who controls it). There is also a tendency to fail to make a clear analytical distinction between private and common property. These points can be seen more clearly in specific examples. Conservatives of the anti-material progress type like the American Irving Babbitt, or the British novelist D. H. Lawrence, were opposed to the socially disruptive effects of *laissez-faire* capitalism rather than property. There were similar attacks on the socially divisive and alienating aspects of capitalism by the American slavery apologists John Calhoun and George Fitzhugh, or by the American poet Ezra Pound. In Germany there has been an especially important tradition of romantic eco-conservatism, which is highly critical of capitalism (Bramwell, 1989; Eppler, 1975). But none were opposed to private property *per se*. And some of capitalism's best known examples of rapacious spoliation occur in relation to common rather than private property. Would the ozone layer have suffered such depletions if it had owners?

This might indicate that private property, rather than capitalism, is the key to the right. Certainly, it is possible to read *The Communist Manifesto* as stating that the abolition of property is the key to communism. However, whilst it is true that support for private property is deeply rooted in ideas of the right, property is seen differently by its various defenders. Private property is almost sacred to conservatives: the accumulation of property, and its passing down through the family are seen as natural developments, vital to social stability. Property is sometimes even seen within a tradition dating from Roman times — and still strong among peasant communities. This views property as an extension of the human body, rather than as a reflection of acquisitiveness, or greed. However, property is not sacrosanct to the conservative in the sense of being immune from interference by the state. As Scruton (1980, p.96) argues:

> A citizens's allegiance requires fixed expectations, a settled idea of his own and others' material status, and a sense that he is not the victim of uncontrollable forces that might at any moment plunge him into destitution or raise him to uncontrollable wealth. In so far as that sense is integral to the authority of the state, then it becomes part of the the the responsibility of the state to settle and uphold the common currency and all the material expectations that are associated with it. But, as conservatives until recently have always realized, this argues not for a free market but for something like its opposite.

For liberals, private property is the basis of society in the sense that it both helps guarantee freedom, and serves as the spur to economic efficiency. For populists property is the reflection of rootedness — the links between man and the soil. Fascist theory had similarities to this, and challenged the implications of the capitalist aphorism, 'what is good for General Motors is good for America'. It believed in a possible disjunction between individual or corporate interest, and the national interest. It could therefore be necessary for the state to control business, though the basic commitment to private property was never challenged.

This returns the discussion to the Marxist view of the right as a defence of capitalism, a view which has even influenced non-Marxists. The argument raises wide-ranging debates about false consciousness, but three points seem central here. First, emphasis on economic issues forces crude Marxism into reductionism when faced with issues such as abortion, or law and order. Secondly, if attitudes to property are the sole, or main criterion, a straight line left–right spectrum produces a picture which puts liberals (in the European sense) to the right of both conservatism and fascism: this stems from the fact that liberals' support of private property is less qualified! Such a conclusion seems difficult to accept and raises a third point. Namely, an economic definition helps divert attention from other potential left–right key concepts, such as authority. Many would argue that there is a strong element of authoritarianism on the left, especially in the Leninist idea of the 'vanguard party' and 'dictatorship of the proletariat' (i.e. the party knows best, and can do with you as it will during some undefined 'transition to communism' phase). Thus focusing on economic issues has been politically useful to the left (though arguably less so today in view of the failure of left–wing economies)

Authority/Authoritarianism

The point about Leninism illustrates a difficulty for those who claim that the right holds a commitment to the need for authority in society, or to authoritarian forms of government, whereas the left is more democratic and participatory. Nevertheless, many see authority, or authoritarianism, as a central aspect of much of the right. Robert Nisbet, an American academic, has written: 'Authority is, along with property, one of the two central concepts in conservative philosophy' (Nisbet, 1986, p.34). And Scruton has written that: 'It is through an ideal of authority that the conservative experiences the political world' (Scruton, 1980, p.19).

Nisbet and Scruton are leading students of conservatism, and there is no reason to challenge their view that such principles have been central to much right-wing thought, but there are serious difficulties if either authority or authoritarianism are seen as the measure of the left–right spectrum. First, all political systems tend to have some form of ultimate source of authority, or legitimation; in communist states it is usually Marxism–Leninism. Secondly, whilst many on the right have stressed the need for authority in society, the source of this authority can differ significantly: it can be seen as stemming from God, monarch, the family, tradition, and so on. More problematically, the form of this authority can differ dramatically. When the new right traditionalists talk of the continued importance of family, or religion, they revive arguments which can be traced back to the critics of the Enlightenment. In particular, they challenge the Enlightenment's belief that man can be remade more perfect, that human happiness can be increased through a life of political debate and questioning. However, unlike many nineteenth-century critics of the Enlightenment, the majority of new right traditionalists accept the liberal democratic state (though see Huntington, 1975; Scruton, 1988, p.12). This is very different to the use of the term 'authoritarian' in connection with right-wing regimes, such as General Franco's Spain (a classic book on 'authoritarian politics' refers only to one-party systems; Huntington and Moore, 1970). It could be argued that such systems are extreme right, but if authoritarianism is the key it seems hard to see how the right can be distinguished from some forms of the left. And liberalism, which some see as a right-wing or centrist doctrine, would be on the left!

Attempting to narrow the concept of authority to one specific area also does not help. At the time of the French Revolution, the right was the defender of king and God, but many on the right have subsequently been neither monarchist nor religious. It is true that there have been especially strong links between religion and the right. Pat Robertson in the United States, or Archbishop Lefebvre in France demonstrate that religiously inspired right-wing views are still very much alive (though Robertson in the 1980s denied that he was a right-winger, a reminder of the continued pejorative sense of the term). During the 1970s and 1980s in America, an important part of the drive behind the Moral Majority came from organized religious groups (Bruce, 1988). However, the connection is not a necessary one, as can be seen by an examination of Christian socialist and other left-wing religious movements. The Church of England was once described as 'the Conservative party at prayer', but in the 1980s some of its leading members took on a distinctly left of centre hue (e.g., see Archbishop of Canterbury's Commission on Urban Priority Areas, 1985). Moreover, there are notable differences even within the right. Some forms of religious right-wing thought, for example, traditional Catholicism, have been highly authoritarian, and often statist. On the other hand, there has been a religious right which is more allied to ideas of limited politics, and individual tolerance.

Freedom/Liberty

The last point might indicate that the key to the left–right spectrum is freedom rather than authority. Thus religions which seek to impose a rigid structure of thought, and reject dissent, could be seen as right-wing; others, which encompass an open-minded attitude, as more left-wing. The right would be the enemy of political freedom, the left its defender. This formulation serves as an excellent example of how key concepts can have more than one meaning — but none resolve the problem of the left–right spectrum.

The negative conception of freedom — the idea of the individual unconstrained by rules or the state — was central to historic liberalism (Berlin, 1967). More recently, it has become central to conservative critiques of the state as Big Brother, but conservatives tend not to believe in freedom as an absolute value. They tend to stress more the need for authority, and the resulting happiness which comes from a natural, ordered society. As Scruton (1988, pp.8–9) argues:

> Conservatism, like liberalism, sees the individual as uniquely valuable...However, it differs from liberalism in two ways. First, it emphasizes the happiness, rather than the freedom of the individual...Secondly...

conservatism regards the individual, his freedom, and his happiness, as the *products* of social order.

This could provide a reason for seeing conservatism as more right-wing than liberalism, or holding that liberalism is not right-wing at all. This view would correspond with many people's perceptions (though not with the belief that the libertarian and *laissez-faire* new right is truly right-wing). However, what are usually seen as left-wing ideologies tend not to place great emphasis on negative freedom; indeed, communism could be seen as its antithesis. Some socialists have recently shown a growing interest in negative liberty in the sense that they have paid more attention to constitutional issues. The British Marxist Stuart Hall has even argued that the left needs to 'reappropriate the concept of freedom', and give it articulation within the context of a 'deepening of democratic life as a whole' (Hall, 1988, p.228). But he is clearly referring to freedom in both negative and positive terms, especially in the context of the claim that a more equal distribution of income and wealth is necessary to enhance personal freedom.

The positive conception of liberty — the idea of freedom actually backed by the ability to do something — is central to much socialist thought. Thus on the negative view, we are all free to send our children to expensive private schools; on the positive view, only a minority of us have such freedom. Or it could be argued that redistributive taxation may restrict the negative liberty of the rich, but it increases the positive liberty of the poor through the resulting welfare schemes. However, in terms of the left–right spectrum positive liberty proves as blind an alley as negative liberty. The basic idea of positive freedom was developed in the late nineteenth century by British Liberals such as Green and Hobhouse. Some conservatives would also be willing to accept aspects of the statism implied by the concept. On the other hand, there would be socialists who would not — anarchists, for example. The situation therefore seems very confusing. Both socialists and conservatives can believe in limiting negative liberty, whereas liberals have stressed both the negative and positive conceptions of liberty! And so on!

It is also important to remember that freedom has another dimension. Many have followed Locke's idea that freedom is an external relationship, between say citizen and state. Others have followed Kant's belief that freedom has an internal dimension, that it is concerned with what today might be called 'self-liberation', or 'self-actualization'. Thus a man could be in prison, but free if he had liberated himself from dominant norms. This idea has been central to many revolutionary ideas, such as Frantz Fanon's theories of colonial revolution. They have also influenced fascist thought (O'Sullivan, 1983). Again, does this mean fascism should be placed on the left?

Equality/Egalitarianism/Elitism

André Siegfried, writing in France at the end of the 1920s, felt that the solution to the left–right division was the competition between the political claims of social hierarchy, and those of democratic equality (Siegfried, 1930, pp.28–34).

This belief that equality is the key has been shared by many commentators. For example, the British financial journalist Sam Brittan attacks most simplistic left–right approaches, but argues that: 'There are particular issues, mostly centring around the concept of equality, to which they can even now be applied' (Brittan, 1968, p. 11). The British academic Raymond Plant (*The Times*, 2 January 1989) has argued:

> Has the Labour Party's post-war commitment to greater equality been rendered irrelevant by a market economy which is supposed to improve the position of the worst off through the trickle down effect rather than government action...[This is the] issue that goes to the heart of the debate between left and right. The right argues that the relative standing of one group to another does not matter; what really matters is that everyone's standard of living is improving.

Equality (or the need for inequalities) has undoubtedly been central to the thought of much of the left and right. For example, during the 1950s the British 'revisionist' theorist Tony Crosland argued in an influential thesis that equality was the linking theme among socialist doctrines.

However, the concept of equality is an elusive one. The ancient Greeks combined a belief in human inequality with the view that men were equal before the laws of nature. The Reformation combined acceptance of inequality in terms of wealth with a belief in equality of all true believers before god. It was Thomas Jefferson, not Karl Marx, who declared that 'all men are born equal', but for a long period most Americans combined this with a belief in the inferiority of blacks. Today at least five aspects of equality need to be distinguished to understand political philosophies fully: equality of 'consideration'; equality before law; equality of opportunity; equality of reward; and equality of wealth.

In terms of equality of wealth and equality of opportunity, there is no contradiction in a libertarian believing in the need to remove traditional privileges, such as inherited wealth, and on the other hand accepting that free market economics would mean inequalities. On the other hand, there is certain classlessness in the liberal ethic, especially in the sense that it taught a common morality, and sense of self-respect. The point can be seen in more concrete terms by considering Margaret Thatcher's Britain. The period since 1979 has witnessed growing relative inequalities of income and wealth. However, her governments have attacked bastions of vested interests — for example, restrictive practices in the legal profession, or the corporatist power of the National Farmers' Union. And there is a sense in which Thatcher aspires to create a classless Britain: everyone will espouse the middle-class, self-help values that are dear to her heart.

Even if consideration is only given to the economic conceptions of reward, or wealth, there are still problems for those who seek to use equality as the key to the left–right spectrum. Some socialists, for example the British Fabian theorists Beatrice and Sidney Webb, have accepted significant income differences. Conservatives of the anti-material progress type, like Melville or Babbitt, have not held a particularly acquisitive view of society. They envisage inequalities, but not vast ones. It is also important to remember that whilst fascism was a hierarchical ideology in some senses, in others it was quite egalitarian. This was not simply through its support of proto-Keynesian economic policies to help the unemployed, or welfare programmes. In theory at least, there was an opposition to conspicuous consumption. Moreover, part of the anti-intellectualism of fascism stemmed from its view that intellectual approaches tended to produce new hierarchies based on education, rather than the old elites based on land or business. Albert Speer, in his last book, held that the Nazi dream was to colonize eastern Europe and establish a society founded upon a return to the land, plus motorways and modern weapons (Speer, 1981). The Nazi celebration of manual work was not just rhetoric; there was a genuinely egalitarian side to it, both in terms of consideration and reward.

Some attempts to use equality as the key to the left–right spectrum also confuse economic and political factors. Thus Bennett has written that 'The Left is egalitarian, the Right is elitist' (Bennett, 1978, p.9). Philosophically, there is no contradiction between being elitist and egalitarian ('early' Leninism), or on the other hand, being inegalitarian and anti-elitist (much of American populism). It could be argued that these points ignore the fact that elitist left-wing ideologies tend to be based on a view of the necessity of elites during the transition to socialism rather than as a long-term feature. This would allow communism to regain a place on the left of an anti-elitist versus elitist spectrum; fascism would fit clearly on the right, whilst liberalism would clearly move away from the right. As such, this produces a spectrum which corresponds closely with common *perceptions*.

However, problems emerge if the concept of elitism is probed more carefully. Firstly, there is the empirical problem that elites have emerged in all advanced societies. In terms of practice, all forms of system would therefore be variations on the right! Even if the left–right spectrum is conceived in terms of philosophical ideal-types, problems remain. Marxism's dialectic makes it non-Utopian. Thus whilst it is possible to talk of communism as involving a withering away of the state, it is at least as reasonable to hold that Stalinist autocracy was not an aberration, but was an inevitable outcome of Leninist thought. On the other hand, a Marxist might argue that liberalism inevitably produces a society based on elites; indeed, Marxism's classic view of fascism sees it as the tool of capitalist elites unable to maintain control in an economic crisis! There are senses too in which fascism is *not* elitist. Fascist political theory is highly critical of existing elites, seeing them as decadent and undynamic. There is also a strong emphasis on popular activism, a view which exists uneasily with the more statist aspects of fascism. More importantly, there is an element of both egalitarianism and anti-elitism in fascism's nationalism, and especially its militarism.

Nationalism/Racism/Militarism

Some have held that support for, or opposition to, nationalism, racism, or militarism can resolve the problem of the construction of a left–right spectrum. However, these concepts can be understood in very different ways, and the connection with the right is far from a necessary one.

Many of the points relating to nationalism can be seen clearly by considering the two main manifestations of fascism. Italy's leading expert on fascism has noted: 'Italian nationalism...is not of the classic, materialistic sort'. Its imperialism was based on the hope (De Felice, 1976, pp.65–6):

> that large numbers of Italians would be able to transfer into new territories to find work, to find opportunities that they did not have in their native land. In short, one does not leave so much with the idea of exploiting the colonies, as with the hope of being able to find land and work.

Racism was much less strong in Italian fascism, and was spiritual rather than biological: thus, there was no necessary contradiction between being Jewish and Italian (the same would be true of American nationalism). This was very different to the racial determinism of the Nazis, and the inherent racial superiority implied by the concept of *Lebensraum*.

It could be argued that Italian fascism was ultimately racist in the sense that peoples in the territories to be colonized were not treated as equals. However, nationalism does not necessarily imply a conception of hierarchy. General de Gaulle, for example, was a great French nationalist, but he accepted the national aspirations of others. Michel Cazenave sees the rapport between the idea of France and the land as central to de Gaulle, as it had been to Péguy and many others before him. However, it was not land conceived in terms of imperialism– *Lebensraum*. It was more an idealization of the peasant as the loyal man-of-arms when challenged; it was more a focus on the land as a reflection of nature and the season — a microcosmic symbol of god's will, and ultimately of the mortality of man (Cazenave, 1988).

Another dimension of nationalism can be seen in the thought of the French high priest of nationalism, Maurice Barrés. He developed the key idea of the *déraciné* — the rootless cosmopolitan, which he harnessed to a mystical nationalism. However, he did not object to socialism as such; the point was more that it should be *French* socialism. There has certainly been no necessary conflict between socialism and nationalism. Nationalism has not only attracted both left and right as a vehicle for mobilizing popular support. It can also be seen as Janus-headed, looking back to a past, in a reactionary sense, but also offering a means to a new future (Kedourie, 1966). Many on the left, especially in the Third World, have seen nationalism as a vehicle both for liberation, and for development. Even in recent Western experience there has been no necessary conflict between the left and nationalism. For example, the 1980s German-central European 'new' nationalism exerted some influence on the left (Baring, 1988).

Racism similarly fails to differentiate clearly between left and right. One problem is that the definition of racism is contested. In the past, it has tended to be associated with ideas of superiority, or a hierarchy between races. In the nineteenth century, such views cut across the political spectrum. Even today it could be argued that there are examples of left-wing racism in this sense, notably in Chinese communist attitudes to the outside world. Some have argued that racism recently has become associated more with natural group solidarity, a view which allows the exclusion of 'aliens' without having to risk the charge of believing in a master race, and suffering association with the damaging Nazi legacy (Barker, 1980). The French Front National leader Jean-Marie Le Pen is certainly fond of family metaphors, and the conception of a natural community has been strong in the writings of some members of the British Salisbury Group. On the other hand, there are some on what is usually seen the right who do not hold this view, most notably the libertarians (for example, they usually believe in free immigration). More seriously, as an analytical tool the new concept of racism has little use, unless the point is to show that almost everyone is racist (which *is* the intention of many in the 'anti-racist' lobby).

Militarism serves little use in helping to distinguish left from right, as there have been militaristic left-wing regimes, especially in the Third World. The concept of militarism has also been widely misunderstood. The term for most people immediately conjures up images of aggression and savagery. However, it is interesting to consider in more depth how many fascists perceived the experience of the First World War. There is no doubt that fascism attracted an element which loved the uniforms, the discipline, the aggressive male company (Theweleit, 1987). But there was another side to fascism's militarism. This involved more a sense of comradeship, of 'blood socialism' forged in the trenches, a belief that fighting for an ideal was more honourable than a society based upon individualism and profit. An aggressive context also provided an opportunity for males to show closeness without connotations of homosexuality. It offered the opportunity for man to rediscover his roots, find his true nature.

Human Nature

Arguably the most helpful essentialist key to the left–right spectrum derives from the fact that a view of human nature is the explicit or implicit base of all ideologies. Thus the British philosopher Roger Trigg has argued that: 'Ideas of human nature are the most potent ideas there are' (Trigg, 1988, p.169).

It could be asserted that left-wing ideologies can be seen as rationalist, and involving a view that man can be remade better: man is a *tabula rasa*, awaiting liberation. For example, Gramsci has argued that the object of socialism is to transform nature (Gramsci, 1973, p.34), whereas the British Conservative academic, Nigel Ashford, has written that: 'The key to government failure lies in a naive view of human nature and a belief in the infinite malleability of man' (Ashford, 1985, p.35). Right-wing ideologies could be seen as holding that man is aggressive, competitive and sinful. This last aspect was especially important in early right-wing thought, which owed much to Christian theology. More recently, such arguments have often been supported by resort to science — for example, Social Darwinism, the view that society is based on the survival of the fittest. Since the 1970s, sociobiologists have tried to show that social features such as aggression, hierarchies or male dominance are genetically determined. Thus any form of society which does not come to terms with these traits is either naïve, or seeks to coerce its members. Socialists often reply by arguing that man's nature is socially determined, or that man is inherently good. The latter is often the position of Christian socialists, whereas the former is held by many Marxists. Such approaches often point to societies where property is held in common, where there are high degrees of equality, although there have also been scientific studies trying to refute the sociobiologists.

At this level of generality, there seems a clear distinction between left and right over human nature. However, this simplistic division can lend itself to very different forms of government. For example, a belief in man's imperfection could justify a system which would suppress man's instincts under a highly authoritarian government. It could, on the other hand, lead more to the idea that it is vital that government remains limited in order to prevent aggressive elites gaining excessive power. The view that man has no inherent nature, but is everywhere held in chains, could also produce very different philosophies. It would be consistent with an elitist view, such as Leninism, of the transformation to the 'good' society. It could also be consistent with a view that man could liberate himself, say through education — a view common among post-war British 'revisionist' members of the Labour party.

Moreover, the distinction between a right which takes man as 'given' and a left which seeks human perfectability begins to creak when examined carefully. Much classic liberal theory, especially as manifested in economic theory, has a view of rational man. Does this mean that liberalism is more a left- than a right-wing theory? It is also possible to find some versions of what are usually thought of as left-wing ideologies which do not place much faith in the perfectability of man. The views of many early British Fabians would be an example of this, in particular their almost Platonic guardian-class belief in technocracy. It could be argued that these examples simply show that Fabianism was not particularly left-wing, and that liberalism (true to its historic situation) is not right-wing.

However, the simple human nature distinction between left and right delineated above leaves other problems unresolved. The idea of man as aggressive or competitive is stronger in fascist, and even some liberal, political theory than in conservative theory. Conservatism tends to have a more fixed view of society, and sees individuals as more deferential to tradition and authority. Indeed, it is possible to think of both fascism and liberalism in revolutionary senses — involving support for dramatic transformations of society. Conservatism and rapid change seem contradictory, unless the context is a country undergoing conservative counter-revolution. Moreover, the fascist theory of human nature, true to its belief that it sought a synthesis, has an element of both the crude view of the left and right's interpretation of human nature. It holds that man has innate traits which undermined any form of pure egalitarianism. However, in other ways man is seen as a product of society. A key idea in fascist political theory is the fall: the fall of the nation from greatness, of the people into decadence. Fascist theory holds that the individual could be reborn by activism and faith within the community, thus restoring the nation (the fall, faith and resurrection are some of the many Christian images in fascist thought). It is here that the crucial distinction lies between fascism and the earlier romantic right. The romantic right tended to see the organic state in terms of liberating an individual who was viewed in fixed terms, especially within the context of a golden past. In fascist theory, the individual is reborn within the group, reaching a higher potential, and thus evolving. For the Marxist, freedom is the consciousness of necessity, an awareness of historical and economic laws. For a fascist, freedom is a consciousness of both nature and evolution. An important part of man's make-up is predetermined for example the ubiquity of struggle, or the need for leadership. It was in coming to terms with these natural laws that man freed himself to achieve a higher potential. The British fascist leader, Oswald Mosley, offers an excellent example of such thought (e.g., Mosley, 1947).

Instead of conceiving the ideological division over human nature mainly in terms of rationalism versus irrationalism, it would be possible to see it in terms of man as a political versus non-political animal. This proves even less helpful. Most left-wing ideologies have a view of man as inherently political, but this is a view they share with that pariah, fascism. It is true that many forms of liberalism and conservatism tend to see man as a non-political animal. Their ideologies are therefore defences of limited politics — of representative government, or elites largely untroubled by mass activism. However, the leading British conservative theorist, Michael Oakeshott, has written that it is: 'not at all inconsistent to be conservative in respect of government and radical in respect of almost every other activity' (Oakeshott, 1962, p.195). The point he is making is that conservatism is essentially a philosophy of limited government, and this philosophy cannot be 'reduced' to a view of human nature, as it is consistent with more than one view. In terms of the split between political and non-political man, it could be argued that defence of limited politics involves an overt, or implicit, view that man is non-political. However, the argument is perfectly consistent with the view that man is political, but in a potentially dangerous way. Hence 'apathy theorists' have claimed that the 'trick' of democracy is to ensure that its participatory and egalitarian rhetoric does not encourage the entry into the political system of the less intelligent, who are associated with views such as racism!

These points clearly show that human nature cannot offer an all-embracing solution to the left–right spectrum, though some of the difficulties disappear if it is again made clear that the task is to offer a *philosophical* analysis rather than one based on popular, or elite, *perceptions*. For example, this could allow fascism to be moved away from the extreme right of the spectrum. Libertarian, or *laissez-faire* approaches could also be moved away from the extreme right given their view of rational economic man. However, this would conflict with other ways of placing these ideologies within the left–right spectrum. Thus in terms of authority, fascism might be seen as truly right wing; and in terms of inequality, libertarianism and *laissez-faire* views might also be thought of as right-wing (though in each case the exact definition of the key-word would be important).

Conclusion

This returns to the basic problems with all essentialist approaches. Firstly, the concepts which are used on unilinear, *x* and *y* axis, or circular models are multi-faceted. Secondly, ideologies are dynamic and need consideration on a much broader front than can be handled by the one or two concepts involved in normal spatial analysis.

The argument can be put in a different way by considering the difference between a necessary and sufficient condition. It could be argued that it is hard to conceive a left-wing ideology which did not place some emphasis on income and wealth equality. As Tony Wright argues: 'Among socialists who have taken values seriously, there has been wide agreement that equality should be regarded as a key socialist value, perhaps even *the* socialist value' (Wright, 1986, p.33). This would make equality a necessary condition of being left-wing. However, it is not a sufficient condition, as there are right-wing ideologies which are relatively egalitarian.

It could be countered that the problem can be largely resolved if the terms 'left' and 'right' are understood within the framework of a series of values relating to a specific socio-political situation. This is especially true if attention focuses on the left, which has tended to have a more overt ideology, centring on change. Thus in a contemporary liberal democracy, the radical left could be characterized by a belief in the need for a break with the existing system in the sense of:

(a) a rejection of capitalism;
(b) a stress on equality (and a defence of the weakest in existing society);
(c) a belief in human perfectability.

However, this returns the discussion to the problems stated at the outset of this chapter: namely, in any list the key terms remain vague, and some can even be found in right-wing thought. Moreover, what is omitted from the list is also important. For example, where do attitudes to the state fit in?

It is true that there is no single form of right-wing thought which encompasses *all* the points covered by (a)–(c), but right-wing thought in general exhibits a diversity which cannot be fully appreciated simply by listing what it is not. Indeed, the best way to proceed towards and understanding of the nature of the right is to consider it in terms of a variety of styles of thought.

References

Archbishop of Canterbury's Commission on Urban Priority Areas, 1985. *Faith in the City*, Church House Publishing, London.

Ashford, N., 1985. The bankruptcy of collectivism, in A. Seldon (ed.), *The New Right Enlightenment*, Economic and Literary Books, Sevenoaks.

Baring, A., 1988. *Unser neuer Grossenwahn*, Deutsche V-A, Gutersloh.

Barker, M., 1980. *The New Racism*, Junction Books, London.

Bennett, R., 1978. The conservative tradition of thought: a right wing phenomenon, in N. Nugent and R. King (eds), *The British Right*, Saxon House, Farnborough.

Berlin, Sir I., 1967. Two concepts of liberty, in A. Quinton (ed.), *Political Philosophy*, Oxford University Press, Oxford.

Bramwell, A., 1989. *Ecology in the Twentieth Century: A History*, Yale University Press, New Haven.

Brittan, S., 1968. *Left and Right: the Bogus Dilemma*, Secker and Warburg, London.

Bruce, S., 1988. *The Rise and Fall of the New Christian Right*, Oxford University Press, Oxford.

Cazenave, M., 1988. *De Gaulle et la terre de France*, Ed. Plon, Paris.

De Felice, R., 1976. *Fascism*, Transaction Books, New Brunswick.

Duverger, M., 1966. *The Idea of Politics*, Methuen, London.

Eppler, E., 1975. *Ende oder Wende*, Kohlhammer, Stuttgart.

Gramsci, A., 1973. *Selections from Prison Notebooks*, Lawrence and Wishart, London.

Hall, S., 1988. *The Long Road to Renewal*, Verso, London.

Huntington, S.P., 1975. 'The democratic distemper', *The Public Interest*, No. 41

_____ and Moore, C.H., 1970. *Authoritarian Politics in Modern Society*, Basic Books, New York.

Kedourie, E., 1966. *Nationalism*, Hutchinson, London.

Laponce, J. A., 1981. *Left and Right: The Topography of Political Perceptions*, University of Toronto Press, Toronto.

Lipset, S. M. and Raab, E., 1971. *The Politics of Unreason*, Heinemann, London.

Lukes, S., 1973. *Individualism*, Basil Blackwell, Oxford.

Mosley, O., 1947. *The Alternative*, Mosley Publications, Ramsbury.

Nisbet, R., 1986. *Conservatism*, Open University Press, Milton Keynes.

Oakeshott, M., 1962. *Rationalism in Politics*, Methuen and Co., London.

O'Sullivan, N., 1983. *Fascism*, Dent, London.

Pickles, W., 1964. Left and right, in J. Gould and W. L. Kolb (eds), *A Dictionary of the Social Sciences*, Tavistock, London.

Scruton, R., (ed.) 1980. *The Meaning of Conservatism*, Penguin, Harmondsworth.

_____ Scruton, R., 1982. *A Dictionary of Political Thought*, Pan, London.

_____ Scruton, R., 1988. *Conservative Thinkers*, Claridge Press, London.

Siegfried, A., 1930. *Tableaux des partis en France*, Bernard Grasset, Paris.

Speer, A., 1981. *The Slave State*, Weidenfeld and Nicolson, London.

Theweleit, K., 1987. *Male Fantasies*, Polity, Cambridge.

Trigg, R., 1988. *Human Nature*, Blackwell, Oxford.

Wright, A., 1986. *Socialisms*, Oxford University Press, Oxford.

5 The Nature of the Right, 2: The Right as a Variety of 'Styles of Thought'

Roger Eatwell, University of Bath

In view of the problems involved in finding a single philosophical key to the left–right spectrum, the question arises as to why the terminology has become so universal. This raises broad ranging questions, but one factor points to a significant way forward in conceptualizing the right. The terms 'left' and 'right' have become almost universal terms of political debate in part because they appeal to major strands in Western modes of thought. Christian monotheism has a clear vision of a world polarized between good and evil, of light and darkness. This duality has been carried into two of the great ideologies of the modern world: liberalism and Marxism. In liberalism the forces of reason lead man in the quest for human perfectability, which liberates. Reason is involved in a battle against prejudice and tradition, which threaten to keep man enslaved to the past. In Marxism, another rationalist ideology, the duality is more the battle between the forces of capitalism and the historic destiny of the proletariat in its quest for liberation. There are also major triadic elements in Western thought (for example, Christianity's Father, Son and Holy Ghost; Marxism's thesis, antithesis and synthesis), but these can be incorporated into the left–right spectrum in the sense that such terminology implies the concept of a centre.

More specifically, dualistic styles of thought, especially liberalism and Marxism, tend to involve a concept of progress. As a result, some have tried to understand the left–right spectrum in terms of progress (e.g., Hebdige, *Marxism Today*, January 1989). This fails because the very term itself is highly contested. The idea of progress is central to the 'American way of life', yet many Marxists would see this as inherently right-wing. They would also reject John Gray's claim that liberalism is the ideology of modernity, because it alone addresses the post-traditional order problem of cultural diversity (Gray, 1986). Even many self-styled 'conservatives' are not opposed to 'progress' in the sense that they accept change in society. Indeed, it has been argued that 'A distinctive feature of the contemporary American Right is its emphasis on progress: moving beyond the past toward a future of unlimited material opportunity and social improvement' (Gottfried and Fleming, 1988, p.vii). There is also the dynamic problem of conceiving ideologies in terms of progress. Thus liberalism has in some ways become more right-wing through time; and left-wing regimes have become, in a way, conservative.

Nevertheless, the association of the left with the concept of progress leads to the conclusion that the right in practice can be most helpfully conceived as a variety of responses to the left. It could be argued that this leaves the concept of the left still undefined. However, as the previous chapter implied, it is impossible to give a brief definition of the left which does justice to its many forms, and its overlaps with what some would see as forms of right- wing thought. The conundrum thus needs breaking by conceiving these responses to the left within an historical framework. In the period since 1789 there have been two broad ideological movements (encompassing significant internal differences) that have attracted major right-wing critiques. These movements are liberalism and socialism/Marxism.

The right's responses can be seen as five styles of thought: the *reactionary right*; the *moderate right*; the *radical right*; the *extreme right*; and the *new right*. The first two emerged as responses to eighteenth century thought, especially to the emphasis in liberalism on freedom and the individual, and more generally to the idea that man and society could be remade more perfect. The third and fourth were more developments of the nineteenth and early twentieth centuries; they sought a specific response to the rise of socialist *movements*, in particular their more economic, end-state concerns. They must also be understood within the context of the emergence of a mass electorate, and the need for the right to exert a broad appeal. The final strand is a response to socialist *governments*, especially their problems in solving questions of both economic growth and the distribution of wealth, problems which have helped undermine the authority of the state.

It is important to stress that it is not claimed that all the arguments used by the varieties of right-wing thought post-date 1789. The terms 'right' and 'left' may date from this period; and the political concept of 'conservative' was coined after the revolution when Chateaubriand gave the name *Le conservateur* to a journal he issued. However, Scruton's book *Conservative Thinkers* (1988) includes Shakespeare; and his magazine has argued that Aristotle is 'the greatest and wisest of philosophers, and the one with the best title to the name conservative' (*Salisbury Review*, March 1989). Clearly, much right-wing thought derives its inspiration from classical sources. Other major aspects of right-wing thought can be traced back to religious doctrines which significantly pre-date 1789. It is also not claimed that each variety of right-wing thought is totally distinct from the others; indeed, there are varying degrees of cross-fertilization. Nor is it claimed that there are rigid categories of right-wing thought, into which it is possible neatly to fit all individuals, groups and ideologies. The argument here is simply that in the period since the French Revolution the right can most fruitfully be conceived within five 'styles of thought'.

The Reactionary Right

This is the right which defends a return to an *ancien régime*, or an idealized past. The archetypal example is the legitimist right which emerged after the French Revolution. This was aristocratic, religious and authoritarian. The old regime had been corporatist, hierarchical, and changed only slowly. People knew their place, and were protected by the inertia of the system, whereas the rise of individualism and market economics threatened a world of dangerous flux. Some on the reactionary right could be uncaring towards the 'lower orders', but the mainstream form of this thought encompasses the feudal view that social position involved obligations as well as privilege.

History has not dealt kindly with the reactionary right. An overly-favourable view of the French Revolution as a 'Good Thing' has meant that those who opposed it tend to be viewed with opprobrium. At best they are seen as individuals clinging to the vested interests of class or religion; at worst they are seen as dangerous fools. However, it is important to stress that the reactionary right has had its great thinkers, men such as de Maistre and Bonald (e.g., de Maistre, 1965; LeBrun, 1965). They argued that the Enlightenment had been founded on a central flaw. It celebrated the centrality of reason, of a life spent in constant questioning. Yet the flux implicit in such a view would break the bonds of society, for society was necessarily founded on tradition and accepted roles. This raises what in some ways has been the central question for the right: how can society be effectively governed in the absence of a consensus, of a stable form of legitimation?

The new doctrine of popular sovereignty was rejected as an answer to this conundrum. It was clearly absurd, as it could legitimize *any* policy for which a majority could be found (or, worse, any policy for which it could be alleged that a majority existed). Taine believed that only the few could truly think (reason was thus on the right rather than left). It was therefore dangerous to preach the new democratic ideas, which were more likely to be manipulated by demagogues than produce heaven on earth. Moreover, no assembly can abolish history; and what is natural is what is historical. Thus the current state has a legitimacy which cannot be voted away (McClelland, 1970).

Central to such reasoning was a view of man. For Rousseau, man was perfectible; society was the source of human ills. For the reactionary right, man was complex and had great capacity for evil — a trait which was often given religious form in the doctrine of the fall and original sin. Critics of the reactionary right have tended to stress its hostility to the rationalism of the Enlightenment. However, its major theorists, like Bonald and de Maistre, believed that their method was *the* science of politics — it was a science founded upon history and hard evidence, rather than *a priori* assumptions. Thus the left may celebrate 1789 for its grand slogans of emancipation. The reactionary right remembers the revolution for the Terror, for the decades of political turmoil which followed. For the reactionary right, these traumas could never be justified by claims that the revolution had led to true 'sovereignty of the people', or the fulfilment of later left-wing aspirations such as significantly increased economic growth, or a radical redistribution of wealth towards the poor. The reality of the republic was rule by self-seeking elites; economically, the revolution if anything set France back in comparison to its great rival, Britain.

Arguably the best twentieth century example of reactionary right-wing thought can be found in the writings of Charles Maurras. Ernst Nolte, a leading German historian, argued in his classic study of *Three Faces of Fascism* that Maurras and his Action Française were part of the fascist tradition (Nolte, 1965). A more philosophical study would reveal major differences. These can be seen clearly by considering the changing relations between Georges Valois and Maurras. Before 1914 Valois was influenced by two main theorists, Sorel and Maurras (Guchet, 1975). He sought to reconcile the working class with order and authority, believing these concepts were embodied in Catholicism and monarchism. Valois was a social Darwinist, who turned Rousseau upside-down: he believed that in the state of Nature man was an ignoble savage until he was forced to be creative by strong leaders. Such views led him to the Action Française, but after the First World War, Valois became increasingly critical of Maurras's lack of dynamism. He believed that the war had shown the great mobilizing power of nationalism, and he sought to amalgamate this with a social programme based on corporatism. This led him in 1925 to found the Faisceau. He had been impressed by Mussolini, but Valois saw fascism in terms of a French tradition — a fusion of Barrès's nationalism and Sorel's attack on the bourgeois state. Valois's fascism did not seek to defend an idealized past. His programme sought a strong government, directing a corporatist economic system which involved real co-operation of workers and management. The ultimate goal was not only social stability, but technical and economic progress. The Faisceau quickly collapsed as a mass movement, partly as a result of Maurras's machinations. However, Maurras's elitism meant that he sought mainly to influence (and thus restore the *ancien régime* through) the church, officers and intellectuals. Action Française, therefore, remained largely ghettoized among fringe elites.

In the late twentieth century the reactionary right is almost defunct in Europe and the United States, though it might (provocatively) be argued that aspects of its critique are of considerable contemporary relevance. For example, how does popular sovereignty square with the fact that only a minority have voted in 1980s American Presidential and Congressional elections? Are there not echoes in 1980s American politics of the Third Republic's endemic corruption, so despised by Maurras? Unfortunately for the reactionary right, some of its key ideas can be found in other traditions. Perhaps the most important idea to carry over into other varieties of thought is the equation of rights with duties. Nisbet has also sought to argue that the focus on family and intermediary units between citizen and state in thinkers such as Bonald, anticipates pluralist thought (Nisbet, 1986). However, this glosses over the intolerant and static nature of much of the reactionary right, especially in its most organic, theological form.

Not surprisingly, the most interesting contemporary manifestation of such right-wing thought comes from the fundamentalist fringes of religion in the form of Cardinal Lefebvre, who advocates the idea of the Christian, confessional state. This rejects the view that all the church should ask from civil society is freedom of action in propagation of its own faith. Some commentators have claimed that elements of the reactionary right have also re-emerged in recent Papal doctrine. However, few Catholics seek to establish a political system which could be seen as truly reactionary. Catholic doctrine has to be seen within the context of Western pluralism; only a small number seek to undermine the liberal democratic state.

These last arguments underline a problem involved in characterizing any style of thought: namely, the difficulties of fitting everything neatly into such schema. The point can be seen clearly by considering whether the many American Nativist movements should be included in the reactionary right. They were backward-looking, celebrating an Edenist society of pioneer values, small communities, and the Protestant religion, which was seen as threatened by the machinations of Catholics and others (Bennett, 1988). On the other hand, they were never aristocratic; they never supported an established church. Their views were also strongly individualistic, and opposed to the authoritarianism and elitism which is central to the reactionary right. Nativism involved a complex mix of values. It had reactionary elements, but its predilection for conspiracy theory is more commonly a feature of the extreme right. And its more Lockean features are central to much of the thought of the moderate right.

The Moderate Right

The moderate right has the same origins as the reactionary right in the sense that it began as a response to eighteenth-century doctrine that the world could be remade a better place by human reason. However, it was not a right that was averse to change. Its most notable early philosopher was the Englishman, Edmund Burke, who coined the famous aphorism that a state without the means of change is a state without the means of its own conservation (see especially Burke, 1973). Burke's views were evolutionary; he sought to temper both the nostalgia of the reactionary, and the imagination of revolutionaries. In their place he preached the value of authority based on tradition, countered by a sense of inevitable progress. Instead of absolutist government on the one hand, or mass activism on the other, he preached the cause of limited government. A particularly important aspect of this form of government were apolitical, intermediate institutions — more truly an early form of pluralist thought, as it was part of a philosophy that countenanced both change and dissent. Indeed, if the hallmark of archetypal reactionaries is intolerance, that of the moderate right is balance — a way between extremes, but never so defined as to become its own form of extremism. Balance is a principle of tolerance, not a new dogmatism.

Burke has been seen as the father of modern British conservatism, which serves as the best example of the moderate right tradition. Nevertheless, similar views can be found in countries such as the United States and in France, though with some differences of emphasis. In America, the moderate right has tended to place greater stress on formal constitutional structures, a reflection of the centrality of liberal-Lockean thought to the American tradition. Aspects of liberal thought can also be discerned in French moderate-right thinkers such as Constant and de Tocqueville. O'Sullivan (1976, p.43) has noted of these two great thinkers that conventionally they:

are classed as liberals, but their deep scepticism about the future of democracy and the absence from their thought of the characteristic liberal ideal of progress make their inclusion as conservative thinkers entirely appropriate.

Constant, for example, sees alienation as an integral part of the condition of modern man, but rejects that this situation can be resolved by radical political action. Alienation stems more from the size and complexity of modern society. Radical attempts to solve it through political action are likely to end in despotism and terror rather than liberation.

The fact that thinkers such as de Tocqueville and Constant have been seen within the liberal tradition highlights the need to separate this clearly from the conservative tradition. In the British context, the links between the British Tory and Whig traditions are complex. Burke and subsequent conservatives owed much to the Whig tradition, though the Whigs had earlier poached aspects of the idea of a balanced constitution from Queen Anne Tories. During the nineteenth century a more clear-cut relationship emerged between conservatism and liberalism. The moderate right rejected liberal philosophy in four main areas: liberalism's individualism; its universalism; its rationalism; and its contractual and utilitarian principles. Many on the moderate right claimed (and continue to claim) that individualism separated possession from responsibility, a view which harked back to the reactionary right. Some even saw (and continue to see) liberalism as almost paving the way to totalitarianism in the sense that individualistic, money-centred society encourages atomized, alienated 'mass' types (this was to become an argument central to the radical right). The moderate right sought to balance liberalism's individualism with a more collectivist perspective, stressing intermediate units such as the family or nation, and the importance of religion — though far from all on the moderate right have been religious. Indeed, the British political theorist, Lincoln Allison, has written that many see religion and conservatism as inextricably linked: 'but there is a long British tradition from Hume to Scruton...which sees conservatism as the only genuine emancipation from religion' (Allison, 1986, p.18).

Some commentators, especially conservative ones, have denied that conservatism is an ideology. Such an approach sometimes stresses the moderate right's pragmatism, sometimes its scepticism towards 'ideologies'. Allison (1986, p.2) begins his book *Right Principles* with the claim:

> The book is an essay in...conceptual scepticism...[this] says that political values and concepts are incoherent: they do not mean anything, at least in the serious sense of 'mean' which requires clarity and substance. As applications of this I will be arguing, for instance, that a belief in human equality is not a belief at all... that a belief in justice can amount to anything at all.

He adds that this often means that conservatism is negative: it is opposed to things more than for them. The most important contemporary conservative philosopher, Michael Oakeshott, holds a similar view, seeing conservatism as a disposition. His views centre around a defence of limited politics and the rule of law, especially against rationalist philosophies which seek to make a better world, remould human nature, rather than see society as a very product of human development (see especially Oakeshott, 1962).

Oakeshott's views illustrate the importance of distinguishing between a British conservative tradition, and the British Conservative party. Hayek has claimed that the Conservatives could not be trusted to defend free society, because they believed in collectivism, and were opportunists (Hayek, 1960). Certainly the Conservative party in the past has presided over a significant increase in the power of the state. This can be seen in nineteenth-century Conservative governments, such as Disraeli's; Disraeli also played cleverly on the collectivist aspects of nation and empire. Collectivism gathered pace during two world wars, which saw Conservative-dominated coalitions. Indeed, some have argued that the major aspects of economic interventionism and the welfare state enacted by Labour after 1945 were envisaged by wartime planning (see Addison, 1975). It could be countered that part of this stemmed from Labour or Liberal initiatives; but the relatively high degree of government economic intervention and the welfare state were maintained in post-war Conservative administrations from the 1950s through to the 1970s (see Aughey and Norton, 1981). Some would argue that, in spite of the rhetoric of freedom, there has been a worrying tendency to increase the power of the state during Margaret Thatcher's post-1979 Conservative administrations.

Such historical events do not negate the fact that conservatism *qua* philosophy has tended to focus on the concept of balance and limited government; as such the archetypal moderate right cannot be truly seen as collectivist. Indeed, the British academic Jack Greenleaf argues that part of the identity of British Conservatism stems from the interplay between its more collectivist and individualist wings (see especially Greenleaf, 1983). Nevertheless, the idea of balance allows for considerable variation, even oscillation, between principles. And it is easy to see how such concepts lend themselves in practice to a Conservative emphasis on 'statecraft', which could easily be seen as pragmatic, or even opportunistic.

The Radical Right

The term 'radical right' is more problematical than the terms 'reactionary' or 'moderate right' in the sense that there is less common agreement about its use. It has been used to describe very different types of thought and movement: for example, McCarthyism and the John Birch Society in the United States, Thatcherism in Britain and the Republikaner Party in West Germany. There is often little in common between these manifestations of the so-called radical right, other than a sense in which they do not fit into what is seen as normal. Indeed, there is a tendency for the term to have a pejorative meaning (for example, the German media began to refer to the Republikaner Party after its 1989 successes as 'radical right', whereas previously it had tended to be referred to as 'national-conservative', or 'right-conservative'; there were clear fears that a new Nazi party was rising).

Nevertheless, the concept of radicalism is important to an understanding of right-wing styles of thought for three main reasons. First, in chronological terms it emerges as a major style in the late nineteenth and early twentieth centuries (though it had antecedents). In particular, it was a response to the rise of socialism rather than liberalism. Secondly, it focused on activism, which was antithetical to previous right-wing traditions. Finally, it was radical because, unlike the reactionary or moderate rights, it sought to justify something which did not yet exist — a task normally associated with left-wing ideologies!

The most interesting manifestation of the radical right emerged in post-1918 Germany. Before considering this, it is necessary briefly to consider the nineteenth century German right-wing tradition. An important aspect of this had been a celebration of the state; in this sense it had similarities with the reactionary tradition. There were echoes of the reactionary right too in its contempt for the masses. However, there were important differences. One concerned the fact that the German romantic right tended to look to history rather than theology as a source of inspiration. This was linked to the idea of *Volksgeist*, or national genius — a term dating back to the eighteenth century and Herder (the idea of a special destiny for Germany pre-dates this; see Poliakov, 1974). This sort of nationalism was not central to the classic reactionary right; indeed, its dynastic and Catholic aspect underpinned a form of internationalism. However, an aggressive and romantic vision of nationalism was vital to what is described here as the radical right. By the early twentieth century, with the onset of universal suffrage, this nationalism had begun to underpin a highly active style of politics.

Some of the best examples of this style of thought can be found in the writings of Oswald Spengler, or those of the essayist and novelist, Ernst Jünger (see especially Spengler, 1926; also Woods, 1982). The German radical right rejected the Greek doctrine of salvation through knowledge, though its view that good citizens produce the good state, rather than the reverse, strongly echoed Plato. The radical right took up the idea of salvation through politics. The stress on activism meant that programmes were seen as relatively unimportant, though this also reflected the difficulties involved in defining a way between socialism and reaction. The result was a tendency to dwell in a romantic, uncorrupted past, though there was no desire to restore the Hohenzollern monarchy; and the radical right was not especially clerical. The present was seen as decadent; there was nothing to conserve. Instead, there was a longing for the strong leader, who would unite the nation, and fuse a sense of true community. The left was strongly attacked for its rationalism, for its failure to see that a true community could not be founded on class politics preached by the extreme left, or as a result of the technocratic social engineering favoured by more moderate socialists.

This style of thought owed much to political theorists such as Nietzsche and Sorel. Sorel argued that action was a necessary part of political activity; thought was a mere rationalization. There was also an important element of catharsis in his support for violence to overthrow the despised, hedonistic, materialist liberal democratic state (see especially Sorel, 1969). Other key ideas were picked up from Nietzsche, though sometimes in confused, even erroneous form. These included Nietzsche's attack on rationalism, and his belief that at rare moments an exceptional leader could emerge, who would transcend problems (see especially Nietzsche, 1969). The radical right also focused on Nietzsche's concept of the will to power; instead of the ancient world's injunction to 'know thyself', the Nietzschean motto was more 'will thyself, and become a self'. However, there are problems involved in seeing either theorist uniquely within the radical right tradition. Sorel, for example, undertook a political odyssey that took him from Marxism, through syndicalism, to mystical nationalism, and Nietzsche was never a German nationalist (see especially Jennings, 1984). Moreover, in many ways the German radical right was influenced by the physical realities of the First World War as much as by works of political theory. Its concept of 'blood socialism' is a powerful reminder of the impact of the shared experience of the war (Jünger was wounded seven times), and of the central belief that community was founded on nationalism and sacrifice, rather than the more internationalist, class-based and 'economic' views of the left.

The philosophy of the radical right, and its theoretical mentors, again raise the question of the relationship with Nazism. In practice as well as theory there were undoubted links, but there were at least two notable differences. First, anti-Semitism was never central to the thought of the radical right. There were elements in the radical right who could on occasion make anti-Semitic references, but this was true of many movements in the pre-Second World War era. Anti-Semitism is deeply rooted in European culture (Mosse, 1978); it is therefore necessary to distinguish between a latent, or erratic, anti-Semitism and political views that focus on racism. In particular, the radical right had little tendency to engage in conspiracy theory. More importantly, the radical right saw activism as a way of rediscovering the true nature of man, which was conceived as essentially fixed. Fascism had a more dynamic view, in which activism was part of a process of evolution.

The radical right was essentially a feature of pre-Second World War politics. Jünger and others continued aspects of the tradition at the level of theory after the war. However, the association with fascism proved damaging. The intellectual differences mattered less than popular perceptions. Moreover, there were crucial similarities, notably the lack of emphasis on the rule of law and constitutional structures. Radical nationalism seemed less relevant to an increasingly inter-dependent western Europe. An element lingered on in Germany, especially in relation to reunification with the east, but the Cold War clearly made this impractical. The radical right was also undermined by changes in the nature of party politics. The age of the mass rally was giving way to the carpet slipper and television. And from a sociological point of view, the radical right was undermined by the diminution of the social groups and tensions which had helped spawn its pre-war manifestations.

Arguably the nearest post-war politics has been to a radical-right movement was 1950s Poujadism, which emerged in a rapidly-industrializing France. The movement was nothing if not activist and nationalistic; but Poujadism was essentially rural and small-town. The radical right, true to its self-appointed task of attracting the working class, was more urban. A further difference stemmed from the fact that Poujadism never spawned a body of serious political theory; as such, it resembled more the extreme right.

The Extreme Right

The terminology 'extreme right' poses problems similar to those raised by the radical right in the sense that it could be seen as referring to any form of right-wing thought which did not conform to a notion of normality. To be of analytical use, therefore, the term 'extreme right' needs to be understood within a very specific framework.

Like the radical right, it has sought to attract working-class support, though its appeal is often across class lines. It shares with the radical right a highly critical view of the left, especially its internationalist and class-based aspects. Communism in particular is attacked, both in its domestic and international form. These arguments are usually presented in crude form; indeed, a defining characteristic of the extreme right is the paucity of its intellectual tradition. The reactionary, moderate and radical rights have produced significant political theorists. The extreme right has tended more to produce propagandists, interested in telling people what to think rather than how to think, and lacking in originality. The radical right was genuinely interested in how to achieve the good citizen; the extreme right has been more manipulative, paranoid.

Like the radical right, it tends not to focus on economic policy. Such concerns are seen as part of bourgeois, money-centred, technocratic society — an important source of the alienation that both the radical and extreme rights seek to combat. To the extent to which they have an economic policy, both have traditionally tended to be statist, though this is not meant to imply a rejection of private property. The point is more that state power is allegedly needed to ensure that the market works in the national interest. However, the growing inter-dependence of economies, and problems with state planning, have meant that some members of extreme-right parties are more sympathetic to the market. Jean-Marie Le Pen, the leader of France's Front National, would be a good example (e.g., Le Pen, 1985).

Extreme-right argument often centres on conspiracy theory. For example, a recurring extremist claim in America since the 1920s has been the charge that there is a communist conspiracy to undermine the 'American way of life', a key element in McCarthyism. Some members of the John Birch Society even held that President Eisenhower was a communist agent! A variation on this theme, dating back to the 'Illuminati' of the eighteenth century, is the claim that faceless men seek to manipulate the nation, and control the world (e.g., Allen, 1971; the 1972 edition's cover proclaimed 'Runaway Bestseller! Over 5 Million in Print'). Conspiracy theory even emerges in debates between factions of the extreme right. A book published in West Germany in 1988 claimed that the failure of the 'nationalist' right stemmed from betrayal by the *iminence grise* of one of its main groups, Dr Gerhard Frey (van Detta, 1988). Frey, it was alleged, publicly claimed to work for the restoration of the greatness of the nation, but in fact encouraged factional division. A particularly virulent form of conspiracy theory involves anti-semitism (Billig, 1978). The Jews are alleged to be involved in a plot to dominate the world and undermine society's bonds. This can take various guises: for instance, it could be by stressing capitalist, money-centred, individualistic values, which will undermine the true community. However, Jews are also seen as the very heart of communism, which is an equal threat to the true community: were not Marx, and many of the Bolsheviks Jewish? Such views are especially associated with the Nazis (Hitler, 1969), but it is important to stress that not all Nazis adopted this form of anti-Semitism (Lane and Rupp, 1978), and many fascists in countries such as Italy and Spain were not in the least anti-Semitic.

Conspiracy theory is a form of political myth. These come in three main forms. First, there are Sorelian ones, which are mobilizing (the classic example is the belief in a general strike as a way for the working class to seize power); these see politics as liberating. Secondly, there are integrating myths (for example, 'log cabin to White House' as a summary of social mobility in the United States); these are perfectly consistent with a passive view of politics. Thirdly, there are *simpliste*-explicatory ones. It should be clear from these distinctions and examples, that myths are not uniquely right-wing, nor confined just to the extreme right (the right sometimes justifies its use of myth by the claim that it needs to counter left-wing ones). Mythology in its extreme right-wing form involves a particular set of views: these centre mainly around nationalism and racism, which can involve mobilizing, integrating and *simpliste*-explicatory myths.

However, in its post-war manifestations the extreme right has tended to use myths not so much to encourage mobilization, as to explain to members why failure had taken place. Deep-laid plots offer a more congenial explanation for failure than the admission that the inherent intolerant and anti-democratic views of the extreme right are seen as illegimate by most citizens. Conspiracy theory also helps provide a common sense of identity through the revelation of having seen the dark forces which run the world in their 'true light'. Conspiracy theory further helps resolve what psychologists call 'dissonance'; how can a belief that the 'Holocaust' was the 'hoax of the century' be squared with evidence of genocide? Answer, the Jews dominate the media and academic life; we have thus been deceived (on the Holocaust denial, see Eatwell, 1990). As such, they require an understanding from the perspective of psychology.

Nevertheless, there is an important sense in which the extreme right has to be seen within the context of Western political thought. Its conspiracy theory can ultimately be traced back to Christianity and monotheism, which simplifies world conflict into a struggle between God and Satan, a tendency which encourages a belief in the existence of a hidden, evil, hand. This is reinforced by a tradition, dating back to the Manichaean heresy and secularized and simplified by the Enlightenment, which portrays the world as a struggle between an in-group and out-group. An important part of this involves a gnostic view of revelation through insider knowledge. More crudely, there has always been a side to the Christian tradition which is anti-semitic. The survival of such styles of thought, therefore, reflects central Western political traditions.

The New Right

The catchphrase 'new right' has been used to encompass very different forms of thought (four are distinguished in Chapter 1). In terms of using the new right as an analytical concept, one linking strand is that its ideas involve an attack on both left-wing philosophy, and the experience of left wing governments. This can be seen most clearly in the ideas of the American and British new right, where the new right has arguably had the greatest impact on politics (see Chapter 1).

Such an attack is also central to the ideas of the key theorist of the French *Nouvelle Droite*, Alain de Benoist. Three themes are central to his thought (see especially Benoist, 1977 and 1979). First, there is a rejection of the Judaeo-Christian tradition. This is seen as having brought monotheism, the belief that there is but one God, one true light — a syle of thought which helped pave the way for totalitarianism. The evils of the Soviet *gulag* feature prominently in this line of argument. De Benoist further argues that the Judaeo-Christian tradition has stressed egalitarianism, when the laws of nature show that man is not created equal. In this sense, Marxism is seen as a form of secular Christianity. Secondly, there is a strong attack on the social and political systems of both the United States and the Soviet Union. In differing ways, each involves a totalitarian narrowing of viewpoints. Each fails to achieve what de Benoist sees as the Indo-European values necessary for a good society. American society is founded on an alienating pursuit of money; the Soviet Union is ultimately based on coercion. The third theme in de Benoist's writing is a quest for identity — a need to define a European community, especially in cultural terms. In order to promote these ideas he has sought to develop a strategy of 'Gramsciism of the right'. Right-wing political ideas would gradually attain hegemony not only through their intellectual force, but also through the cultural sphere, and more surreptitiously by a careful infiltration of individuals in key institutions.

De Benoist's thought is interesting not just in its own right, but as another example of the problems of producing neat styles of thought typologies. It is possible to see affinities with the extreme right, in particular the almost mystical references to racial culture. Some critics have even heard echoes of fascist theory in the attack on capitalism and the left as equal evils. However, the charge is misleading as de Benoist's strategy is intellectual rather than mass mobilizing (though there are others within the new right who have adopted aspects of the radical right's emphasis on activism).

Nevertheless, these arguments could be seen as pointing to the fact that the term 'new right' is a gross misnomer. Should not the epithet be 'new rights'? And should not some within the new right, for example the libertarians, be classed as something other than right-wing: how can they be associated with theorists such as de Benoist? The problems of defining the right have already been discussed, but three points can be made here. First, with the exception of some mainly within the libertarian and the *laissez-faire* new right, there is little emphasis on the idea of limited politics in the sense of constitutional structures. In part this can be explained by a tendency among some right-wingers to play down the importance of such devices. For example, it could be argued that American politics is better understood in terms of its traditions and values than in terms of Bills of Rights or Constitutions: how else can the treatment of blacks be explained in a country where 'all men are born equal'? However, there is another reason for the underplaying of constitutional issues, which constitutes the second broad similarity within the new right. This is a belief in the need to remould human nature. The libertarians and *laissez-faire* supporters continue their pursuit of a society based on rational economic and political man. Members of the traditional and mythical new right retain the view that man cannot be made perfect, but they see a society in which alienation is growing, in which there is a significant loss of respect for authority. They therefore seek to restore the values of community, based on a natural order, rooted in the past. A third similarity can be seen by noting that during the early twentieth century there emerged a crisis in right-wing thought, marked by self-doubt and a tendency to compromise with other principles (O'Sullivan, 1976). During the 1970s and 1980s there was a notable revival of both right-wing political theory and self-confidence in its attack on the failures of the left. The new right 'came out', it dared to speak its name (an allusion which should appeal to libertarians more than traditionalists).

However, by the late 1980s there were signs of doubt among some right-wingers, both in terms of their intellectual analysis, and of the public support for *laissez-faire* policies in particular. Symptomatically, some American right-wingers began to call themselves 'progressive conservatives'. This could point to the need to view the new right in more dialectical terms, and see it as part of a struggle in which some form of synthesis, or balance, will emerge. As such, it would take its place more clearly in the moderate right tradition. Indeed, there are already some within the new right who might fit into the moderate right tradition. The American neo-conservatives would be prime examples (though their style of debate and writing can be remarkably intolerant of other points of view). If such a synthesis emerges, it would probably have as its focus a more sophisticated view of the exact role of the state. A pointer in this direction can be seen in the comment of Daniel Bell (who grew to disdain the label 'neo-conservative', though without drifting back to the left): 'the national state has become too small for the "big" problems of life (e.g., the tidal waves of the capital and currency markets) and too big for the "small" problems (e.g., the problems of neighbourhood and community) (Bell, 1989, p.55). However, this raises vast new questions — which will be examined in a subsequent volume in this series, *The Future of the Right*.

Conclusion

The British Conservative politician Ian Gilmour has claimed that the right 'cannot be exactly defined [but], it is, like the elephant, easily recognized when it is seen' (Gilmour, 1977, p.12). The discussion in the opening chapters of this book casts serious doubt on this common sense approach (an approach very much in keeping with the tendency of British conservatism to play down abstract or theoretical thought). It is especially difficult to understand the nature of right-wing thought if an essentialist answer is sought. Seeing the right in terms of a series of responses to the left, as different styles of thought, does not completely resolve the problem. As has been argued above, it is impossible to fit every single movement, thinker or ideology neatly into five varieties of the right. There are blurred edges between the categories; and some individuals and movements seem to transcend the categories. Moreover, each style of thought involves more complexities than has so far been implied. Brief descriptions of each style tends to create a picture of thought which is relatively cut and dried, which does not engage other principles. There have been elements of the right-wing tradition which lack theoretical sophistication, notably much of the extreme right. Other aspects, especially the moderate right, can at times be pragmatic, and reactive rather than creative. However, as a whole the right wing tradition is multi-faceted, far from static, even imaginative.

In order fully to appreciate these points it is therefore necessary to consider the five styles of thought in more detail. The following chapters, each written by a leading expert in the field, seeks to further the task of understanding the nature of the right.

References

Addison, P., 1975. *The Road to 1945*, Jonathan Cape, London.

Allen, G., 1971. *None Dare Call it Conspiracy*, Concord Press, Seal Beach.

Allison, L., 1986. *Right Principles*, Blackwell, Oxford.

Aughey, A. and Norton, P., 1981. *Conservatives and Conservatism*, Temple Smith, London.

Bell, D., 1989. 'American exceptionalism' revisited: the role of civil society, *The Public Interest*, No. 95.

Bennett, D. F. H., 1988. *The Party of Fear: From Nativist Movements to the New Right in American History*, University of North Carolina Press, Chapel Hill,

Benoist, A. de, 1977. *Vu de droite*, Copernic, Paris.

_____ Benoist, A. de, 1979. *Les idées a l'endroit*, Libres Hallier, Paris.

Billig, M., 1978. *Fascists*, Harcourt Jovanovich Brace, London.

Burke, E., 1973. *Reflections on the Revolution in France*, Penguin, Harmondsworth.

Eatwell, R., 1990. The Holocaust denial, in L. Cheles *et al.* (eds), *Neo-Fascism in Europe*, Longman, London.

Gilmour, I., 1977. *Inside Right*, Hutchinson, London.

Gottfried, P. and Fleming, T., 1988. *The Conservative Movement*, Twayne, Boston.

Gray, J., 1986. *Liberalism*, Open University Press, Milton Keynes.

Greenleaf, W. H., 1983. *The British Political Tradition, Volume Two, The Ideological Heritage*, Routledge, London.

Guchet, Y., 1975. *Georges Valois*, Editions Albatros, Paris.

Hayek, F. A., 1960. Why I am not a Conservative, in *The Constitution of Liberty*, Routledge, Kegan Paul, London.

Hitler, A., 1969. *Mein Kampf*, Hutchinson and Co., London.

Jennings, J. R., 1984. *Georges Sorel*, Macmillan, London.

Lane, B. and Rupp, L. (eds), 1978. *Nazi Ideology before 1933*, Manchester University Press, Manchester.

LeBrun, R. A., 1965. *Throne and Altar: the Political Thought of Joseph de Maistre*, University of Ottawa, Ottawa.

Le Pen, J-M., 1985. *La France est de retours*, Carrère-Lafou, Paris.

McClelland, J. S. (ed.), 1970. *The French Right (from de Maistre to Maurras)*, Jonathan Cape, London.

Maistre, J. de. (trans. J. Lively), 1965. *The Works of Joseph de Maistre*, Macmillan, London.

Mosse, G., 1978. *Towards the Final Solution*, Howard Fertig, New York.

Nietzsche, F., 1969. *Thus Spake Zarathustra*, Penguin, Harmondsworth.

Nisbet, R., 1986. *Conservatism*, Open University, Milton Keynes.

Nolte, E., 1965. *Three Faces of Fascism*, Holt, Rinehart and Winston, New York.

Oakeshott, M., 1962. *Rationalism in Politics*, Methuen and Co., London.

O'Sullivan, N., 1976. *Conservatism*, Dent, London.

Poliakov, L., 1974. *The Aryan Myth*, New American Library, New York.

Scruton, R. (ed.), 1988. *Conservative Thinkers*, Claridge Press, London.

Sorel, G., 1969. *Reflexions on Violence*, Free Press, Glencoe.

Spengler, O., 1926. *The Decline of the West*, Allen and Unwin, London.

van Detta, G., 1988. *Gerhard Frey: Ohne Maske*, J. Fischer Verlag, Nuremberg.

Woods, R., 1982. *Ernst Jünger and the Nature of Political Commitment*, Academischer Verlag, Stuttgart.

PART II
Varieties of the Right

6 The Reactionary Right: The French Revolution, Charles Maurras and the Action Française

J. S. McClelland, University of Nottingham

Approaching the Reactionary Right

For many people, the term 'reactionary right' conjures up images of the past, in particular of declining social groups, unable to come to terms with the legacy of the Enlightenment, and more specifically the French Revolution. However, the reactionary right has encompassed many major political theorists, as well as disgruntled aristocrats, monarchists and others with a hypertrophied nostalgia for an *ancien régime*. In the eighteenth and nineteenth centuries, these theorists included men such as Bonald and de Maistre (McClelland, 1970). In the twentieth century by far the most important such theorist has been Charles Maurras.

Being radical means being prepared to dig up the roots; being reactionary in a country with an entrenched radical tradition means much the same thing. Charles Maurras's great service to the French right was to exercise an intellectual domination so complete that right-wing thinking which was different from his always looked incomplete by comparison. Maurras's attack on entrenched republicanism was a root and branch attack. His *Enquête sur la Monarchie* (Maurras, 1909) contains all the arguments a royalist, anti-semitic, anti-democrat could wish for. It was sumptuously republished in the 1980s, proof of its continuing importance as a source-book of reactionary ideas. The purpose of Maurras's polemics is reactionary in a straightforward sense, because he wants to turn the clock back to monarchy, but there is nothing backward-looking about his method. There is no mystical appeal, no warm-hearted and misty-eyed medievalism. If Voltaire were to re-appear as a monarchist he would probably think like Maurras. The centrepiece of Maurras's political thought is his account of royal authority in the very modern sense of political leadership. He believes that the republic has consistently failed to produce dynamic leaders of its own, and he sees in this a failure of political legitimacy. It is as if republican leaders do not themselves believe in their own right to govern. Maurrassian monarchy is about highly visible authority embodied in one man, just as Maurrassian Catholicism is about visible moral authority embodied in priests and bishops. When Archbishop Lefebvre insists on the full panoply of the Latin mass, and on his authority to celebrate it, the spirit of Maurras lives on.

The French Revolution and the Right

The French right has been complaining about the French Revolution ever since it happened, and it is easy to see why. The revolution expelled France's natural rulers from their rightful place in the state. Dispossession puts all conservatism at a disadvantage because, being the champion of order, its attack on institutions, however revolutionary in origin those institutions are, can easily be seen as disorderly. The natural place for a right is within existing institutions, and its natural function is to defend those institutions from the inside against the insurrectionary thrust of a politics of the left. To be able to do that convincingly, which means being able to do it without becoming reactionary, or wilfully obtuse, requires a ruling class confident of its own legitimacy and of its political skills. These political skills must be of a high order, and must be of two kinds, manipulative and deflectionary. A ruling class has to be able to make institutions work, and work in such a way that the urgency of demands for a re-modelling of those institutions can be dismissed as the self-interested jealousy of an out-group which uses the cry for reform or revolution as the cover for its own, essentially selfish, power hungry motives. In short, a ruling class has to deliver. A ruling class which is an ancient aristocracy proud of its tradition of service to the state and its kings should be in an ideal position to defend itself. If that state has reasonably stable frontiers, possesses a reputation for military greatness, a church capable of controlling its own Jansenist and ultramontane tendencies, and a population decently fed in more years than it starves, then it is hard to imagine the circumstances in which that aristocracy could be dispossessed and its king (let alone its queen) sacrificed. Hard to imagine before 1789 that is, but horribly easy to imagine afterwards.

The French right has always had to confront that original and startling victory of the left. Monarchy, and the political system which went with it, was written off. French right-wing political thinking has always had something of the post-mortem about it and the verdict has always necessarily been murder not suicide, and certainly not natural causes. It was in England that another conservatism pin-pointed the *theoretical* problem of the causes of the French Revolution for all conservatism. Burke was already sifting through the possible right-wing explanations for the great event before the terms 'right' and 'left' had properly entered the political vocabulary. Burke was one of the first to realize that the French Revolution could not be confined to France, and he also knew that the British revolutionary settlement of 1688 was beginning to look like the tarnished victory of an entrenched oligarchy whose handling of the Jacobite Rebellion of 1745 had been none too confident, and whose handling of the crisis in America had forced the colonists into a rebellion the outcome of which was the founding of a new English-speaking state within what had once been a united empire. English malcontents could begin to wonder whether the time might not have come for another version of 1688, this time more radical, and using 1789 as a precedent. Burke's defence of the British constitution, and of the structure of the society which had produced that constitution and made it work, depended on his being able to convince his audience that the English ruling class possessed the wisdom necessary to keep the political system working by amending it as necessary from time to time. The settlement of 1688 was a precedent for Burke, but a precedent of a very different kind from the precedent it was taken to be by English radicals. The Glorious Revolution was successful precisely because it was confined to the ruling class itself, a triumphant vindication of the ruling class's capacity to solve problems by coping with a lawful but lawless king without invoking grand principles of elective monarchy and the right to choose forms of government, and certainly without any of the 'appeal to the people' nonsense which had caused so much trouble in Cromwell's time. Burke's message was that the English ruling class could hold the fort against anybody and anything provided that it kept its nerve. That meant believing in its own ability to govern without making concessions to ideas about republicanism and an ultimately popular sovereignty, and having the intellectual courage to see, after nearly a century's intermittent war with France, that the cause of the French monarchy and aristocracy was England's cause. (Nothing could have been easier for Englishmen to believe than that the French monarchy in 1789 was being paid back in its own coin for the decisive help it had given the American rebels in their War of Independence.)

Burke's *Reflections* can easily be read as a covert condemnation of the French monarchy and aristocracy, which is perhaps why they made so little stir in France when the monarchy was restored after the defeat of Napoleon in 1815. Beneath Burke's rather flowery lamentations about the death of chivalry in France, which allowed the rude multitude to lay hands on the queen, there lies the clear message that the French aristocracy cannot have been much good to allow it to happen. (Burke may have filched the idea from Dr Johnson, who remarked during his *Tour of the Hebrides* that the Scottish aristocracy deserved its subservience to the English crown because it had not stopped Elizabeth executing its own Mary Queen of Scots.) Burke pretends that in 1789 France had the rudiments of a good ancient constitution which only needed improving, but that, unlike the British constitution, it had not been improved by its own ruling class and the consequence was the revolution and the brand-new constitution produced by the Constituent Assembly. Of course, Burke cannot cry up the failure of the French aristocracy openly to a world in which it is obvious that the revolution is going to be exported to other European countries (and eventually in its Napoleonic phase to Malta, Egypt and Syria, though Burke could be forgiven for not predicting that), so that counter-revolution was going to need all the allies it could get, the French aristocracy included. That failure of the French aristocracy to get a grip on its own political system before the revolution was to lie long and heavily on the conscience of the reactionary right in France, and especially on the conscience of Charles Maurras.

Nobody understood better than him that the central paradox of monarchy was that in normal times the natural opponents of kings are aristocrats, but that when monarchy is threatened, aristocracy is supposed to rally round the king on the principle: No King, no Aristocracy. Maurras takes an essentially Burkean, that is to say implicity critical view, of the failure of the French aristocracy, so that if France is to be rescued from the revolution and all its works, which effectively means Bonapartism and the republic, then all his

hopes had to be centred on the return of the king. Maurras converted Action
Française (a political group, with a journal of the same name, formed at the
time of the Dreyfus Affair) to monarchism. This conversion has often been
seen as the cause of Action Française's failure. Maurras, it is sometimes said,
condemned Action Française by nailing its hopes of success to a romanticized
kingly totem which could only be absurd in the modern world, but it is hard
to see where else Maurras could have pinned his hopes. If the republic was the
revolution's legacy he could not hope for anything from its citizens; if
Bonapartism was the joint creation of a usurper and his plebiscitary rabble,
and if aristocracy was a broken reed, then that left only the king. Of course,
Maurras liked aristocrats provided they were royalists, but the royalism of
post-revolutionary aristocrats had to be clear-thinking enough to recognize
that their political resurrection depended on the resurrection of monarchy,
and not the other way round.

Like Burke, Maurras could not harp publicly on the failure of the French
aristocracy to protect the monarchy in 1789, and so, again like Burke, he is
forced on to attack that aristocracy's enemies. As a traditionalist, though a
very unsentimental traditionalist, Maurras is very conscious that the one thing
he cannot say is that tradition failed, or that tradition has a gap in it. For
traditionalists tradition never dies, so that when something untoward happens
to a tradition its causes cannot be internal to the tradition itself; traditions
never suffer internal bleeding except when that internal bleeding is caused
from the outside. So Maurras is forced to seek the causes of the French
Revolution outside France, and the fact that Rousseau was born in Geneva is
a godsend. Rousseau caused the French Revolution, and Rousseau was not
even French, therefore the French Revolution cannot really have been French
at all, and neither can anything that follows from the revolution. The worm in
the bud became the canker in the flower. What is alien can always be got rid
of, though the process by which this is to be done may have to be drastic, at
least in the beginning. Maurras is adamant that foreign imports into a culture
remain foreign: the spirit of Rousseau can never be assimilated, though it can
taint everything else. It will not do to ask: Did Maurras *really* think that
Rousseau caused the French Revolution single-handed? Rather we should say
that, being the kind of traditionalist he was, Maurras could not have thought
anything else.

Maurras made his name during the Dreyfus Affair; he died in 1952 without
ever having changed his mind about anything important. It was the affair
which alerted him to the dangers which continued to deny to France her
rightful place as the great nation. The defeat by Prussia in 1870 was a
symptom, not a cause of national decline. The real enemies were within, and
a divided France was never going to be a match for the Anglo-Saxon egotisms
which surrounded her. The establishment of the House of Hohenzollern as
emperors of the Second Reich added a permanent external threat to the moral
affront of the expanding British Empire and rise of American super-capital.
The lost provinces of Alsace and Lorraine gave Germany a bridgehead on the
left bank of the Rhine from which another attack could be mounted on Paris.
After 1870, France would have to live in an increasingly hostile world, and
would more than ever need to be united to make up the lost ground both

literal and metaphorical. Events prior to the Dreyfus Affair were not encouraging. Defeat by Prussia was followed by the Paris Commune and its brutal suppression by the republican government of Monsieur Thiers. National defeat, followed by the spectacle of Frenchmen tearing at one another's throats, which even the occupying Prussians found hard to stomach, was not a good beginning. A certain economic prosperity made it possible to pay off the war indemnity to Germany in record time, but no sooner was that done than another German invasion occurred, this time in the form of Marxism.

The French Revolutionary Tradition

The left in France was socialist long before it was Marxist. There is nothing particularly surprising about that. Marx's own socialism derived in part from his contacts with French socialists in 1848, and it was under their influence that he wrote the famous *Communist Manifesto*. Usage of the terms 'socialist' and 'communist' was firm enough in France by 1848 to distinguish between them. To be a socialist was to believe that the world should belong to those who worked, St-Simon's *industriels*. There was no place for the parasites (which in that simpler age meant the idle rich, not the idle poor); everyone who worked had a natural affinity with each other and could be expected to share a natural antipathy to those who produced nothing. This was a socialism which could look back to the French Revolution's extirpation of the aristocracy with a certain satisfaction; the fact that France worked after the *émigrés* had left, and worked better, was proof that aristocracy was merely an embellishment. Of course, not all aristocrats were idle in the extended sense of the term; theirs was the business of war and government, and so politics came to be seen as an expensive aristocratic game for which the rest of the nation paid the price. On this view, buyers and sellers of labour have no necessary quarrel with each other; they can make common cause against their class enemy, and there is no contradiction involved in workers accepting bourgeois leadership in their political struggle. A socialism from the top downwards, to be achieved through parliamentary mechanisms, with legally constituted political parties with bourgeois leaders, is one obvious political strategy of this kind of socialism. On the other hand, being a communist in 1848 meant to see the class divide between the toilers and everybody else; that everybody else included the buyers of labour, so that the toilers would be well advised to look suspiciously upon all bourgeois sympathizers and to realize that the working class would have to accomplish its own emancipation. That distinction between socialism and communism was not always put in those terms, and many who continued to call themselves socialist thought like communists, but those two attitudes have persisted on the French left right up to the present. What has to be emphasized is that they are not attitudes that derive from an economic analysis of French working conditions, though care has always been taken to keep the category of 'worker' broad enough to include peasants, but from an analysis of French politics, and particularly from an analysis of French republicanism since 1789.

French socialists have in general always accepted that the revolution of 1789 was a bourgeois revolution by the simple test of *cui bono*. The great revolution's leadership came from disaffected members of the bourgeoisie leading a rank-and-file *sansculotte* revolutionary army; it was the working people of Paris who supported the revolution when it was at its most revolutionary during the Jacobin Terror, and it was in the name of those same working people that Gracchus Babeuf tried in his celebrated Conspiracy of the Equals to return the revolution back to its original Jacobin purity. This may not be very good history, and it certainly would not satisfy the truth criteria of 'bourgeois' scientific history, but it does provide the perspective which encourages socialists in France to see every regime after the Jacobins as a betrayal of the part played by the toiling masses in the great events which ushered in the modern world in France and in the rest of Europe. The Directory, the Consulate and Empire, and the Restoration of the Bourbons in 1815 were all straightforwardly reactionary. The problem for French socialists, if they were still revolutionary, was how to proceed from there. Events after 1830 left them no clearer than before. The revolution of that year, which left as its great memorial Delacroix's *Liberty Leading the People*, promoted the Orleanist branch of the French royal house to constitutional monarchy with a Chamber elected on a property franchise. Louis-Philippe went walkabout in Paris wearing a bowler hat, while his government obligingly sent out troops to put down strikes, so that, from the socialist point of view, another revolution had been betrayed.

The compulsion to repeat (constitutional monarchy was what Mirabeau had wanted before Jemappes and Valmy, when Louis XVI's head was still on his shoulders) continued in 1848, which was to become the text-book case for French socialists (and for Karl Marx) of how their bourgeois allies would always turn on the workers to show that the republic would never be theirs. Nothing keeps the idea of revolution alive like frequent changes of regime. Perhaps Lamartine was right when he said that by 1848 France was bored. Bourgeois monarchy lacked the charm of the real kings elsewhere in a Europe which was still ruled by divine right. Constitutional monarchy still had to be invested with the anodyne progressivism which was Prince Albert's contribution to the arts of modern government. Monsieur Chauvin was keeping the memory of Napoleonic panache alive in the Parisian music halls, and it was easy to think that almost any regime was preferable to an Orleanism which could not do much more than invite Frenchmen to enrich themselves. The revolutionaries of 1848 went through their by now well-established rituals: speeches; barricades; *Hotel de Ville*; Republic, proclamation of; *fraternité* all round; Constituent Assembly; new Constitution; elections under same; and then they waited to see what would happen, which meant seeing Who would betray Whom this time. From the socialist point of view it was a guess made in advance, as ritualistically predictable as it had always been: the bourgeoisie would betray their worker allies. Against all the odds, French socialists had kept themselves faithful to the dream that *their* republic might arrive one revolutionary day, the social republic, with work and bread for all. The political equivalent of universal social provision is universal suffrage. Universal suffrage might not be the cause of a sufficiency of bread (in

England the Chartists were much criticized for their ignorance of political economy which led them to believe that annual parliaments would improve the harvest), but the French working class, instinctively Marxist, never doubted that there was a connection. The insurrection of the June Days in Paris in 1848 was an attempt to keep the bourgeois revolution moving in a proletarian direction (Marx was to draw the same theoretical lesson from the revolutions of 1848 in general: unless the communists made the revolution 'permanent' they would be picked off by their erstwhile revolutionary allies). Repression followed; Louis Bonaparte was elected President of the republic on universal suffrage, a clear signal that Bonapartism was again about to take up its historic role of stopping revolution in its tracks. The scenario was complete once again when the President of the republic made himself the Emperor Napoleon III with the *coup d'état* which Marx wittily called *The Eighteenth Brumaire of Louis Bonaparte*.

Marxism, which was later to become the subject of exotic and esoteric exegesis, was at its beginnings little more than the theoretical statement of that sense of betrayal forced upon the politically advanced sections of the French working class by its understanding of its own revolutionary experience. Bourgeois counter-revolution even followed the heroic, all-republicans-together, Gambetta-inspired defence of Paris after the new, but smaller, Napoleon had failed to revenge Waterloo by losing to the Prussians in 1870. The repression of the Paris Commune was the last example in a long series of bourgeois betrayals of the working class at a time when betrayal did not mean reneguing on electioneering promises but rather the bayonet and the fusillade at the wall at *Père Lachaise*. Marxism came into France in the 1880s at exactly the time when the French working class needed a theoretical statement of its own sense that, since the Jacobin dictatorship, its republican allies had betrayed it in the name of a republic which would always be bourgeois. Of course, the French working class would always be republican because so many of the republic's enemies were its enemies: clericalism, for instance, or the insolence of rank. Regimes which had not been republican had outlawed the working class's own institutions, allowing only bourgeois-sounding mutual self-help rather than real trade unions, which could so easily become centres of revolutionary conspiracy.

So the republic which Maurras saw being torn apart by the Dreyfus Affair was itself already divided. Maurras saw what the republic's socialist enemies saw, that the republic was little more than a special interest claiming, in the way of all special interests, that its own interest was the interest of the whole. Much more was involved than the mere instability of a regime which was only twenty years old when the Dreyfus Affair began in 1894; rather the affair, which showed how unstable the regime was, was itself part of that deeper *malaise* which had begun in 1789. Maurras believed that, unlike the Engish or the Germans, the French were incapable of learning the lessons of their own history. In his special sense, France since 1815 *had* no history. The regimes thrown up in the period from 1789 to 1815 — constitutional monarchy, republic, Jacobin dictatorship, oligarchic Directory, Consulate and finally Napoleonic Empire — exhausted the alternatives to traditional monarchy. Since 1815 French politics had simply been variations on those themes, and none of them could be any more stable in the future than they had been in the past. For the right the republic is the most divisive of the alternatives to monarchy because it is the most fraudulent. The Rights of Man, Liberty, Equality and Fraternity, and the Republic One and Indivisible are the grandest of all political slogans, but the reality of republican politics gives them the lie. Politics in a democratic republic like France appeared to be spectacularly corrupt and scandalous — witness the Wilson scandal and the Panama Canal scandal; republican politics does not seem to be able to produce strong leaders or long-lived governments because of the deals which governments have to make with groups of politicians in the Chamber who seem to be able to make and unmake governments at will. The political freedoms which the Rights of Man promise produce a mendacious press and a multitude of parties, no one of which is a truly national party with a will to govern; the economic freedom promised by the Rights of Man produces a world of high finance in contrast to which the underworld is a model of probity. In the Panama Canal Scandal, the Chamber, the press and the financiers took the country to the cleaners. Was this the direction in which Liberty had been leading the People? The Rousseauist vision of the republic as a voluntary union of free men giving themselves a new moral character does not sit easily with what the republic is actually like.

As a radical, Maurras has to believe that there must be something wrong with the idea of the republic at its roots in Rousseau: his fraudulence must be the republic's fraudulence in embryo. Rousseau perpetrated a massive confidence trick when he persuaded the modern republic to dress up in the toga. The classical past was appropriated at one fell swoop for subversion, and the proof of Rousseau's success was that even the great anti-historian of the revolution, Hippolyte Taine, had been taken in to such an extent that he blamed the revolution on an *esprit classique* which had so infected the culture of the *ancien régime* that the *ancien régime* almost connived at its own destruction (see Taine, 1876–94, esp. Vols. I and II). The classical spirit was far more than just a simple-minded desire to imitate the ancients, though there was plenty of that: Rousseau's own bedside reading was Plutarch's *Lives* as well as the Bible. Rather the classical spirit was a particular way of looking at the world which saw virtue in all simplicity, including intellectual simplicity. This view of the world shared with Rousseau the idea that the real world had become unnecessarily complicated. With that complication came an analogous complicatedness of the minds of the people living in the world. Increasingly sophisticated societies needed increasingly sophisticated theories to understand them. Rousseau thought that both these instances of complication were evidence that the world had lost sight of the much simpler truths of ordinary human goodness, justice and patriotism. What the classical spirit did was to try to get behind the complexities of the societies in which people actually lived to something which was common to all men living in all societies. It did not matter how obscure the things they had in common had become as different societies developed in their own separate directions. There *had* to be something which all men had in common, a basic human nature which wrote a different story in the different geographical and social landscapes in which it happened to find itself. Despite its concern for what men had become under the influences of different societies and locations, this was an enterprise with profoundly anti-historical implications. Differences between separate national traditions would always be secondary. Part of what made what we would now call comparative sociology so interesting was exotic difference of detail between societies, but these differences would always be thought of as being accidental, as having to be thought away so that the basic and fixed human nature lying behind them could be brought to light. The social science of the Enlightenment would always welcome accounts of simple societies, the society of the South Seas, for instance, or of North American Indians, because, being simpler than European societies, human nature was more likely to show through. America after its War of Independence (a war which Americans might have lost had it not been for the help of French sea power) was a particularly interesting case because there for the first time a race of men from the corrupt societies of old Europe was to have the chance to re-write its own history in a virgin moral landscape. It came as no surprise to advanced thinkers in France that the Americans should choose a republic as their political form: perhaps men were republicans by nature.

Taine came to believe that this simplifying spirit was responsible for the French Revolution. He was struck by the fact that the revolutionaries spoke the language of a new beginning symbolized by the new calendar which began the republic at the year 1. The spirit of Jacobinism he called 'geometrical', by which he meant that the political programme of the Jacobins was worked out by deductions from the universal principles of human nature discovered by enlightened political thinking. Being universal, human nature was the basic constitution of the universe, and the political constitution was simply an extrapolation from it. Such a constitution's merits would depend in large measure on its being as unlike the constitutions which preceded it as it was possible to be. How could it be otherwise, when the way France was ruled before the revolution was just another example of human history's playing false with the constitution of man? Like Rousseau in his account of himself in the *Confessions*, the Jacobins believed that everything which was reprehensible about human beings was the fault of the world which corrupted them, and everything which was good about them stemmed from their own inner selves. *Liberté*, liberation, meant tearing down the whole social and institutional superstructure which was the cause of man's inhumanity to man in order to give the real man within his chance. That this had to be a universal programme was true by definition: natural man everywhere suffered from much the same constrictions. When Rousseau wrote that man was born free but was everywhere in chains, he meant that 'everywhere' to be taken literally. The new dawn had broken at Paris, and it was up to the revolutionaries to spread its rays until the last king was hanged in the entrails of the last priest. Kant had said two years before the fall of the Bastille that the age was the Age of Enlightenment but was not yet an Enlightened Age. By this he meant that, while most of the great discoveries in the sciences had already been made, including the human sciences, those discoveries had yet to make their way properly in the world. The revolutionaries took Kant's dictum seriously: revolution, which was the spirit of Enlightenment made flesh, could not be

confined to France, and French political history up to the defeat of Napoleon
was to be largely a quarrel about who was to be the revolution's agent-at-large
in the rest of Europe. Napoleon has come to be seen through Anglo-Saxon
eyes as the Corsican ogre, or as a particularly modern kind of tyrant, or as the
failed Hero of Carlyle, but that is not how the powers of old Europe saw him.
The kings and emperors feared him as Jacobin trying to found a dynasty, and
they were hard put to it to decide which was worst. Napoleon represented a
combination of efficiently centralized state power, the career open to the
talents and the culmination of the desire to abolish the frontiers of Europe
which had been the revolution's original promise.

Taine's great *Origins of Contemporary France* (Taine, 1876–94) therefore
saw the whole revolutionary experience as peculiarly and typically French.
The much-vaunted classicism of French culture, distorted a little, but not
much, by Rousseau, was responsible not only for the revolutionary events
themselves but also for the unprepared state of those whose job it was to cope
with them in 1789. The Rousseauist illusion of the virtues of simple folk (even
Marie Antoinette used to pretend to milk cows) left the French ruling class
astounded and shocked by the peasant savagery of the *jacqueries*. M. Necker
was advising their 'good king' to trust to the simple goodness of the people
when those same people were lynching aristos all over France. Taine is enough
of an elitist to know that revolutions are not insurrections springing from
nowhere. Regimes fall when one elite is replaced by another, and what
interests him is the conditions under which the elite in place allows itself to be
replaced, and his view is that Rousseauism made such headway among the
natural defenders of the existing order that they quite literally did not know
what was going on in the revolution until it was too late. Taine saw three
cutting-edges to Rousseauism: it infected all sections of literate French
society, including the ruling class, before the revolution; it served very well as
the ideology of a new would-be elite, the Jacobins, on their way to political
power in the name of liberty, and it served equally well as the ideology of that
Jacobin republic based on the Terror which Professor Talmon long ago taught
us to regard as a prototype of totalitarian democracy (Talmon, 1952).

Taine's history was appearing from 1876 to 1894 (the last volume was
published posthumously) and it was intended to subvert eulogizing accounts
of the revolution like Michelet's. Maurras could therefore not ignore it. Any
attack on the revolution and its republican legacy was bound to elicit his
sympathy and a full-bloodedly positivist attack like Taine's suited Maurras's
own unsentimental temper very well. The scientific history of Taine's *Origins*
was poles apart from earlier, Catholic attacks on the revolution. De Maistre's
and Bonald's view of the revolution and its horrors as God's punishment for
the atheism of the Enlightenment now began to look a little quaint, if not
antiquated. But Maurras had to tread warily. Taine saw the revolution as
coming naturally out of the last century of the *ancien régime*, which made the
revolution French in a sense which Maurras would not allow. For Maurras,
the revolution had to be the great break with tradition. Maurras's position
in relation to Taine was further complicated by the fact that Taine singled out
Rousseau as the special incubus of the revolution, a view which
Maurras shared. Whichever way Maurras looked he seemed to see

the figure of Rousseau, but, after Taine, there had to be not one Rousseau but two, the Rousseau who really had caused the revolution and the republic, but a Rousseau who couldn't be Taine's Rousseau, because that would be to admit that Rousseau was French and that the revolution itself was French, part of native tradition, regrettable in some ways no doubt, but part of France for all that.

A reluctant acceptance of Rousseau, the Rights of Man and the republic was available to anti-Dreyfusard conservatives like Maurice Barrès. Barrès is something like a French conservative after the manner of Burke, or after the manner of those Englishmen who were against 1688 to begin with, but who became reconciled to the Hanoverian Succession with the passage of time. Barrès's position is the position of the honest conservative who could say that he would probably have been against the revolution when it happened, but that there is so much republican water under the bridge by the time of the Dreyfus Affair, that the republic and the Rights of Man are now so much part of our national culture that it is absurd to pretend that they could possibly be foreign (see McClelland, 1970, pp.143–211). Like those who opposed the Constitution of the United States before it was ratified but who accepted it afterwards, the Barrèsian conservatives would in the future not attempt to undo what had been done in the republic's name but would settle down to ask themselves what it meant to be a republican in the present.

Charles Maurras and the Action Française.

Not Maurras. Again, the matter rested on the particular view of Rousseau that one took. Maurras's way forward was clear. He had to argue that Rousseau's classicism was a fraud; that what passed for an admiration of the ancient world in his thinking was nothing of the kind. The ancient republics which Rousseau affected to admire were the pure figments of an over-heated imagination. Like most of Rousseau's enemies, Maurras makes straight for the *Confessions* as a central doctrinal statement. In them, Rousseau makes his view of the world perfectly clear. Rousseau plainly knows what a little shit he is. Hume was right when he said that Rousseau wasn't fit to sit down at the same table as decent men. Rousseau insists that all his unpleasantnesses are the fault of circumstances; his is a goodness dying to show through in a world which relentlessly tries to corrupt him. He congratulates himself for the goodness which remains. What is monstrously egotistical about Rousseau is the way he takes the condition of his own wretched soul for a paradigm of the whole human condition. The whole world is doing to human goodness what it has already done to him. Therefore the whole world must be re-made in order that he, Jean-Jacques, can be happy in it. This is easily recognizable as the egotism of Romanticism, a view of self so inflated and self-centred as to be positively insane.

When Maurras wrote his famous attack on Rousseau in the preface to *Romantisme et révolution* (Maurras, 1922), interest in Rousseau's personality was already more than a century old, but the late nineteenth century had added a new twist (see also McClelland, 1970, pp.239-263). The connection between Rousseau and the French Revolution was taken so much for granted that the questions came to be asked whether there might not be some inner connection between Rousseau's own disturbed personality and the more horrific revolutionary events, particularly the guillotinings of the Terror, the lynchings and the September massacres. Nothing was easier to say than that during the revolution the world had gone mad, but advances in the sciences of depth psychology and group psychopathology, and an awareness of the connections between them, made some thinkers begin to wonder whether there might not be a degree of scientific literalness which could be added to the old conservative idea that the French had gone collectively insane in 1789 and turned themselves into a pack of ravening wolves. The great French criminologist Gabriel Tarde had already argued that Rousseau's was a classic case of the internal duality of the insane — what we would now call paranoid schizophrenia (Tarde, 1912, p.160f.). Tarde contrasted the innocent, trusting, nature-loving and lovable Rousseau with the guilt-ridden, morbidly suspicious, unbearable-to-live with Rousseau, the denouncer of his imagined enemies. This unquiet spirit, now serene and now vicious, was exactly what Maurras thought had caused the revolution. To call it classical seemed to him to be a horrible mistake. The classical virtues were the virtues of order, the order of a statue, of law, of a line of poetry or of a constitution. The political order of classical times was certainly not based on any false notion of political equality. Greece and Rome had been frankly elitist, distinguishing between free man and slave, civilized man and barbarian, and always celebrating the outstanding man as leader. Classical civilization had been successful precisely because it had been able to keep private and popular passions in check. Rousseau has confounded classical civilization's enemy with classical civilization itself. The enemies of order within: slaves threatening revolt, *demos* and *plebs* temporarily insolent with the strength of numbers, and the enemies without: barbarian peoples, restlessly on the move, are the true progenitors of the Rousseauist spirit. Not forgetting the Jews, enemies of the Roman order, irreconcilables either to the Roman Empire or to its successsor, the Roman Catholic church.

Maurras can now pinpoint Rousseau's historical mistake. Rousseau simply failed to see that the vehicle which carried the classical heritage from the ancient world to the modern is the Catholic church in France. When the barbarians established their kingdoms on Rome's ruins, the aristocratic prelates of the church lay in wait to play Alcuin to Charlemagne and civilize the barbarian kings. Rude and destructive vitality was converted by degrees into ordered and civilized monarchy as Rome triumphed through Christ's church. France was classical before Rousseau imported an invented pseudoclassicism from Protestant Geneva. The Catholic church preserved Latin in its public ceremonies and taught it to children in its schools. Christianity itself became civilized; what had begun as a subversive religion of Jews became part of the order which controlled men's lives and gave them meaning. France's greatness was royal and Catholic greatness, and its enemy is Protestantism in all its forms. Rousseau's Genevan origins speak for themselves (Maurras conveniently forgets that Calvin was French). Maurras's Catholicism is the reverse of theological. He has no interest in dogma, and

and even less in the Gospels written by four obscure Jews. Maurras's church is the church of the institutionalized authority of popes and bishops and the authority of doctrinal statement; not the Apostles but the apostolic succession. Maurras himself was probably never a *bien pensant* Catholic. His Catholicism is intensely empirical, speaking to a great fact of French national life at a time when organized religion was the most obvious institutional continuity with the *ancien régime*. The republicans had achieved a majority in the Chamber in 1876 and there seemed to be very little possibility that the king would be invited back quasi-constitutionally. Maurras knew as well as James I that No bishop meant No king. The necessary connection between Catholicism and absolute monarchy had been a cliché of political thought since the Reformation so that anti-anti-clericalism was a sound political tactic in a republic prepared to continue the revolution's drive towards *laïcité*.

The body of the faithful was the real France waiting only for its king (Maurras, 1909). This was the France which remained untouched by the revolution and by Rousseau, the France which Rousseau had the effrontery to deny existed. Rousseau and the revolutionaries wanted to replace this real community with the fictitious community of *The Social Contract*, as if it was a matter of choice what community one belonged to. The France of the *ancien régime* had been corporatist and hierarchical. Status was closely related to function. The three estates had separate legal status; economic life was regulated by guilds and supervised by the state; everyone knew who he was and knew his place in the scheme of things. Authority extended naturally to every aspect of social life, and each aspect of authority, from fathers of families right up to the king, co-operated with the rest. The revolution had torn men from their natural places and allegiances, leaving them defenceless against big government and big capital. Rousseauist romantic individualism had room for only two personalities, the self-defining moral individual inhabiting the natural self, and the new moral person, the state. Nothing was to come between them, and every social institution which attempted to mediate between the individual and the collectivity was at best a diluter of pure patriotism and at worst a conspiracy against virtue. Everything which stood in the way of the individual's solitary contemplation of the collectivity, every counter-loyalty, to family, priest, locality, *patron*, seigneur, class or order, came to be seen as delusion, the result of the operation of sinister special interests opposed to the interest of the whole. As a new moral person, the republic could make claims on its citizens undreamed of by the theorists of absolute monarchy. In particular, it could call for sacrifice in the republic's defence, because all men could be called upon to defend the public thing in which they all equally shared. Rights imply duties. A right without a corresponding duty is a privilege, something which is valuable because it brings benefits without costs and which is valued because others do not possess it. According to the revolutionaries, the *ancien régime*, riddled with privilege, could not be saved by the grace of *noblesse oblige*. The One and Indivisible Republic drew up a much starker list of the virtues of a citizen than any absolute king would have dared. The life of virtue is lived in a properly constituted republic; outside that republic there is no virtuous life, no life worth living; therefore you owe *your* life to the republic in its wars against organized privilege elsewhere (and it goes without saying that dissenting life within the republic is automatically suspect).

Of course, Maurras insists that the nation is the only collectivity which matters because it is the only collectivity of which Frenchmen are already members, and of course he insists that of all the people in the world not to spot it, the most likely one is Rousseau, the metic (the word is Barrès's), the man who was at home nowhere, not in Switzerland, or France, or Italy or England. Rousseau is a typical *déraciné* (again the word is Barrès's), one of those cosmopolitan intellectuals without roots who, without a mandate, wish to legislate for the whole human race, appealing only to others like himself who have no place in the ordinary course of a nation's life. France did not need a new pretend community, the abstract republic, and a new pretend religion, the farcical cult of the Supreme Being. The republic is really a foreign import, alien to the nation's real life, and the transmutation of Robespierrist civic religion into the cult of Marianne and *laïcité* threatens to poison the wellsprings of the nation's religious life. The republic is a state within a nation, and Maurras believes they are alternatives. It might be objected that Maurras never considers how deeply the idea of the republic had penetrated into the life of the nation itself. The republic, it might be said, is the political idea against which all the other possible regimes in France define themselves. Does this not show just how tenacious the idea of the republic was? Surely a true conservative would have to take some account of that? Not Maurras. The Dreyfus Affair convinced him that the republic was simply another, and the worst, political alternative in a France in which any regime which was not monarchist was always going to be the regime of a faction. The only difference about the republic was that it claimed that the republican state belonged to everybody, a classic example of a dishonest interest masquerading as the interest of the whole.

And not just the whole of France, but the whole of mankind. The Dreyfus Affair saw the formation of rival political leagues, the League of the French Fatherland against the League for the Defence of the Rights of Many, France against Humanity. According to the right, the pro-Dreyfusards were calling for justice for Dreyfus after Dreyfus had *got* justice. Dreyfus was a French staff officer (and being a Jew, lucky to be one) and had received French justice. What other justice was there? The Dreyfusards countered by saying that the justice which Dreyfus got failed by the standards of a universal justice founded on an immutable idea of human rights which had been the bedrock republican principle at least since the eighteenth century. No doubt, the Dreyfusard argument was partly tactical. France was, after all, a republic when Dreyfus was condemned by military justice, so it seemed to be a good move to appeal to the republic's government for a re-trial in the name of the republic's own principles, but the controversy did not stop there. Barrès and Maurras, in their over-intelligent way, saw that the Rights of Man argument was leading right back to the eighteenth century origins of the French republic. In 1789, an insurrectionary republicanism had torn France apart in the name of the Rights of Man and Citizen; now France was being torn apart (not perhaps the whole of France, but certainly the France that mattered) by the Dreyfus Affair in the name of those same principles. Where was the justice to be found in whose name Dreyfus had been unjustly treated, except in the kind of abstract principles which Rousseau and the revolution long ago had launched in their disruptive career in the modern world? To pretend that there is another, universal standard of justice, and then to attack French justice in its name, is to begin the French Revolution all over again.

The circumstances in Europe at the turn of the century made the Dreyfus Affair especially damaging for France. The fact that secret military intelligence had indeed been passed to an enemy power showed that something was wrong with the army at General Staff level. The condemnation of the Jew Dreyfus had enabled the right to say that the morally pure French army had been betrayed by a foreigner who should not have been a staff officer in the first place. But if Dreyfus was innocent, then somebody else in the army must be guilty, and that would most certainly be a Frenchman, because there were not enough Jewish staff officers to go round for a second investigation and trial. And if, as seemed increasingly likely, Dreyfus had been condemned by procedures which at best were somewhat irregular and at worst faudulent, then the right would have to face the fact that the French army was both corrupt and inept. That mattered terribly at a time when France looked to its army to restore the territorial integrity of the nation through the reintegration of the lost provinces of Alsace and Lorraine after some future war of *revanche* against Germany. The fact that France was looking to an army whose only recent victory, a few colonial successes apart, had been against fellow Frenchmen of the Commune, made it all the more imperative to believe that it really was a good army, really capable of avenging its own defeat by the Prussians in 1870. The consequences of 1870 had been the rise of the German Empire, and disaffected persons, especially on the left, were muttering that the French army was responsible both for the civil war of 1871 and for German domination of central Europe, the two great disasters of recent French history. Whatever had been true in the past, the right had to argue that in the present the army was France's best hope.

Action Française, and Maurras in particular, was consistent in its fear of Germany, even though this led to certain apparent inconsistencies in its own doctrine. Integral nationalism meant seeing everything as being connected to French greatness, and did not require acknowledgement of national greatness elsewhere in Europe. Action Française could argue endlessly for a restoration of the monarchy at home and for the restoration of the national territory, while at the same time arguing after the First World War that the German imperial house should be abolished, and that some German national territory should go to the victors. What mattered was France first. That was the only guiding principle, and it meant consistency, because if it was true that only monarchy could be relied upon to secure a stable and strong state, and if Germany was the enemy, then it followed that France in her own national interest should do all she could to abolish imperial monarchy in Germany. The record of French kings had been exemplary in this respect. They had always been expert at keeping Germany divided, realizing that a patchwork of mini-monarchies across the Rhine was the ideal condition of French security and greatness. That policy had meant war from time to time, but it had been essentially defensive war to preserve a state system dominated by France.

Conservative, kingly war was to be sharply distinguished from the series of aggressive wars begun by the young republic in 1792, and which had continued ever since. Despite the glory and victories, these had all been disasters from the national point of view, orgies of expenditure of blood and treasure, which left the restored monarchy of 1815 a second class power in Europe. Louis-Napoleon's wars merely continued the decline. Action Française was nothing if not pragmatic about foreign policy. Maurras's watchword *La politique d'abord!* enabled him to tread a confident path through the difficult area of foreign policy controversy in the aftermath of the First World War and the rise of European fascism, and in the even more difficult circumstances of the rise of Hitler and the era of the Popular Front. Germany would have to pay for the First World War, not because of some high Wilsonian rant about war's wickedness, but on the ages-old principle of: 'to the victor, the spoils!' (Action Française campaigned for a generous war-bonus for ex-servicemen — not for them the Jacobin rhetoric of a 'pure' patriotism). The peace settlement had either to be severe enough to make sure that the German economy would never again be able to finance a drive for European hegemony, the position Action Française took, or it should not be so severe that it would feed a resentment against the victorious powers which would automatically lead to a drive for revenge analogous to French revanchist feeling after 1870. In Action Française's view, the peace settlement seemed nicely calculated to cause the minimum amount of damage to Germany for the maximum amount of national resentment. Action Française pressed for exact payments of reparations, and moved away from France's erstwhile allies as Britain and America went soft on reparation payment deadlines. (This even meant that, for a time at least, Action Française went soft on Bolshevism. The East was a long way away, and anti-Bolshevism could easily distract attention from the real enemy, Germany). Italian fascism caused Action Française no problems. Italy was Catholic, had been an ally in the war, Mussolini was bent on destroying a corrupt and feeble parliamentary regime and Italy still had a king. Italy re-born would always be a useful counterweight to Germany, a perception re-inforced when the rise of Nazism raised the possibility of *Anschluss* and German troops on the Brenner.

Maurras had to believe that German politics was romantic because French politics in the Action Française version was classical. Maurras saw Wagner every time he looked across the Rhine; when he saw Nazism he saw an ages-old Germanic drive towards some kind of mystically conceived national destiny. Maurras was sure enough of his own reading of German culture to be certain that Nazism would succeed in Germany, but his essentially backward view of Nazism as a thing from the past made it difficult for him to see the full implications of Nazism in terms of modernity. The higher lunacies of Nazi ideology blinded him to what a Nazi victory could mean in purely secular, that is political, industrial and military, terms. Maurras's own clarity as a political thinker in the classical tradition led him to suppose that a political leader with Hitler's cloudy mind could not also grasp the principle of *La politique d'abord*. French fascist groups of the era of the Popular Front did not admire Hitler because he could turn them all into little French Siegfrieds; they admired him as a national leader particularly successful at solving domestic and foreign policy problems which seemed to be common to all the European states. Hitler the problem-solver (however short-term the solutions now appear with hindsight to be) just could not figure in Maurras's intellectual universe where the kinds of political positions Nazism stood for were universal problem creators. Part of the tragedy of Maurras is that in the long term he was probably right about the Nazis. We can now see that they *were* a menace to civilization, that they were capable of taking their anti-semitic and anti-Bolshevik rhetoric seriously to a degree which would have been inconceivable to a routinely anti-semitic and anti-communist conservative *anywhere* in the 1930s. Maurras's instinct about Nazism was right, but it did not help Action Française at the time. His position on Germany in fact played into the hands of that part of the French left which was untainted by the pacifism of the Popular Front. Fascists on the French right never tired of pointing out to Maurras that continuing hostility to Germany would eventually mean war, and a war which on Maurras's own account of the matter an enfeebled French republic could not win. The revival of the German national spirit and its prudent futurist investment in the latest military technology were a recipe for a French national disaster compared with which Sedan would appear to be a little local difficulty.

And Maurras appears never to have thought about where a victory of German arms would leave him. He was clear enough in his own mind that there was no contradiction between his anti-Germanism and his anti-anti-Nazism. The Nazis were anti-semitic, anti-communist and anti-liberal, and so was he; the Nazis' enemies were his enemies, though not always for the same reasons, but Maurras was anti-Nazi and anti-German as well. Maurras's intellectualism prevented him from seeing that what was crystal clear to him would not be crystal clear to everyone else. It was emphatically not going to be clear to his political enemies after France was occupied and then liberated, the more so because Germany had been the ally of an Italy with whose fascism Action Française had sympathized and whose army had been allowed to occupy part of southern France in 1940. This problem was part of the larger problem of how Action Française was ever going to get its programme implemented. Implementation mattered because Action Française's monarchism prided itself on its lack of sentimentality. There was absolutely nothing Jacobite about Maurras. *La politique d'abord* meant feasibility; monarchy had to make sense in a country where so many alternative regimes were being canvassed. Monarchism could not make much headway in electoral politics because republican politicians controlled the parties, the legislature, and the process of politics. Maurras continued to think that most Frenchmen were royalists at heart and that the republic was what stopped that royalism getting out. That was why the returning king would have to establish a dictatorship, at least in the beginning. The king could not do that by himself; he would have to be brought back and the most obvious candidate for bringing him back was the army. Somebody would have to be found who would play General Monk. That was perhaps a possibility just after 1871, but the victory of the Dreyfusards made that repetition of the return of Charles II increasingly unlikely. As the vision faded of a king brought back by a general, welcomed by his adoring people, and perhaps welcomed, or at least not scorned, by the Assembly, it became obvious that only some kind of real revolution, or at least some great national disaster, could be the occasion for the restoration.

The problem for the Pretender was always that he wanted to return to the throne of his ancestors with some show of legality, which meant that some great national institution had to give him an invitation, otherwise he would come into France as one of her conquerors (as Louis XVIII had been brought back by the powers which had beaten Napoleon and as Vichyites were to look upon General de Gaulle's return to France with the invading armies in 1944). In the era of fascism it was always going to look as if Action Française was tending in the direction of the kind of rabble-rousing politics of the right which an older, Legitimist right looked down upon with patrician contempt. This parting of the ways between Action Française and its monarchy (and also its church) could be prevented for a time after the First World War when Action Française could ride high on the anti-German nationalism common to almost all French parties and politicians, so that for once Action Française could be seen to be on the government and winning side, but it could not last. Just as the church saw through the essentially instrumental nature of Maurras's Catholicism, the Pretenders and their closest advisers saw through the essentially instrumental nature of Maurras's monarchism. Time was not on Action Française's side. If what Maurras had to say about the republic was true, that it was alien to the spirit of France, corrupt and feeble, and therefore could not last, then every passing year of the republic's survival had to be explained. Maurras never changed his mind about anything important, and things which he was saying in the 1890s when the republic was relatively new were bound to have a different resonance in the 1920s and 1930s when the republic was half a century old. The republic just refused to die. Of course, Action Française did have an explanation of what kept the republic going. It was kept in being by the secret forces of Freemasonry, the money power, and the Jews in whose interest it was to keep the democratic facade intact so they could hide behind it. The state itself was effectively self-perpetuating. The army of officials which the Jacobins and Napoleon had unleashed on the French people held on to their offices no matter what government pretended to rule in Paris, little caesars accountable to no one but themselves. The national system of education incestuously produced a steady stream of new recruits; nothing better to produce bureaucrats than bureaucratically controlled education. The longer the republic lasted the more urgently Action Française had to plead its case until the shrillness of its denunciation of France's internal enemies became indistinguishable from fascist voices denouncing those same enemies all over Europe.

There was always something parasitical about Action Française's apparent successes. Those moments when it appeared to be speaking for the whole right and perhaps for the whole nation were typically moments when the nation was acting up nationalistically for foreign policy reasons. Action Française was faced with the problem which revolutionary movements always have when they are opposed to a system part of which is electoral politics. Action Française could not easily say on the one hand that electoral politics was a sham and on the other hand field candidates in its own name. Its obvious strategy was to try to penetrate *real* institutions — army, church and bureaucracy — but that left the question of who or what was going to change the regime unanswered. The regime in fact overturned itself at Vichy after the defeat, and the result was the collaborationist rule of Marshall Pétain. That was the final irony of Maurras's career. The thinker who had done more than anyone else to rescue patriotism from the Jacobins and their political descendants would find himself compromised through his ideological associations with a regime which had come into being as a direct result of the victory of German arms. Maurras simply could not win.

It is easy to say that Maurrassism is now of the past, but that would be a mistake. What Maurras left in place was a radically intelligent critique of French republicanism. Many of Maurras's criticisms (though they were made by others besides him) have become the commonplaces of politics. If I were to single out one, it would be his insistence that the governing institutions in France consistently fail to deliver, what in the language of political science has come to be called 'institutional failure'. Central to Maurras's argument is the failure of political parties, which, in his view, are adept at producing weak governments and at exercising veto powers on those governments. Maurras rightly diagnosed the cause: monarchy apart, there was no natural party of the majority in post-revolutionary France. Nobody understood that better than General de Gaulle. A regime of the parties would be a repetition of all France's political troubles in the Third Republic, which French political experience after 1945 and before the General's return to power seemed to confirm. Gaullism's contribution to French politics is that for the first time a majority was cobbled together which seemed to have some hope of permanently institutionalizing itself. This in its turn has led to Mitterrandism, the hope that a majority can also be cobbled together on the left. The recognition of the need in France for stable, mass, electoral party followings, without which democratic politics cannot work effectively, comes out of exactly the kind of analysis of French politics which Maurras had been engaged in since the Dreyfus Affair.

References

Note: this essay is based on an extensive reading of Maurras's works; the most important source has been his *Enquête sur la monarchie* (1909). As the vast majority of Maurras's voluminous works have not been translated into English, an extensive bibliography of his works has not been included. It is also worth noting that Maurras has attracted little in the way of scholarly secondary literature. The following list therefore includes only works specifically cited in the text, together with some of Maurras's other main works and the main secondary sources in English.

McClelland, J. S. (ed.), 1970. *The French Right (from de Maistre to Maurras)*, Jonathan Cape, London.
Maurras, C., 1909. *Enquête sur la monarchie*, Nouvelle Librairie Nationale, Paris.
_____ 1912. *La politique religieuse*, Nouvelle Librairie Nationale, Paris.

_____ 1916. *Quand les français ne s'aimaient pas*, Nouvelle Librairie Nationale, Paris.

_____ 1922. *Romantisme et révolution*, Nouvelle Librairie Nationale, Paris.

_____ 1937. *Mes idées politiques*, Fayard, Paris.

Nolte, E., 1969. *Three Faces of Fascism*, Mentor Books, New York. Original German edition, 1963.

Taine, H., 1876–94. *Les origines de la France contemporaine*, 6 Vols., Hachette, Paris.

Talmon, J. L., 1952. *The Origins of Totalitarian Democracy*, Secker and Warburg, London.

Tarde, G., 1912. *Penal Philosophy*, Howell, Boston.

7 The Moderate Right: The Conservative Tradition in America and Britain

Arthur Aughey, University of Ulster

Approaching the Moderate Right

The word 'moderate' is (as someone like Hayek might argue) a weasel word. Its use in politics is most frequently for practical rather than analytical purposes, a characteristic which tends to devalue it as a meaningful category. It is the contention of this chapter that moderate right does have some meaning. But first one must examine those expressions which are analytically illegitimate. There are two major forms of usage which fall into this category. First, 'moderate' may often be a definition applied by political opponents to those features of thought and practice of an opposing ideology congenial to their own objectives and practices. For instance, in Britain socialists have been keen to accord the accolade 'moderate' to that style of 'consensual' Toryism which conforms most closely to collectivist assumptions. Clearly this understanding fails the test of objectivity because it is part of political practice and not a reflection upon it. Second, there is the very common assumption that moderation is a condition or style of politics which predisposes the advocate of that style to always seek the 'middle way' between 'extremes' of ideology. However attractive this definition might appear, even as self-ascription, it too is inadequate. What it suggests is a tradition of politics which is inert, without imagination or vision; a tradition of politics which is distinguished entirely in terms of responses to stimulation from those outside it. Conservatives who tend to accept this understanding get themselves into all sorts of bother when they wish to argue that, in fact, they do have something distinctive and purposeful to say. To proclaim, as Goldwater did, that he was 'extreme in the cause of moderation' was an attempt to square the definitional circle — not to break out of it.

An analytically useful definition of the moderate right may be approached by another route. French conservatives have often suggested a distinction between the *pays légal* and the *pays réel* (a distinction which finds a certain echo in the Marxist separation of 'base' and 'superstructure'). The *pays légal* denotes the structure of political and judicial institutions and the agencies designed to enforce their authority; or what is collectively known as the state. The *pays réel* denotes the true sentiments or spirit of a people expressed in traditional observances, pieties and social relations. Moderation, therefore, is political thought and practice rooted in the recognition of the correspondence between the legal and political order of the state and the sentiments, customs and practices — the character — of the people. Respect for constitutional procedure is central to this designation of moderation. For those on the left, constitutional form provides adequate avenues and possibilities for gradual reform. For those on the right, respect for constitutional procedures is the fundamental basis of stability and order. In both cases there is a recognition of the limits of the political over the social. Extremism of the right or left, by contrast, is rooted in the perception of the disseverance of state and society — either the foul usurpation of power by unrepresentative or unnatural leaders or the exploitation of the many by a self-perpetuating political elite — and that, therefore, constitutional practice is an illegitimate sham.

British conservatism is usually taken as the paradigm of the moderate right precisely because of the so-called massive continuity of British constitutional practice. American conservatism is rarely accorded the same respect. Indeed its exponents have expended an inordinate amount of energy trying to come to terms with the question of whether it forms part of the American political tradition or not. This has been wasted effort. Constitution 'consciousness' and the focus of ideological debate on its interpretation speak eloquently for both moderation and conservatism in American political life. The experience of the moderate right in America and Britain is examined below.

The Conservative Tradition

The lament of the moderate conservative might well be summed up by Stendhal's Lucien Leuwen, who questioned his fate thus: 'Am I doomed to spend my life between mad, selfish, and polite legitimists in love with the past, and mad, generous, and boring republicans in love with the future?' Dismissing the claims of both reactionary nostalgia and revolutionary imagination, which would seek to make over the established order in terms of either an ideal vision of what once was or an ideal vision of what ought to be, the conservative advocates a necessary caution and limitation.

Conservatism is partly an 'idealism of nostalgia', as Bob Berki argues, concerned not to celebrate the present alone but to achieve a moral and valuational anchorage in some definite, well-known and not too remote historical experience. The political good for a conservative is essentially taken from the past 'and no conservative of any distinction has ever thought that the past can or ought to be recreated *in toto*, or that past standards do not need any reformulation' (Berki, 1981, pp.199–200). Thus the distinction between the reactionary and moderate is not as simple as the distinction between nostalgia and satisfaction with what is. Conservatives and reactionaries both share a fascination with the past as a repository of fundamental wisdom. But whereas the conservative is willing to identify with the accumulated achievements of a political order, if not all of its contemporary values, the reactionary does not. For the conservative, as Ian Crowther puts it, an interpretation of the past is a means to 'elucidate what is rational in the "given"'. By contrast the reactionary comes to share a common disposition with the revolutionary (as

Leuwen clearly recognized) for the 'given' is 'invariably a source of envy and alienation and therefore to be swept aside and replaced by a new order of things more transparent to the (simple) mind' (Crowther, 1987, p.55). In short, the conservative recognizes the limits of nostalgia and in a profound sense recognizes that, on the one hand, the past is another country (it cannot be recaptured) but that, on the other hand, its values are to be found (however obscurely) in the enduring institutions and practices of the political order. It is that sense of reverence for the permanent vitality of the achievements of history which informs the conservative disposition. In its heroic mode, conservatism will understand itself to be the defender of the values of civilization. In its more prosaic, though less self-conscious mode, it will present itself as a set of political principles concerned to preserve continuity in the state.

Similarly, conservatism is not without imagination, though it can never expect to reach the heights of speculation of radicalism nor the sentimental depths of reaction. There is a heavy ballast within conservative thought which tends towards inertia, which is prepared to defend even the uncomfortable and the inconvenient simply because it has become part of a settled and predictable form of social life. Indeed, there is a tendency to make a virtue out of recognized evils because in some mysteriously intricate way they have deep inner relationships with what is good. The practical lesson though, according to conservative wisdom, is not that the delicate inter-relationship between aspects of the social and political order enjoins absolute fatalism or immobilism. As O'Sullivan points out conservatism is not committed to the absurd idea of opposition to change as such or to preserving all existing institutions (O'Sullivan, 1976, p.9). It is that there are limits to what can be done to change the human condition by conscious political action. This being the case, political activity ought to concern itself with specific abuses and not with grand visions. It matters little what reasons are cited to support this contention — human nature, common sense, law of unintended consequences, imperfection. The conclusion remains that revolutionary optimism is not just destructive but irrational for it attempts to step outside history. That is the sphere of the divine, not the human. And when men cast themselves in the role of gods they end up behaving like beasts.

This is hardly an inspiring admonition. It is certainly not a message which appeals to the apostles of dynamic transformation, to those who have faith in the boundless capacity of human reason and technique. Since their optimistic doctrine has exerted a powerful attraction upon the Western imagination in the last two centuries, conservatism is likely to appear timid, bloodless and incorrigibly defensive. In some ways it is. Berki is quite correct to assail the often 'ritualistic inexorability' of this feature of conservative thought, its readiness to 'erect "imperfection" into a kind of pseudo-perfection', its tendency towards a smugness and complacency in the face of both specific and general abuses (Berki, 1981, p.201). Such criticism is particularly apt at times of general crisis like the Wall Street crash when nations seemed trapped by their history and conventions, when conservative common sense often resembles worthless platitudes. But that is not all there is to be said about the conservative imagination (or the lack of it).

Berki is fully aware of this and his book is a masterly exercise in doing justice to both the realism and partiality of conservative thought. For moderate conservatism is not without the resources to criticize the existing nor to appreciate the inadequacy of current practices. Conservative thinkers may identify with the life of the state; their ideas are not thereby totally absorbed in the elaboration of the total perfection of that life, its harmony and grace. The notion of 'harmony' may be an important element in the calmly reflective idealism of conservative thinkers, that Tory strain which is almost religious in sentiment and tone (and therefore unpolitical). In the British and American experience mainstream conservatism has not suffered the anguish of utter severance of the *pays légal* from the *pays réel* which tormented and demented conservatives in France after the revolution and traditionalists in much of western and central Europe after the First World War. But the notion of a self-satisfied and complacent conservatism insensitive to the moral claims (to use a Greenian term) made of the state; or of a doctrine constantly trembling on the edge of concession or repression is nothing but a caricature. It is the product of the sort of thinking which assumes conservatism to be ideology of the ruling class or, which is more or less the same thing, a 'situational' ideology. For instance, Eccleshall, following Mannheim, claims that the intention of conservative ideology is 'to make the existing authority structure' acceptable to the masses and so 'provide a defence of class rule *per se*' (Eccleshall, 1977, p.66). And Huntington gives the impression that conservatism is some sort of ideological commodity or service to be taken up when the going gets rough, a notion which would be laughable were it not so influential (Huntington, 1957, esp. pp.470–3). The assumption of both explanations is that conservative thought is without substantial philosophical value. To adapt from Péguy, they propose that conservatism '*commence en mystique et finit en politique* — through mysticism and politics of a most conspiratorial and philistine kind. But that is bad history and bad politics. Principally it confuses the conservative tradition with a wider tradition of which it is part, a point to which we shall return.

The conservative imagination may be limited to suggestions for amelioration and reform. Yet this is also a creative if imprecise exercise and presupposes a sympathy for and an apprenticeship in a concrete manner of behaviour. The purpose and legitimacy accorded to change is that of conserving or advancing the rights and liberties of an actual political order. Its spirit lies in a sort of incremental consolidation which is why conservatism is usually taken unawares by a deep and general crisis. The logic of imaginative change for the moderate right in Britain and America is thus figurative rather than scientific. Whereas political logic in the latter sense implies the application of exact principles in advance of activity, the former suggests recognizable conditions which arise as a result of practical engagements, historical circumstance and public convention. As Anthony Quinton has it, for conservatives 'political action and institutions should be adjusted to accommodate changes which have come about in an extra-political way' (Quinton, 1978, p.20). Of course such an 'organic' view of political life, one tied to a certain ill-defined social naturalism, does not prescribe any particular solutions. 'Remedying the incoherences' of a political order or pursuing its 'intimations', to use the vocabulary of Oakeshott, depends not upon philosophical precision but upon judgement, calculation and often faith. Nor does it rest upon some theory of an inexorable linear development vouchsafed to only a few. Neither the British nor the American conservative tradition has had much time for philosopher kings.

Now there is quite a respectable tradition of argument which accounts for the accommodating nature of conservative politics in America and Britain in geographical terms. Britain's insularity and America's isolation, it is held, permitted these traditions to develop in a peculiarly civil fashion without the authoritarian militarism of western European states. Britain's empire and America's frontier relieved conservative forces in both countries from having to confront head on the political demands of newly emerging interests and classes. Geographical breathing space created a vital cultural *Lebensraum* and helped to establish a political tradition of concession and reconciliation. There may be something to this argument but in itself it is clearly inadequate. Britain's was not the only empire and America's was not the only frontier. What gives a reasonably coherent identity to conservatism as a political ideology is its engagement with opposing political principles, its intellectual and cultural contention with radical idealism. This relationship gives content to the empty categorization of 'situational' and reveals that there is more to the moderate right than the materialism of class interest. And rather than the British and American experience determining the character of conservatism, the engagement of conservative and radical ideas *is* the American and British experience.

In this sense conservatism may be understood as the *inner vision* of the political life of a state. It looks within the authoritative traditions, customs and conventions of political community for its imagery and inspiration. What it seeks are recognizable and stable landmarks to orient it in the flux of the present. In feeling thus engaged with the continuity of the social world one 'stands in the current of some common life' (Scruton, 1980, p.21). One's individuality is filled out by participation in this common life and this common life is modified, significantly or infinitesimally, by individual contributions to it. Thus to try to discover one's real self, as some radicals claim to do, by removing all 'artificial' social influences and accretions or by removing oneself, actually or metaphorically, to some naturally primitive state is a romantic nonsense. The only self we can discover is our social self. Similarly, freedom is not to be found in liberation of the individual from every social restraint except those which are self-imposed. Freedom understood in this sense can only lead to anomie and chaos. Freedom lies in living responsibly according to the morality of one's society. Of course this criticism of radical individualism does not imply a preference for the egalitarian sovereignty of the mass. For the conservative both the individual and the mass are unreal polarities of political discourse. Just as the individual cannot be understood except in terms of the vital social membranes which give meaning to personal liberty, so the mass cannot be understood except in terms of its inherited national character — which is none other than those 'age-old customs, dignities, considerations and gratifications' of the established social order (Blackham, 1961, p.54).

This starting point helps to explain the conservative concern for what Burke called the 'small battalions', its professed interest in social diversity. Certainly it is easy to translate the expression 'social diversity' into 'economic inequality' and thereby accuse conservatism of defending the privileges of wealth. The accusation would have to be upheld; but it does not necessarily signify anything very profound. The importance of the variety of social institutions, like the church, the family, the school, the club, the business, private property, lies in their moral and civic educative function. The radical denigration of such institutions and the passion to liberate individuals from their dulling thrall undermines not only order but liberty as well. For since order and social discipline are essential to any functioning community, what is not acknowledged from within must be imposed from without. As Robert Nisbet (1986, p.186), the American sociologist who has been preoccupied with — some would say obsessed by — the fate of what he calls the intermediate groups in society, portentously argues:

> the conservative vision is made distinctive by premonition that out of mass democracy and boundless social and moral liberalism would come not greater freedom and justice, but a new and terrible form of society characterised, on the one hand, by the kind of absolute and ubiquitous political power that Burke saw as the chief contribution of the French Revolution and, on the other, by the incessant generating of what Burke called an 'unsocial, uncivil, unconnected chaos of elementary principles...one homogenous mass.'

Oppressive conformity imposed by political convenience could only be avoided by maintaining the spontaneous vitality of a diverse social life. That was the foundation of a proper civility. With one illuminating insight in a thesis which is generally wrong, Morton Auerbach notes the conservative ideal of 'nonrepressive self-control', which is conducive to the integration of a community 'by tradition and institutions handed down from the past' (Auerbach, 1959, p.1). Yet for Auerbach this ideal was an intolerable attempt to frustrate the inevitable course of history towards greater individual freedom and was doomed to fail. None the less, the fear outlined by Nisbet and the ideal outlined by Auerbach have been common currency in moderate conservative discourse throughout the nineteenth and twentieth centuries.

In that now rather quaint yet powerfully suggestive phrase of the English Idealist F. H. Bradley, conservatism identifies with both the mundane and the philosophical meaning of 'my station and its duties' (Scruton, 1980, p.34 has also understood the significance of the phrase). This is not just an instance of incorrigible conservative antiquarianism. The reasoning is that theories of individual rights or social justice, general radical exhortations to emancipation of the individual or the mass, cannot tell us how to behave as responsible and intelligent citizens. For the conservative they are abstract, worthless and therefore dangerous. In short, they are an escape from thought. It is only when we recognize ourselves to be involved in a larger life which demands of us an education in civility and morality; only when we acknowledge the authority of their duties are we citizens in any real sense of the word. To be parent, teacher, property owner, club member and so on entail performances and commitments which are not self-imposed but which must be learnt and accepted. To recognize that one has a certain station and certain duties and to come to know them is, for the conservative, the only rational way in which creative social experimentation can take place. Conformist, silly, pointless and spiritually deadening are what institutions and practices appear to those who only care to look in from the outside. To 'reject what exists without having tried it, and merely because it has not been self-imposed', argues O'Sullivan, 'is a response to the world which is unique in Western history' (O'Sullivan, 1976, p.21). It is a response characteristic of the radical thought to which conservatism is fundamentally opposed.

What is true of social life is equally true of political life. Conservatism locates political values in the existing institutional form, in the inner workings of a political community. As Oakeshott stresses, for the person of a conservative disposition political activity 'springs neither from instant desires, nor from general principles, but from the existing traditions of behaviour themselves' (Oakeshott, 1962, p.21). On the other hand, the radical erects an index of abstract principles with which to measure political life. The greatest happiness of the greatest number; liberty, equality, fraternity; social justice are the crusading simplifications which must uproot all existing form, systematically or violently, in the process of realization. The institutions and mechanisms which conservatism take to be the repositories of value and principle are seen as nothing more than obstacles to rationality and righteousness. This transcendent vision of the radical is dismissed by the conservative as a dramatic misconception, an ideal index, the standards of which no political order, however just and benign, can hope to satisfy. What is more, humble and imperfect citizens cannot satisfy it either. Conservatism holds that political ideals are not divorced from the real but presuppose it; and to deny the latter in the glory of the former is to mistake shadow for substance. The abstract claims of radical idealism have no vital independence. They are nothing but 'a mere index of concrete behaviour' (Oakeshott, 1962, p.136). In other words, radical idealism erects a standard of rational criticism which is taken to be universally correct but which turns out to be the life of the state understood without its accidents, contingencies and non-rational attributes.

The values which the radical seeks to realize already have currency. They are to be found within the institutional life of the political order itself which accounts somewhat for the conservative regard for constitutional propriety and the majesty of the law. What to the radical appears as either stuffy formalism or the masking of oppressive power is for the conservative the efficient secret of political liberty. Institutional form is no horrid irrationality but an achievement of civilization. It is not something to be overthrown lightly for it embodies and preserves the political genius of a people. Thus there is an organic relationship between principle and the practices of the state; and like all living things the organism must be imperfect. For Burke (1973, p.120), this relationship had its own natural rhythms and:

> moves on through the varied tenor of perpetual decay, fall, renovation and progression. Thus, by presenting the method of nature in the conduct of the

state, in what we improve, we are never wholly new; in what we retain we are
never wholly obsolete.

The correspondence with nature, the sense of the God-given, stressed the
limits of politics and asserted the divine purpose, though not the divinity of
the state. This latter argument was both irrefutable and unprovable; and
though the religious idiom may still find its way into conservative discourse,
especially in America, it is not a necessary justification for the temper of the
moderate right. In secular times, if mankind can no longer understand itself as
an instrument of the divine neither need it understand itself to be capable of
divinity. Mankind can be creative but it can never be the Creator. Like the
artist the politician works within a general tradition which limits and
disciplines but which allows for inventiveness and originality. Of course,
conservative thought is most often concerned with, and sometimes obsessed
by, limit and discipline and seldom with inventiveness and originality.

   This is the very source of the insufficiency of conservative 'truths'. They do
not do full justice to that complexity of political life which they claim
uniquely to recognize. There is something too dogmatically certain about its
denunciation of dogmatic radical certainty. Its iteration of the accumulated
wisdom of historical experience is only a limited perspective on that historical
experience. For the general tradition which conservatism claims to affirm is
not its tradition alone. Conservatism is political tradition seen from the inside
and is therefore a partial and circumscribed vision. Conservatism appropriates
the historical achievements of a polity and ascribes them to its own sagacious
insight. This is at best a half-truth. It ignores the very necessary contribution
to the public good of the very radicalism which it opposes and draws a discrete
veil over those features of conservative politics which do not fit the benign
self-image.

   Very simply and perhaps obviously, the moderate right in Britain and
America is part of a wider tradition of political life and cannot be understood
apart from it. The inner vision depends upon the transcendent vision and vice
versa. The philosophy of limits, gradualness and hard-headed pragmatism is
the counterpart of the philosophy of limitless human progress, dynamic
enthusiasm and impatient principle. As Kenneth Minogue stresses, 'the
elements of one country's political tradition lean heavily on each other and
form part of a single political experience'. And to say that we cannot escape
from tradition, he goes on, is 'simply another way of saying that we cannot be
other than we are — a statement which would be entirely vacuous were it not
that the illusions of practical life so constantly tempt us to think differently'
(Minogue, 1968, p.287). So while the character of the right is defined in
opposition to the character of the left neither the right nor the left inhabit
entirely distinct and exclusive worlds. A political tradition, as Oakeshott has
warned, is a very tricky thing to get to know. The ideological abstractions of
conservatism and radicalism do reveal certain features of a tradition but only
in the form of a caricature. And within a tradition of politics, as Hegel
observed, the philosopher can rarely detect the clash of right against wrong
but the tragic clash of right against right. But then the philosophical mind, like
the religious mind, is *hors du combat*. It is the very partiality and one-

sidedness of political conviction which gives to an ideology its passion and purpose.

A tradition, the concrete experience of a political community, can be interpreted in terms of liberal progress. It can also by interpreted in terms of conservative stability. The same historical fortunes may be understood by the reactionary as a chronicle of usurpation; and by the revolutionary as a tale of frustration and betrayal. Understood in this light, Minogue thought that conservatism, confronted by the dramatic inspiration of radical optimism in the nineteenth and twentieth centuries, had resolved itself into 'little more than a timid appeal to caution' (Minogue, 1968, p.308). A similar interpretation could be put on the conclusion of R.G. Collingwood's *The New Leviathan*, where conservative politics is allotted the role of acting as a necessary restraint upon and limitation to the progressive thrust of modern radicalism (Collingwood, 1942). It is correct to see the spirit of the moderate right expressed in terms of caution and limitation. It would be incorrect to understand the influence of conservative politics as a mere break on developments, the course of which it cannot influence. That is to understand a political tradition in a mechanical fashion which does not effectively capture its ideational complexity. It makes the same sort of error as Eccleshall or Huntington, only this time in reverse. The only difference is that radicalism has replaced conservatism as the ruling ideology situated in defence of a dominant view of the world. Political relationships are not so rigidly fixed, not so neatly packaged for academic consumption. In truth, a Tory might well steal the Whigs' clothes while they are bathing and vice-versa; for both conservative and radical can draw upon a vast range of political ideas which are neither intrinsically conservative nor identifiably radical. And in so far as political life is carried on within generally accepted rules of traditional civility — however fluid they may appear on occasions — both will share many assumptions and prejudices, be part of the *Zeitgeist*.

Moreover, conservatism does not just engage in a forlorn delaying operation dishing out concessions when required. Conservative values contribute definitely to its character. For instance, a recent and influential thesis advanced by Martin Wiener attempted to account for the rather poor performance of the British economy since the late nineteenth century by reference to the inherent conservatism of the notion of 'the English way of life'. In his opinion the 'idealisation of material growth and technical innovation that had been emerging received a check and was more and more pushed back by the contrary ideals of stability, tranquility, closeness to the past and "nonmaterialism"' (Wiener, 1981, pp.409–11). And such is the variety of a political tradition that in the mid-1970s conservative politics should be associated with a crusade designed to shake the British economy out of that traditionalist torpor. An examination of the justification for what has become known as Thatcherism reveals both the partisanship of tradition but also the limits which tradition imposes. Thus, Sir Keith Joseph once talked about the 'ratchet effect' of socialism which had inexorably taken Britain to the left since 1945. No distinctive measures derived from conservative principles had been stamped upon British society. Conservative compromise had become a euphemism for capitulation to the idealism of the left. The purpose of conservative politics, therefore, ought to be to reverse the trend, to launch a crusade, as Mrs Thatcher put it, not just to put a brake on socialism, but to stop its onward march once and for all. This was effective party politics but historical nonsense. (Those, like Sir Ian Gilmour, who thought that elements of Thatcherism were philosophically unconservative had some justification for their suspicions. Politically, though, Thatcherite radicalism served well the interests of the Conservative party.) The nature of the British polity is the outcome of the interaction of conservative, liberal and socialist values and the mosaic of policy since 1945 has generally been laid on the firm foundation of common political ground. The rather cautious and limited reform of the Thatcher years reveals the simplicity and partiality of the original assumption as well as the resistant character of the British political tradition.

Now what has been said so far about the politics of the moderate right may appear unexceptionable as a description of the British case. What may appear exceptionable is the extension of the foregoing analysis to the American experience. The point I wish to make is not that British and American versions of conservatism are identical; it is to argue that the moderate right in Britain and America both share that general vision of politics which I have defined as a concern to defend the substantial inner life of the state against exogenous and/or transcendent challenges. Before exploring some of these concerns — and in order to establish this point — it is necessary to examine briefly the nature of the American political tradition.

American Conservatism

First, Leuwen's lament might appear distinctly inappropriate in the American case because there has never been an *ancien régime* to restore and the concept of progress, of a limitless future, has been the central idea of the 'American way of life'; in other words, it has no feudal past. Secondly, the 'classlessness' of American society may be held to make nonsense of the notion of station and duties. Thirdly, it could be argued that the naturalness and divine 'givenness' which conservatives have attributed to the political order is irrelevant in a country where the state has been established by men and grounded in their self-evident rights. Finally, traditions congenial to the conservative mind are exactly what Americans lack. The rich history which British conservatives can plunder to advantage contrasts severely with the barren inheritance of the United States. As Oscar Handlin notes, efforts to 'locate a conservative tradition ran up against the blank wall of the American past, which offered men no heritage but that of change' (Handlin, 1963, p.446). That evidence would appear to point conclusively against any vital conservatism in American politics, a view which has exerted a powerful influence in American scholarship.

One example is Louis Hartz, who advances the argument that *the* American political tradition is a *liberal* tradition. Liberalism and Americanism can be used interchangeably. There is no inner vision and no transcendent vision. There is only a universal Lockenism, a triumphant, inarticulate doctrinal homogeneity. As he puts it (Hartz, 1955, p.141):

When a nation has cause for political philosophy, nothing can stop it from producing it, and the clue to its absence in America lies in the absence of its cause. The absence of 'opposing principles', the fact that beneath its political heroics the nation was of the 'same mind' on the liberal formula, settled in advance the philosophical question.

For Hartz, American history only revealed 'the fixed dogmatic liberalism of a liberal way of life'. However, it is this very fixed dogmatism which begins to worry his critical intelligence, for Hartz has an intimation that it represents the weakness of his thesis. For American political life has exhibited flux and controversy, dissent and upheaval, not just dogmatic certainty. He notes a tension in politics between the claims of 'variety' and 'equality' and suggests, but does not explore, the historical contradiction of American liberty producing the threat of conformity. Since he does not allow this tension to have any concrete issue, the only resort is to suggest a conflict of emphasis within dogmatic liberalism itself (thereby, of course, rendering it *undogmatic* and a very uncertain guide to its practitioners). The 'ironic flaw in American liberalism', he writes, 'lies in the fact that we have never had a real conservative tradition' (Hartz, p.57). Apart from what he calls the 'Reactionary Enlightenment' of the feudal South which flourished in defence of slavery and is represented by the writing of Calhoun and Fitzhugh, Hartz has no place for ideological conflict in his view of the American experience.

But the real irony of Hartz's liberal tradition is that its supposed universality, which embodies both affirmation and criticism, can readily turn into its opposite. It does not take much for dogmatic liberalism to transform itself into dogmatic conservatism and still be faithful to a unique interpretation of American history. According to Boorstin (1953, p.6), the history of the United States has fitted its citizens uniquely:

> to understand the meaning of conservatism. We have become the exemplars of the continuity of history and of the fruits which can come from cultivating institutions suited to a time and place, in continuity with the past.

Like Hartz he believed that the lack of political philosophy was the result of a settled tradition. Of course, for Boorstin (1953, p.176), this American way of life:

> is conservative: it presupposes a certain national character or destiny as always in a sense given, given by the circumstances of geography and history. Its corollary is a suspicion of grand schemes which seek to make over the character of men and institutions.

A more succinct exposition of the limited style of conservative politics, of the 'inner vision' of the moderate right, would be hard to find. Hartz and Boorstin cover the same ground and make more or less the same observations yet place different ideological labels on the nature of Americanism. How do we account for this?

Part of it is due to the intellectual atmosphere of the early 1950s which stressed the 'end of ideology'. The impact of this was to render the study of political history and culture arid and lifeless. The liberal tradition of Hartz and the conservative tradition of Boorstin, because they claim universal application, lack precision and definition and therefore cannot really explain the divisions and contentions of political life. It is like arguing that nineteenth- and twentieth-century British history is an essay in Burkean stability; or equally that it is an elaboration of Mill's *On Liberty*. Either of these interpretations would have a certain truth. But neither of them would be the whole truth. It is also blandly contradictory. Hartz's liberalism is a thoroughly conservative tradition; Boorstin's conservatism is a mere abridgement of the liberal idea. More significantly, part of the explanation is also due to the weight put upon America's historical uniqueness, its lack of a feudal inheritance, the absence of an aristocratic, hierarchic social order. Since Americans rebelled against the impositions of such an order in the name of liberty and rights and established the 'first new nation' as a republic, there has been an assumption that they also rebelled against the whole ethos of conservative thought. In so far as conservatism is taken to be only the expression of aristocracy and the feudal inheritance, this would be so. Moreover, what has given this interpretation greater force is that a number of modern American intellectual conservatives, like Kirk and Nisbet, have tended to subscribe to that notion as well. This has often meant that systematic studies of American conservatism have looked in vain for the political influence of the *urtypisch* Burkean 'model', aristocratic and feudal, and conclude that something must be amiss with their subject.

Thus, Clinton Rossiter argued that the reason the American right was not conservative was because it had not been for most of its history. His questionable original assumption was that conservatism 'first emerged to meet the challenge of democracy', an assumption which ignores a whole web of principled opposition to the ideas of the French Revolution. Liberalism has been suspicious of democracy as well. However this may be, Rossiter's point was that the early triumph of democracy in America 'was a disaster for genuine, old-country Conservatism'. This goes to the heart of the matter, for genuine, old country Conservatism' is something which the American moderate right — by definition — could not espouse, even if there was an initial Federalist hankering for a political order founded on something more substantial than simple republican 'virtue'. Rossiter's conclusion, though, was that American conservatism has always been out of touch with the 'nation's ideals' and that outspoken conservatism has been doomed to political failure (Rossiter, 1962, pp.201–2). It is a conclusion that echoes throughout much of the subsequent literature. Ronald Lora traced the poverty of the conservative ideal in America to its lack of compassion, hostility to science, its 'antagonism toward the very premises on which modern Western civilization, and particularly the United States, rests', its opposition to individual freedom and finally its suspicion of the idea of progress (Lora, 1979, ch.13). This denies too much, for the absolute judgements made by Lora really reveal his own ideological prejudices rather than the alien character of conservatism in America. The substance of his criticism reduces itself to the rather obvious truth that — abstractly stated — the American conservative understanding of compassion, science, civilization, freedom and progress is at odds with the relevant liberal valuation. Ultimately, he too must resort to some notion of 'genuine' conservatism which conveniently solves his difficulties (of course, by Lora's own definition, genuine conservatism must be definitely unAmerican) and prop up his conclusions with the old crutch of Hartz's universal liberal tradition. In both cases the fascination with the substantive distinctiveness of the American political tradition has concealed the real character of conservatism. It has become lost in the very special idealism of the 'American way of life'.

Now it is undoubtedly true that the language of American idealism sounds curiously radical and enthusiastically optimistic to the ear of the world-weary European right. The 'spirit of '76' is a heady spirit. But it too can mean different things to different people. It too has an inner and a transcendent vision, though the similarity of language can often confuse. Novelists have captured this atmosphere more accurately than academics. As Vida Sherwin told Carol Kennicott in Sinclair Lewis's *Main Street*:

> I'm afraid you'll think I'm conservative. I am! so much to conserve. All this treasure of American ideals. Sturdiness and democracy and opportunity. Maybe not a Palm Beach. But, thank heaven, we are free from such social distinctions in Gopher Prairie. I have only one good quality — overwhelming belief in the brains and hearts of our nation, our state, our town. It's so strong that sometimes I do have a tiny effect on the haughty ten thousandries. I shake 'em up and make 'em believe in ideals — yes, in themselves.

Vida Sherwin is a great exponent of conservative wisdom. She advises the radically-minded Mrs Kennicott, who cannot encounter a current practice without wanting to reform it, that the only way to change is reform from within. 'Think how much better you can criticise conventional customs if you yourself live up to them scrupulously' (Lewis, 1985, pp.66 and 344). In the saga of Gopher Prairie there is much to be learned about the nature of the inner vision of heartland American conservatism; what liberty, democracy, progress and the pursuit of happiness mean as a definite way of life. 'Genuine' conservatism there is. But it is not a British import. It is a product of the American way of life, which also produces the radical ideas against which it defines itself.

An instance may serve to make this point. In a recent history of the United States Peter Carroll and David Noble develop a radical and revisionist view of their subject. Their intellectual premise is a sound one in that they reject the ideological simplicity of both the 'consensus' and the 'conflict' historians. The course of American politics, they believe, can only be understood in terms of a 'dynamic' relationship of groups and ideas. However, they too fall into the trap of rigid abstraction and often fail to see the real dynamic interaction between opposing ideas. Thus for Carroll and Noble (in Barnes and Noble, 1985, p.16):

> the history of the American people may be seen as the attempt by transplanted Europeans to impose Western values on nature and society in the face of spreading opposition from within — from Native Americans, blacks, ethnics, women and, most recently, young people.

The truth is that the opposition of which Carroll and Noble speak is incomprehensible except in terms of transplanted Europeans and their imposed values. The counter values which all these so-called 'out' groups espouse are none other than Western values in another guise. In particular, the idealism of the counterculture which challenges the materialism of American society is inconceivable without that materialism. The 'Easy Rider' culture depends on motorcycle workers in Milwaukee, motorway construction workers, oil corporations and the whole socio-economic and political order which makes it possible. Similarly, the advancement of minority rights presupposes a whole philosophical, political and legal tradition which recognizes claims made in the name of right and justice. Carroll and Noble can express well the themes of American radical idealism and its transcendent values. They reveal its historical impact and suggest its unfinished business. On the other hand, they cannot grasp their subject as a dynamic whole and acknowledge the equally compelling insights of the 'inner vision' of American conservatism.

Linking Themes

Full justice cannot be done to the range of argument within the moderate right in America and Britain in the space of part of a chapter. Enough may be suggested to indicate the common concerns of, as well as the differences in, the two traditions. In the nineteenth century, conservative thought engaged the problems of revolution and constitutional government, democracy and progress. In the twentieth century, conservatism has been concerned with establishing a firm foundation for individual liberty against the challenges of socialism and libertarianism. Each epoch raises distinctive political questions for which answers must be sought. These preoccupations tend to impart to different periods of history a definite atmosphere. But it is important to remember that no single question can exclusively occupy any political ideology. Therefore the conservatism of each political generation will amount to a reworking of the whole of that tradition of which it is a part. In that reworking the meaning of some principles will change as will the significance of particulars of faith. Others may be abandoned entirely even though their spirit may linger as a poetic romance — for despite its association with hard-headed realism, conservatism is acutely prone to the romantic idiom. Therefore it is not true to say that the 'substance of conservatism is essentially static'; that it is 'without tradition' or 'without history', a simple repetition of a basic 'catechism' universally applicable (Huntington, 1957, p.469). Jacobins or Bolsheviks in power may have something to conserve but they are not part of a conservative tradition.

Tom Paine had declared in *Common Sense*, a treatise which has been seen as steeling the American colonists for revolution, that men had it in their power to begin the world over again. The revolutionary force of Paine's belief did not make itself felt in the America of 1776 nor in 1787. It was the dramatic and wondrous course of the French Revolution which startled the world with the profound political implications of that idea. It provoked a response which has since been acknowledged as the birth of political conservatism. In the face of the challenge of this unprecedented revolutionary idealism opposition emerged to the idea that the world could be made over at will. It stressed the limits of human reason, the solid wisdom of tradition and therefore the limits of political action to change the human condition. Specifically it opposed the subversion of the institutional framework of society and the concentration of political power in the pursuit of some absolute and transcendent principle. The vast inheritance of constitutional form ought not to be squandered on this speculative bond of radical optimism; nor should the variety of human purpose, endeavour and achievement be reduced to the levelling and monomaniacal instincts of the *philosophes*. Conservatives looked instead to the ideal of constitutional balance which had a place for everything and everything in its place. Unsurprisingly, they found the substance of that ideal in current form.

In England Edmund Burke looked to the Revolutionary Settlement of 1689 as having bequeathed a constitution which effectively balanced interests and estates. In America John Adams contrasted the 'wild philosophy' of the French Revolution with the conservative wisdom of the American embodied in the Constitution with its federalism, its checks and balances and its separation of powers. But unlike Burke, Adams could shed no tears over the *ancien régime*. The French had a right to reform their institutions and to attain constitutional liberties. He believed that they happened to be misguided in their attempt (Peterson, 1976, pp.57–75). Yet both held that the principles of the French Revolution were not just subversive of bad government but subversive of all government and so at odds with political reason. But in attacking the naïvely optimistic delusions of the revolution, Burke and Adams tend to transform the idea of the constitution into prescriptive formalism, of balance into permanent rigidity. Burke assumed a harmony between the political and social orders which revealed a state of constitutional perfection. Adams paid so much deference to the English model and its ideal symmetry of monarchy, aristocracy and democracy that he was too often blinded to the social conditions and too pessimistic about the political character of his own republic. However they were clear on one point; namely, that the passionate elevation of one or more principles, such as democracy or equality, over and above or subsuming all others was destructive of limited constitutional government whether monarchical or republican. And for both men limited constitutional government was no mere notion but an achievement of civilization. On the other hand, the abstract index of revolutionary principle was an instrument of permanent revolution that could find no institutional form for the values it claimed. In its frenzy of Virtue it could only destroy those settled virtues of constitutional government necessary for the enjoyment of liberty, property and civilized life.

Certainly the seventeenth-century British aristocratic order and the relations of American colonial society could not be the last word on liberty, property and civilized life. Conservative politics had to adapt to the forces of change working within the state. In the American case, the adaptation was more abrupt. Indeed the position adopted by the Federalists at the turn of the century was at odds with the spirit of the new republic. Almost echoing the

Cromwellian lament they were suspicious of the world they had helped to create and longed for something monarchical — and aristocratic — in the structure of government. Those like Alexander Hamilton and Fisher Ames may have been expressing a belief which was common to students of the classics; and feared, like Montesquieu, that large states were incompatible with republican virtue, that liberty needed its natural guardians. But this was not to be conservative according to the nature of American society. It was to be conservative according to the nature of European society. The defeat of the Federalist transatlantic nostalgia in the early years of the republic perforce transformed the character of native American conservatism. As Lipset (1979, p.85) argues:

> American conservatives during the first half of the nineteenth century had to come to recognize that, like it or not, they must operate within the context of a society in which egalitarian values were dominant, and in which the right of the people to govern, and of the able to succeed, must be accepted as inviolable.

Many of the most articulate and cultured members of the right did not like it at all. Hofstadter notes that the coarse, materialistic civilization that emerged in the middle of the nineteenth century 'produced among cultivated middle-class young men a generation of alienated and homeless intellectuals'. Frustrated by politics they took to scholarship, their tender consciences finding 'wistful expression in the writing of history' (Hofstadter, 1966, p.206). Henry Adams's nine volume *History of the Administrations of Jefferson and Madison* (1885–1891) was a tribute to an aristocratic ideal of public service, which served as a contrast to the corruption of contemporary democratic practice. His brother Brooks was notoriously pessimistic about the quality of American public life and both were dismissive of popular paeons to progress and social evolution. Similarly A. J. Nock attacked the superficial utilitarianism of his society which despite all its technical efficiency was deficient in moral qualities. What was the point of dramatic mechanical progress if it were unaccompanied by the spiritual improvement of mankind?

Santayana too saw 'no special ideals of life' embodied in American political democracy and feared that the levelling of society 'would leave no room for liberty. The only freeman in it would be one whose ideal was to be an average man' (Santayana, 1905, p.307). Of course such interpretations involved a conservative theory of mass society and its consequences, a society without the necessary virtue or will to protect its liberties. It expressed those specific reservations about democracy in America that had been advanced by de Tocqueville fifty years earlier. De Tocqueville acknowledged that democracy in America had its dangers of the tyranny of the mediocre and observed the problems of establishing 'a spirit of honourable devotedness'. He wrote that democracy in America was not conducive to a 'brilliant society' but was in the process of creating a society diverted to 'the production of comfort and the promotion of general well-being' (de Tocqueville, 1972, pp.252–3). Of course it was these very 'unheroic' and 'inglorious' developments which fostered the disenchantment of conservative critics. Huntington is quite justified in labelling all of them 'malcontents'. But he is wrong to assume that discontent is no part of conservative thought for discontent is essential to thought (Huntington, 1957, p.472). It is true to say that it was not a programme for action. Santayana (perhaps unwittingly) caught the real mood of this style of 'sensitive conservatism' by writing that its exponents were reluctant 'to embrace the fertile principles of life' in America, that the 'good laggards had not the courage to strip for the race' (Santayana, 1905, p.307). Which is not to say that their criticisms had no impact whatsoever upon American culture. They helped to keep alive an ideal of civilized values which is not reducible to calculations of utility.

Nevertheless conservatism in an active guise *was* in the political race. As Lipset further argues, conservatives 'concentrated their egalitarian enthusiasm on the need to make opportunity possible, as distinct from an emphasis on actual equality in social relations' (Lipset, 1979, p.85). Here the ideological similarities with British conservatism become more sharply focused even though the context is different. Towards the end of the nineteenth century conservatism in Britain began to turn 'from the defence of liberty as guaranteed by property' (an aristocratic ideal) to 'the defence of property in the name of liberty'. It represented an acceptance of Dicey's opinion that 'if you once desert the solid ground of individual freedom, you find no resting place till you reach the chasm of Socialism' (Southgate, 1977, p.197). In the British case there was no absolute triumph of the second idea of liberty, but rather a distinctive blending of the two. In America it was accepted almost without qualification and became inseparable from the whole revolutionary declaration of the progressive pursuit of happiness. Looking to the future in the security of the permanence of national institutions became a profoundly conservative and peculiarly American ideology. It was a complacent optimism which could celebrate the genius of its political achievements while at the same time glossing over the deficiencies of the present in the name of an even more glorious future. For Americans, as Handlin observes, 'there was always the future to redeem the shortcomings of the present' (Handlin, 1963, p.180). Defending property in the name of liberty meant defending a society differentiated in terms of wealth and achievement in the name of equality. The aristocratic tinge of the cultural conservatism of the Adamses and Santayanas — the idea that the advance of civilization has consisted in the diffusion and dilution of habits and values arising from the lives of the privileged and cultured few — transformed itself into its materialist *alter ego* which has been part of the character of the American right. It is also to be found in the writings of some British conservatives. The argument is that the material well-being and progress of the people depend upon the mass dissemination of the life-styles of the rich; and that what the few have today the many will have tomorrow. That was the real conservative achievement in America, a reconciliation of the future with the past in terms of popular accommodation with the present. Such a reconciliation was also the aim of British conservatism.

Conservatism in Britain, according to Lord Hugh Cecil, was not the effect of purely conservative tendencies which he believed disposed one to rest, safety and the familiarity of the known. Instead it was like a great river 'the waters of which come from many converging streams' (Cecil, 1912, p.23).

Cecil indicates the adaptive and responsive character of that tradition as it encountered the major challenges of industrialization and democracy and tried to reconcile them to the idea of constitutional balance. The justification of the political dynamic of these two challenges was to be found in a larger notion. The nineteenth century had inherited and developed an alternative idea which threatened the secure and settled features of the Burkean inner vision. This was the idea of progress which has been clearly outlined by Sidney Pollard in a way congenial to the interpretation of inner and transcendent visions. In his view the idea of progress (Pollard, 1971, p.184; our emphasis) has emerged as the:

> only one firm island *outside* the temporal and biased perspective of each separate interest: the continuous improvement, that is to say, the progress of humanity itself. It is a yardstick against which the separate contributions of men, of classes, and of theories, can be measured, and it can give moral reassurance to those who are well aware of the relativity of their convictions, but who yet require, psychologically, the assurance of a firmer morality. Conversely, without the conviction of progress, there is *no alternative* to an inevitable despair in reason and in a rational scientific approach to society, and to the decline into the mythology of nihilism.

That single external yardstick to which there is no rational alternative, whether it is called utility, individual right or social equality, has been rejected by conservatives in the name of the inherited values of the traditional order. Whereas American Federalists had only recourse to the classical texts of political philosophy, British conservatives could idealize the 'real' values of a 'true' aristocracy.

It is now easy to dismiss much of this conservative response in the first part of the nineteenth century as the political response of minds out of touch with the developing spirit of the age, and threatened by it. It can also be put down to the simple defence of an aristocracy whose power depended upon the maintenance of a unreformed constitution and a socio-economic order which deferred to the priorities of the landed interest. There is some truth in both of these views. After the mid-century, especially after the repeal of the Corn Laws, medievalism begins to wane and hostility to industrialism loses its edge in the era of settled Victorian prosperity. But it is not the whole truth for it neglects the importance of the *idea* at the heart of the criticisms of liberal utility. Nor was this idea without some impact on the traditions of British public life. Nor was it without an impact on the ideological inheritance and political appeal of the Conservative party. As Ian Crowther (1987, p.56) succinctly puts it:

> we can now see that the selfish materialism of early Victorian England desperately needed an infusion of the 'irrelevant' feudal principle that property has its duties as well as its rights...Socialists and liberals bid us go unresisting into the future. And without an articulate conservatism there would be no appeal against their religions of progress.

For instance, Coleridge's strictures against the state of his own day involved the necessity to establish a new balance between the forces of progress and the forces of stability, commercial wealth and the land. This was a two-way process. The accommodation of the old identity to the claims of the new also demanded of the new an acceptance of the traditional duties of the old. Interpenetration of both ideas would ensure the continuity of the balanced constitution while giving proper rein to the worth of each. Coleridge clearly defended the character of the traditional hierarchical order but the value of what he had to say is not confined to that defence. His was a vision deeply aware of the totality of political life, a unity that could not be contained within the confines of rigid nostalgia nor fulfilled by the simplicities of radical dogma. Disraeli had less philosophical insight than Coleridge and what he had he tended to borrow from Carlyle. But his romantic novels and his Young England fantasies involve a critique of liberalism which has inspired Tory rhetoric ever since. The central notion is that liberalism in its crusade to undermine traditional authority in the name of liberty and progress elevates self-interest into the highest principle of life. What liberals want to do is to separate possession from responsibility, privilege from duty. It was the neglect of responsibility and duty which created the 'Two Nations' and the 'Condition of England Question'. Disraeli has often been taken to advocate a return to feudalism. It is easy to see why, though this interpretation is mistaken. England's greatness, he recognized, also depended on her manufactures. Rather like Coleridge he was looking for a way in which Tory principles which he praised could infuse and in turn be invigorated by the energies of the new industrial and urban Britain.

Only the most uncritical Tory would argue that Disraeli's political career was one in which he set about transforming the values of his novels into the policy of the Conservative party. Only the peddlers of partisan 'good cries' would claim that humanitarian social reform was only the result of conservative opinion. A more sensible interpretation would be that by 'bringing the romantic tradition into the service of Toryism, he was instrumental in bringing the party up to date to suit the needs of the modern world' (Mendilow, 1986, pp.169–70). Disraeli helped to accommodate conservative thought to the social and economic character of late nineteenth-century Britain. On the one hand it could claim to represent order, property and stability and on the other it could claim to acknowledge the need for reforms in society, as Disraeli understood it, 'in accordance with its acquired and inherited character, and at a given rate'. Patriotism (the maintenance of national institutions), imperialism (defending Britain's interests abroad and extending its power) and social reform (giving self-help a paternal push) were woven into a balanced appeal to order and liberty, to stability and progress. It was a reworking of a number of familiar Tory themes in a fashion consonant with the temper of Victorian pride and its spirit of improvement.

One of the elements of 'Beaconsfieldism' was the elevation of the condition of the people symbolized by the slogan 'One Nation'. Of course the essence of this slogan was that there really did not exist any fundamental conflicts in British society (so long as, that is, a dutiful electorate returned Tory MPs). From that rather complacent disposition emerged the notion of Tory Democracy, a quite sanguine view of the possibilities of ensuring popular deference to the established authority of a balanced constitution. Not all were so optimistic. Two intimately related threats were perceived by reflective conservatives: a liberalism that would, in the name of individualism and personal freedom, grind down every distinction and difference in society — what Leslie Stephen called the 'macadamisation of society' — and in the process destroy individuality; and a socialism which would appeal to the dull mediocrity of mass man, encouraging him to abase himself before the image of his collective power (which is also the revelation of his personal impotence), the state. Hostility to the absolute claims of democracy were rooted in these fears. The coming of universal suffrage does not mean they were ill-founded; nor does it mean that conservatism 'lost' the ideological battle. That is far too superficial a view. In the main, conservatives like Lord Salisbury, well noted for his realism and his pessimism, were prepared to accept the inevitability of *procedural* democracy; but that was not the same thing as offering no resistance to the idea that the democratic state should have absolute power. Resisting the claims of democracy in the name of limited constitutional politics was easily transformed into the slogan of resisting the 'state' in the name of 'liberty'. This was *not* what conservatives were really concerned to do but it was a convenient ideological shorthand. Therefore conservative political thought at the end of the nineteenth and the beginning of the twentieth centuries increasingly concerned itself with the questions of individuality and liberty. This change of emphasis is often understood in materialist terms to represent an accommodation to the 'prevailing priorities' of capitalism. Again that is not the whole or even the significant truth of the matter. Confronting on the one side liberal individualism and on the other socialist state collectivism, conservative thinkers believed both to be abstractions (of liberty and order) from the substantial inner life of society. The problem for conservatives in the twentieth century was how to make this rather sophisticated idea intelligible to a democracy fed on a diet of political programmes.

Hannah Arendt captured a truth of the twentieth century when she wrote that 'distinction and difference have become private matters of the individual' (Arendt, 1959, p.38). This simple insight has profound implications for conservative political philosophy. Nineteenth-century conservatism held that distinction and difference were *public* matters essential to a limited style of politics, the inculcation of a sense of duty and responsibility and the nourishment of liberty. It was at the heart of the idea of a balanced constitution. A number of commentators have suggested that conservatism was concerned to maintain a set of mediate institutions between the individual and the state. The intuition is correct but the mode of expression is wrong. The idea of the balanced constitution supposed that the individual was part of, and had meaning in, a definite class or station and that the state was the authoritative expression of that arrangement. In other words the state was not absolute for it presupposed the life of its parts but neither did its authority exist solely to protect the rights of individuals nor could it be reduced to one or more of those rights. For those rights were meaningless without relation to the entire life of the state. The trend towards 'privatization' which Arendt explored could only disorder that notion. It made it easy for the state to absorb the vital functions of social institutions — a facility which has potentially unlimited political consequences. Similarly, it also made it easy for the individual to retire into a private world abandoning civic duty to the care of 'professionals'. Both tendencies would be mutually reinforcing and would contribute to a centralization of power, a social vacuum and selfish individualism. This is indeed a trend which conservatives have observed and their response to it has taken a number of forms.

One might have expected that American conservative thought would have been a fruitful source of reflection on these problems. The experience of the United States, as de Tocqueville clearly revealed, has been an anticipation of developments in Britain and Europe. Curiously enough, some extremely influential American conservative thinkers in the twentieth century tended to dismiss their own political inheritance and circumstances and look wistfully to the Old World. They set up their shrines to Burke and worshipped before them in tones of sepulchral incantation. Thus Russel Kirk presented six canons of conservatism most of which sounded rather quaint rather than perceptive. In particular his conviction that civilized society required orders and classes was alarmingly irrelevant to the average American (Kirk, 1953, p.17). The lesson of conservative America, which is also its continuing problem, is how civilized society and constitutional order can be maintained without recognized orders and classes. Similarly, Robert Nisbet's prolific writings showed great erudition and wisdom. Nevertheless, the force of what he has to say about the dangers of mass society has tended to get lost in his nostalgic romanticization of feudal society and its mediate associations (Nisbet, 1986b, esp. pp.33–47). But American society has never had these 'feudal' associations and it is pointless to advance a philosophy of politics founded on the assumption of their benign legacy. The history of the United States has been one of people constantly choosing their 'communities' and 'associations' rather than being born into them. That experience of civility is a substantial one with valuable lessons for modern conservative thought. The failure of this very prominent style of American conservative scholarship is that it is not in touch with the inner life of American society and can never engage its sympathies. It can only remain as an intellectual affectation. As O'Sullivan (1976, p.148) has noted, cutting themselves off in this manner:

> from the American tradition of dynamic change and dedication to material gain, the new conservatives were bound to appear as reactionaries who could, in the last resort, find refuge only in moral, aesthetic and religious appeals, rather than in concrete political and social performances.

A more appropriate understanding on the moderate right in America is to be found in the writings of people like Irving Kristol, Nathan Glazer and Daniel Bell who form part of what has become known as 'neo-conservatism'. Neo-conservatives have attacked the over-optimistic interference of government, the growth of a 'new class' of officialdom intent on preserving their own interests in the name of public welfare, the weakening of individual self-reliance by a paternalistic state. As Ashford's acute and succinct study (1981, p.360) reveals the:

neo-conservatives concern about government failure is not primarily motivated by questions of efficiency and waste but with how it has undermined confidence in the American political system and in those values they perceive as the basis of American society.

The implication of these writings is that the *pays légal*, the world of Federal Programs and Presidential initiatives, has got somewhat out of joint with the *pays réel*, the real America of self-reliance based on a self-discipline fostered by family, school and local community. However, this neo-conservative analysis is not populism of the mindless kind, a populism excellently characterized by Harvey Mansfield Jr (1987, p.201) as that of:

> honest individuals with good upbringing who do not need fancy constitutional contraptions in order to be honest, much less to restrain them from acting on what an honest people honestly sees.

It acknowledges the limits of government but also the requirements of order. Therefore neither is it simplistic free-market economics masquerading as politics. The Whiggery of Hayek is more prominent than the liberalism of Friedman. It aims to protect what is of value in the American tradition from the fashions of the new class and to encourage a proper reflection on and appreciation of the political achievement of the Constitution. The political vision of the neo-conservatives is one which can be readily shared by all citizens and not just the cultured few.

In Britain the notion of ordered liberty had become something of a conservative cliché. It was also easy to assume that if you wanted to know what ordered liberty looked like all you had to do was consult the policy of the Conservative party. That was a substitute for thought. The importance of the writings of Michael Oakeshott derive precisely from their fabrication of an intelligent and distinctively modern philosophical argument which provided conservatism with something more intellectually substantial than either the pieties of party propagandists or the repetition of Burkean sentimentality. Oakeshott's well-known attack on rationalism in politics and his articulate exploration of the idea of tradition of behaviour in which politics is a 'pursuit of intimations, not of a dream or a general principle' made it easy to interpret what he had to say as only the 're-orchestration of traditional conservatism' (Quinton, 1978, p.184). Certainly he emphasized the view that 'governing is a specific and limited activity, namely the provision and custody of general rules of conduct' and therefore 'something which it is appropriate to be conservative about' (Oakeshott, 1961, p.184). He was also concerned to re-assert against the engineers of human souls the variety and multi-dimensionality of experience, thus laying himself open to charges of mystification, that heresy relentlessly pursued by all transparent radicals.

All of this is familiar stuff. But what is really significant about Oakeshott's contribution to conservative discourse has been his attempt to adjust the ideas of tradition and diversity to the insight of Arendt and thus accommodate the claims of modern individuality to authority. This is much more obvious in his *On Human Conduct* published in 1975. Oakeshott here investigates political life in terms of civil association, a rule-articulated association within which all agents pursue their own self-chosen satisfactions. He contrasts this with enterprise association in which all must subscribe to a common purpose or interest. In Berki's words (1981, p.212) he:

> emphasizes that the relationship of civility consists in relative strangers (in the personal sense) being 'just' to one another, i.e. tolerant of diversity, respecting one another as free agents, ordering their activities in such a manner as not to hamper the satisfactions of others, etc., and that consequently the state cannot be turned into a giant factory, a church or a brotherhood.

This captures Oakeshott's formulation admirably and while it may be philosophically inadequate it has provided modern British conservatism with a theoretical understanding of individuality and authority which can more than hold its own against that advanced by the left.

Not all conservatives would find Oakeshott's understanding congenial. He may be suspected of being a little too individualistic for comfort. They would probably find greater comfort in the style of Roger Scruton who has taken the weight of conservative advocacy off Oakeshott's shoulders. In doing so Scruton has become the conservative whom every radical loves to hate and he has revelled in that role with an intellectual *jeu d'esprit*. The balance of Scruton's argument may be more concerned with authority than liberty but it is silly to suggest that he is a reactionary authoritarian. His work is an important contribution to the modern conservative attempt to locate personal freedom in a way which neither glorifies the state nor celebrates individual liberation. For instance when Scruton writes that 'Anglo-Saxon privacy which we esteem is in fact nothing more than the public order seen from within' he is not denying freedom in favour of order but recognizing it as but one relation in a 'substantial and enduring' life (Scruton, 1980, p.187). Freedom is the consequence of settled arrangements which set limits to both authority and personal liberty. Contributions to Scruton's *Salisbury Review* may be erratic and often wildly nostalgic. But his own considered academic work is fully within the tradition of the moderate right. Scruton has confronted the British new class on their own territory — especially in the column he wrote for *The Times* — and analysed its unspoken assumptions and hidden agenda in a way that has given intellectual respectability to what he has called the rather inarticulate 'conservative point of view'.

One piece of work which deserves special mention for linking up the modern themes of liberty and order in the American and British moderate right is the essay by Shirley Letwin *On Conservative Individualism* (1978). Letwin herself might claim to have a foot in both traditions being a student of Hayek and a disciple of Oakeshott. Her essay is an attempt to reconcile the apparent conservative dilemma — the choice between 'order' or 'freedom'. Far from being contraries, she argues, they are inseparable. Hers is a portrait of a world in which 'there is no need to repress the endlessly changing variety of the human world — it can be respected and enjoyed as the product of rationality' for individuality 'is displayed not in egoism, wilfulness, or in rebellion but in the integrity of a man's personality'. Society, therefore, is the cradle rather than the enemy of individuality. In its diversity (and here Letwin repeats a conservative truism as old as the balanced constitution) it is more friendly to liberty than the single universal truths of radicalism. The conservative individualist wants a kind of security which 'can only be found in an order that rests on tradition and authority' (Letwin, 1978, p. 62). That tradition and authority can encompass the Declaration of Independence and the Federal Constitution just as easily as Crown, Lords and Commons.

Letwin's essay represents a synthesis of responses to what O'Sullivan has called the 'crisis of conservatism' in the twentieth century. If it is in itself incomplete at least it indicates the sort of considerations which conservatives might fruitfully explore. It would be tempting to conclude that we can already witness the outworking of these ideas, however tangentially, in the politics of Reagan and Thatcher, however different their styles and circumstances. For as radicals constantly remind themselves in their house journals, 'Reaganism' and 'Thatcherism' will long outlive the political careers of the two leaders. So perhaps the crisis of conservatism is not as severe as O'Sullivan estimated in the mid-1970s. What we can be sure of is that there can never be an absolute triumph of the conservative attitude. Since it recognizes the diversity of thought and experience, an intelligent conservatism must also recognize that it is only a part and not the whole of a political tradition.

References

Arendt, H., 1959. *The Human Condition*, Doubleday, New York.

Ashford, N., 1981. The neo-conservatives, *Government and Opposition*, Vol. 16, No. 3.

Auerbach, M. M., 1959. *The Conservative Illusion*, Columbia University Press, New York.

Barnes, P. N. and Noble, D. W., 1985. *The Free and the Unfree*, Penguin, Harmondsworth.

Berki, R., 1981. *On Political Realism*, Dent, London.

Blackham, H. J., 1961. *Political Discipline in a Free Society*, Blackwell, Oxford.

Boorstin, D., 1953. *The Genius of American Politics*, University of Chicago Press, Chicago.

Burke, E., 1973. *Reflections on the Revolution in France*, Penguin, Harmondsworth.

Cecil, Lord Hugh, 1912. *Conservatism*, Home University Library, London.

Collingwood, R. G., 1942. *The New Leviathan*, Oxford University Press, Oxford.

Crowther, I., 1987. The uses of the past, *Salisbury Review*, Vol. 5, September.

Eccleshall, R., 1977. English conservatism as ideology, *Political Studies*, Vol. 25, No. 1.

Hartz, L., 1955. *The Liberal Tradition in America*, Harcourt, Brace and World, New York.

Handlin, O., 1963. *The American People*, Penguin, Harmondsworth.

Hofstadter, R., 1966. *The American Political Tradition*, Vintage Books, New York.

Huntington, S. P., 1957. Conservatism as ideology, *American Political Science Review*, Vol. 51, No.2.

Kirk, R., 1953. *The Conservative Mind*, Regnery and Gateway, New York.

Letwin, S., 1978. On conservative individualism, in M. Cowling (ed.), *Conservative Essays*, Cassell, London.

Lewis, S., 1985. *Main Street*, Penguin, Harmondsworth.

Lipset, S. M., 1979. *The First New Nation*, Norton, New York.

Lora, R., 1979. *Conservative Minds in America*, Greenwood Press, New York.

Mansfield, H. C. Jr, 1987. Pride and interest in American conservatism today, *Government and Opposition*, Vol. 22, No. 2.

Mendilow, J., 1986. *The Romantic Tradition in British Political Thought*, Croom Helm, London.

Minogue, K., 1968. Revolution, tradition and political continuity, in P. King and B. Parekh (eds), *Politics and Experience*, Cambridge University Press, Cambridge.

Nisbet, R., 1986. 1984 and the conservative imagination, in *The Making of Modern Society*, Wheatsheaf, Brighton.

Nisbet, R., 1986b. *Conservatism*, Open University Press, Milton Keynes.

Oakeshott, M., 1962. *Rationalism in Politics and other Essays*, Methuen, London.

O'Sullivan, N., 1976. *Conservatism*, Dent, London.

Peterson, M. D., 1976. *Adams and Jefferson: a Revolutionary Dialogue*, University of Georgia Press, Athens, Ga.

Pollard, S., 1971. *The Idea of Progress*, Penguin, Harmondsworth.

Quinton, A., 1978. *The Politics of Imperfection*, Faber, London.

Rossiter, C., 1962. *Conservatism in America*, Vintage Books, New York.

Santayana, G., 1905. *The Life of Reason*, Constable, London.

Scruton, R., 1980. *The Meaning of Conservatism*, Penguin, Harmondsworth.

Southgate, D., 1977. From Disraeli to Law, in Lord Butler (ed.), *The Conservatives*, Allen and Unwin, London.

Tocqueville. A. de, 1972. *Democracy in America*, Alfred Knopf, New York.

Wiener, M., 1981. Conservatism, economic growth and English culture, *Parliamentary Affairs*, Vol. 34, No. 4.

8 The Radical Right: The 'Conservative Revolutionaries' in Germany

Roger Woods, Aston University

Approaching the Radical Right

Characterizations of the radical right generally have to explain what marks it off from the traditions of the reactionary and the moderate rights. Most typically the radical right marks itself off from tradition through its commitment to an all-embracing, authoritarian concept of right-wing politics. The moderate, conservative, concern for the preservation of institutions also gives way to a rejection of the 'alien' institutions of modernity such as pluralism and parliamentary democracy. For the radical right the whole of the existing social order is decadent and needs to be removed. The position has been summed up as 'a revolt against existing institutions in the name of authority' (Muller, 1987, p.20). However, what is envisaged is not the return to the *status quo ante* of the reactionary right.

Traditional conservative disregard for organized political activity is replaced by the drive to articulate a political programme. And what forces the pace of this politicization and the consequent emergence of the radical right is primarily the need to provide a counterargument to socialism: much of the radical right's theorizing is clearly based on an inversion of the brand of social analysis which takes class and radical reform of the social order as its starting point. The need to combat class-based socialism generates a set of beliefs and values which touch upon every aspect of human existence.

An outlook which is primarily based upon negation of the existing order is particularly inclined to stress the spirit of any new political order rather than its content, and here we find the source for one further feature of the radical right: its activism.

All these features of the radical right are to be found in nineteenth- and twentieth-century Germany, particularly in the period between the world wars. Traditional conservatism was rejected as beyond repair and unable to counter socialism. The alien institutions were embodied by the Weimar Republic — an order attacked as having been imposed upon a nation in defeat. This perspective brought a further feature of the radical right to the fore: its nationalism. A problematic relationship with tradition, the need to rescue some meaning from the lost war, a rejection of the present and an inability to formulate a genuinely new political stance all contributed to the rise of activism within the radical right at this time.

The most articulate spokesmen of this position of the radical right in modern Germany were to be found in the movement which went by the paradoxical name of the 'conservative revolution'. It is an especially important manifestation of the radical right, not least because it helps illustrate both the common roots with, but also important differences from, fascism.

What Was the Conservative Revolution?

The conservative revolution has often been described as part of the great counter-movement to the French Revolution (see Mohler, 1972, pp.10f.; Bracher, 1973, p.183; Sontheimer, 1968, p.120; Schüddekopf, 1960, p.248). By this definition it extends back beyond the twentieth century, and it is clear that the radical right in the crucial Weimar years was able to carry forward from the nineteenth century a tradition of militaristic, authoritarian nationalism together with a rejection of liberalism, socialism, democracy and internationalism. These attitudes, which had taken shape not least as a reaction against the French Revolution, and the alienation of German political thought from western European traditions, had been consolidated by the failure of the 1848 Revolution in Germany. At the start of the nineteenth century Fichte had maintained that Germany had a 'special mission...which set it apart from the hitherto much admired and imitated French' (Bracher, 1973, p.39).

Yet today the notion of a fatal continuity of thought from the start of the nineteenth century to the Nazi takeover in 1933 is largely discredited: study of the inspirational and causal effect of ideas has generally given way to an examination of why, in the more immediate pre-Nazi period, these particular strands of German political thought were revived.

In this chapter the emphasis will be on the Weimar period of German history, a period in which the conservative revolutionaries assumed the role of 'intellectual vanguard of the right' (Struve, 1973, p.227), producing a flood of radical nationalist writings in the form of political journalism, manifestos, theoretical tracts outlining the development and destiny of political life in Germany and the West, war diaries and works of fiction. Their common goal was 'new' or 'revolutionary nationalism'.

The conservative revolution embraced academics, writers, journalists, politicians, philosophers. Throughout the Weimar years they strove to realize their visions of a strong Germany united beyond class antagonism, controlled by an authoritarian state and freed from what they condemned as the crushing burden imposed upon the nation by the Treaty of Versailles.

Although the term conservative revolution predates the First World War it only became an established concept in the Weimar period, passing into the cultural and political vocabulary of the day via the writer Hugo von Hofmannsthal and the publicist Edgar Jung (Mohler, 1972, pp.9f.). Modern historians have rightly referred to the term as a paradox (Bracher, 1973, p.183), even a semantic absurdity, and suggested 'neo-conservative' as a more easily justifiable label for the movement (Struve, 1973, p.224). The important point here is to understand what the term was meant to convey in the Weimar period. It was advocated by those radical right-wing thinkers who emphatically denied any allegiance to the traditional brand of conservatism which had its roots in Wilhelmine Germany. Most of these thinkers were equally scornful of the political parties of the right, and in the firm rejection of all thoughts of a political restoration and in the arrogant dismissal of all political parties as Western imports unsuited to the German people we see two of the major strands of conservative revolutionary thought. Equally important was the need to come to terms with socialism, not by embracing it in its existing form, but rather by reworking it into a 'German socialism', a 'socialism of the blood'. To examine the problems unearthed in the course of defining this German socialism is also to examine the dilemma of German conservatism in the post-1914 period.

The conservative revolutionaries also projected themselves as the young generation of German nationalists: many of them were born in the last decade of the nineteenth century, and this generational bond was strengthened through the First World War which so many of them had experienced directly in their formative years. The war looms large in their minds, for they see it and the November Revolution which followed in its wake as achieving a clean break with the past, liberating German political life from the constrictions of Wilhelminism and challenging the young generation to create a 'new nationalism'. The writer Friedrich Georg Jünger (1926, pp.5f.) explains just how fundamental this break with the past was felt to be:

> The November Upheaval confronted it [nationalism] with new, vital issues. Changed in its essence, forms and goals, it emerged from the collapse of the Wilhelmine State, no longer bound by the throne and inhibited by it, and consequently freer in itself, more aggressive, more dangerous than ever before. It had gone through such a transformation that it could no longer be compared with what people called nationalist before 1914.

The conservative revolution was not a tightly-knit movement with formal membership and a fixed programme. It certainly did embrace political organizations such as the Berlin Juni-Klub under Moeller van den Bruck and the Politisches Kolleg established in Spandau in 1920 by Martin Spahn to promote German nationalism and encourage the development of a ruling elite, yet no single organization included all the conservative revolutionaries.

The task of defining the conservative revolution is further complicated by the fact that its unity was often founded on negation: conservative revolutionaries were outspoken in their total condemnation of the Weimar Republic and its acceptance of German's 'colonial status'. Other targets range from the communists to political parties such as the Nationalists, who are said to be clinging to all those articles of traditional nationalist faith abandoned by the new nationalists.

Yet it is possible to list goals and attitudes common to most, if not all conservative revolutionaries: Weimar democracy is to be swept aside and replaced by a dictatorial order modelled on the military hierarchy and the 'front-line socialism' of the First World War. This national community (*Volksgemeinschaft*), it is argued, transcends the conventional divisions of left and right, and is the only true German heritage. More importantly, it is the only way for Germany to attain a position of strength in a world where nations have effectively discarded more standards in their dealings with each other and are guided only by 'natural' self-interest. Conservative revolutionaries' scorn for all who operated within the framework of parliamentarianism marks them off, if only in a formal sense, from the National Socialists. They can also be viewed as a group by virtue of their middle-class backgrounds.

The following account includes those figures who regarded themselves or who were regarded by their contemporaries as conservative revolutionaries, as well as those who shared a certain set of political beliefs, in particular the belief that it was necessary to break with traditional conservatism and come to terms with socialism. This approach suggests what is meant by a conservative revolutionary 'movement', but it does not mean uncritical acceptance of the movement's understanding of its position in the political spectrum, its aims or its motives. As will become apparent, it is often the discrepancy between an individual's subjective and objective positions which is so revealing about aims and motives, and about the conservative revolution as a whole.

Significance of the Conservative Revolution: Some Methodological Matters

Students of the conservative revolution generally see it as historically significant because it helped prepare the ground for National Socialism. For Martin Broszat the ideas of the conservative revolution served to weaken the German bourgeois academicians' intellectual resistance to Nazi ideology (Broszat, 1966, p.40). Bracher sees its main influence among the semi-educated middle classes and in the universities, where its 'anti-democratic ferment' found a receptive audience (Bracher, 1973, p.184), and Walter Bussmann argues that the ideologies of men such as Moeller van den Bruck spread notions of authoritarian leadership instead of a government responsible to parliament among the educated, indeed most gifted of Germany's youth (Bussmann, 1960, p.77). Sontheimer argues that anti-democratic thought in the Weimar Republic succeeded in alienating Germans from the democracy of the Weimar constitution and making large groups receptive to National Socialism (Sontheimer, 1968, pp.13f.).

It is true that some of these accounts of how the conservative revolution encouraged Germans to turn away from Weimar democracy and towards National Socialism are vague, and that more research on the transmission and dissemination of ideas needs to be undertaken, yet it is clear that the movement did make its mark on Weimar Germany. Oswald Spengler, a leading figure of the conservative revolution, is generally regarded as one of the most influential political writers in Germany after 1918, a view supported not least by the very popularity of his major work, *Der Untergang des Abendlandes*, which went through forty-seven editions in four years. More generally, the publishing activities of the conservative revolutionaries were conducted on a massive scale (Sontheimer, 1968, pp.32–4; Petzold, 1978, p.12). Historians looking at public opinion in the Weimar period have rightly referred to the upsurge in demand around 1929 for conservative revolutionary writings on the First World War as evidence of the spread of militaristic thinking which reduced the Kellogg–Briand Pact outlawing war to a mere piece of paper and helped the Nazis into power (see Wette, 1979, pp.94–9).

The direct links between conservative revolutionaries and mass organizations were numerous. The ex-soldiers and writers Ernst Jünger and Franz Schauwecker were brought into the paramilitary organization Stahlhelm and given their own journal, *Die Standarte*, in order to inject new life into the debate over the league's ideals. *Die Standarte* appeared as a supplement to *Der Stahlhelm*, with a circulation of 150–170,000. This was in the mid-twenties when Stahlhelm had an estimated membership of 300,000. Larger still at this particular time was the 400,000 strong Jungdeutscher Orden led by Artur Mahraun, a key figure in the debate over new nationalism, and especially the leadership principle (estimates of the size of these, and other combat leagues vary considerably; see Diehl, 1977, pp.293–7). Sontheimer is thus correct in saying that the conservative revolution is no esoteric affair for an elite group of ideologues, but rather at the productive heart of antidemocratic thought in the Weimar Republic, providing parties and other political groups with their ideology. Sontheimer refers in particular to the new nationalism of the conservative revolution and links this with the combat league Wehrwolf, Bund Oberland, Bund Wiking, and various youth leagues (Sontheimer, 1968, p.27).

It is clear that the conservative revolution was far from being an exclusively intellectual movement with no involvement in everyday politics (as early studies tended to suggest it was). It is also clear that there are ideological continuities between it and National Socialism. Yet Helga Grebing sums up the problem for anyone seeking to explain the significance of the conservative revolution and its predecessors when she writes that the question of the susceptibility to and preparation for National Socialism is not the same as the question of the roots and ideological precursors of National Socialism (Grebing, 1964, p.75).

Acknowledging this means that the conservative revolution must be placed alongside rather than above the host of other influences which undermined the Weimar Republic and brought the Nazis to power. This more modest assessment of the significance of the conservative revolution has helped to direct attention away from straightforward presentations of ideas and towards a consideration of the social, political and economic circumstances which produced those ideas. Thus, recent research has looked at how the combat leagues helped create not only the intellectual climate but also the physical environment in which the violence of the NSDAP could come to be accepted (see Diehl, 1977, p.ix; also see Struve, 1973). At another level Joachim Petzold has examined the financing of conservative revolutionary activities in an attempt to shed light on motives, and to question the revolutionary character of the movement (Petzold, 1978). The general concern of this research is to look at the sociopolitical base of antidemocratic ideas. Thus, Struve sees conservative revolutionary ideology as an expression of the 'status panic' of the major strata of the middle class after the First World

War, a period when they felt crushed between organized labour and capital, when the differences in economic circumstances of white- and blue-collar workers had been eroded, when the free professions were severely overcrowded, when inflation and depression reduced the income of broad sectors of the middle class (Struve, 1973, p.13). For Herf the social base of the conservative revolution was the middle class — small and medium-scale farmers, artisans, shopkeepers, white-collar workers in big industry and the civil service, and the professional middle class — lawyers, doctors, professors, higher civil servants and engineers. Herf argues that these diverse groups were bound together by common reactions to the rapid development of industrial capitalism in Germany. They were 'anxious and afraid of large capital on the one hand and the organized working class on the other'. In this situation the nation-state is projected as being above narrow class interests (Herf, 1984, p.22). Yet if this work, carried out primarily with methodologies taken from the social sciences, has brought new insights, it has also brought new problems. The element of reductionism in arguments based on social, economic and political context has encouraged observers to overlook the evidence of the immediate context of ideas. Ideas and ideology do not receive sufficient analytical attention — generally because they are seen as surface phenomena which are unlikely to yield as much information about motives as a consideration of the circumstantial evidence.

What can one do then with ideas and ideology? Recently there has been a call to 'give ideas their due'. In *Politics, Language and Time* Pocock (1971, pp.37–8) argues:

> Under pressure from the idealist-materialist dichotomy, we have been giving all out attention to thought as conditioned by social facts outside itself and not enough of our attention to thought as denoting, referring, assuming, alluding, implying, and as performing a variety of functions of which the simplest is that of containing and conveying information...

> the paradigms which order 'reality' are part of the reality they order...language is part of the social structure and not epiphenomenal to it, and...we are studying an aspect of reality when we study the ways in which it appeared real to the persons to whom it was more real than to anyone else.

Dominick LaCapra refers to the historians' habit of reducing texts to mere documents and not paying sufficient attention to the ambiguous structure of complex texts (LaCapra, 1983, p.14). Robert Darnton has pointed back to the challenge from social historians who have posed questions not answerable through traditional techniques or narrating or analysing ideas, but he has also pointed forward to the growing doubt among historians about treating thought as an epiphenomenon of social organization. Instead, historians are becoming more interested in showing how thought 'organized experience and conveyed meaning among the general citizenry' (Darnton, 1980, pp.327f.). Even if one regards ideas as surface phenomena, one should be aware of the possibility of a dialectic of surfaces which can often tell us something about the underlying motives of those producing the ideas. The main elements of

conservative revolutionary thought need to be examined not as static ideology
but rather as ideas worked out in response to a series of conflicting pressures,
as ideas which cannot simply be portrayed as if they were a political
programme, but rather as expressions of tension. The tension is everywhere in
evidence, whether it be over the question of how to find meaning in the
sacrifices of the First World War, how to establish links with a tradition of
German political and cultural thought, what the contents of 'new nationalism'
should be, how to rid Germany of the Weimar state, and whether National
Socialism is the movement which will transform Germany according to
conservative revolutionary ideals. Let us examine these issues one at a time.

The First World War

Crucial to an understanding of radical nationalism in the Weimar period is an
understanding of how nationalists sought to come to terms with the First
World War. It is widely thought that the conservative revolutionary view of
the war is based upon a myth of heroic self-sacrifice for the good of the nation
(Sontheimer, 1968, pp.95–100; Greiffenhagen, 1971, p.277; Herf, 1984, p.72).
Yet this simple categorization of the conservative revolutionary view, a
categorization which places it in direct opposition to the pacifist view of the
war, does not take into account the complexity of the productive tensions at
the heart of much conservative revolutionary writing on the war.

The most important conservative revolutionary interpreter of the war
experience was Ernst Jünger. Jünger had enlisted as a volunteer on the first day
of the war at the age of nineteen and by the end of the war he had reached the
rank of temporary company commander. He was wounded some seven times,
and in 1918 he was awarded the *pour le mérite*. After the war Jünger remained
in the Reichswehr until 1923. He attracted the attention of the reading public
with his first account of his war experiences, *In Stahlgewittern*, published in
1920 and reaching sales of around a quarter of a million by 1945. He followed
up this first work with many more accounts of the war, ranging in form from
war diaries and a novel to edited collections of essays and essays in political
journals.

Within this body of work, Jünger's thinking undergoes a radical
development. In its first phase this is a development from expectations of a
glorious war to the disillusionment which sets in when he is confronted with
its reality. He and his fellow conservative revolutionaries describe the
enthusiasm with which they greet the news of the outbreak of war in terms of
'intoxication' (Jünger, 1920, p.1); the transition from civilian to soldier is a
radical switch from a confused and aimless existence to a simple and
disciplined life in which every movement is precise, clear and purposeful
(Schauwecker, 1926, pp.21f.). Yet Jünger writes that after a short period with
the regiment he and other new recruits had lost nearly all the illusions with
which they had started out: instead of encountering the dangers they had
hoped for, they found 'filth, work and sleepless nights' (Jünger, 1920, p.6;
similarly, Hesse, 1922, p.30; Schauwecker, 1926, p.49). This profound
disillusionment, coupled with an awareness of the possibility of meeting a

meaningless death in the form of battle where the enemy may not even be glimpsed, marks the conservative revolutionary view of war off from the traditional nationalist view of war, which had been captured and propagated in countless war diaries and military memoirs of the time.

What is more, the conservative revolutionaries went through a systematic rejection of all conventional sources of meaning which the more tradition-bound nationalists were intent on upholding during the Weimar years. Meaningless death was not for example rendered meaningful by recalling Germany's war aims. The conservative revolutionaries actually spent very little time contemplating what the political aims of the war had been: Ernst Jünger recalls that soldiers greeted discussions of war aims with an ironic smile, and Rudolf Huch, writing in the pages of the new nationalist journal *Deutsches Volkstum* is tempted to go along with Remarque's perspective when he recalls a meeting of 1917 at which politicians told businessmen of the need to secure certain territories without which, comments Huch sardonically, the Germans had got on well enough before the war (Huch, 1928, pp.598–603).

These psychological problems have their political equivalent. The nagging doubts about whether random death in a totally impersonal form of warfare could be seen as having any meaning were accompanied by doubts about whether a lost war could be seen positively. Kurt Hesse, a lieutenant in the Reichswehr set out the problem and moved towards an answer: in *Der Feldherr Psychologos* he asks whether the fact that the war was lost is sufficient reason to see this episode in the history of the nation as a negative experience. One must try, he argues, to establish what positive aspects of the war remain. After listing just how much Germany did lose in the war, he asks whether there must not be some gain to emerge from a struggle which was kept up with so much spiritual and physical effort. His suggestion of where meaning is to be found helps explain a key feature of the radical right's view of the war: if the war was lost there must be a new battle-cry: 'So be it, we must annexe spiritual values' (Hesse, 1922, p.135). In this suggestion we see how failure in the world of actual military power prompted the conservative revolutionaries to *internalize* the war experience, why for example Ernst Jünger called his war book of 1922 *Der Kampf als inneres Erlebnis* (Fighting as *Inner* Experience). In this 'inner experience' the best qualities of the soldier — courage, heroism, selflessness — become ends in themselves. Franz Schauwecker describes the situation of the Germans in the war and concludes that they were fighting against hopeless odds. In such a situation there is 'no point' in fighting on. Yet if fighting on has no point, says Schauwecker, it does have a 'meaning'. This meaning resides in the courage and commitment of the soldiers who fight the losing battle (Schauwecker, 1926, p.132). The radical nationalist Werner Best describes how new nationalism sees the world as dynamic, consisting of tension, struggle and turbulence. He quotes Friedrich Nietzsche on 'the world which is perpetually creating and destroying itself'. And he quotes Ernst Jünger's dictum: 'the essential thing is not what we are fighting for, but how we fight'. Extending the 'logic' of his thinking, Best concludes that the aims of any struggle are ephemeral and ever-changing, and for this reason the success or failure of the struggle is not crucial (Best, 1930, p.150–2). Here we

see one of the main roots of the activist style of politics which lay at the heart
of conservative revolutionary thinking: the search for meaning in the face of
a chaotic war which ended in defeat leads the conservative revolutionaries not
to wonder whether the war should have been fought at all but to seek meaning
in action for its own sake.

On the political level there were conflicting images of the war. At one point
it could be seen as an event in which 'social issues took a back seat, even among
the workers'. In the place of class division there arose a consciousness of
national unity (Hesse, 1922, p.142). At another point, however, the
conservative revolutionaries were aware that there was another way of
viewing the war. Franz Schauwecker calls the war an imperialist war, and he
asserts that while nationalists are prepared to fight for the German nation they
are not interested in fighting a war for money (Schauwecker, 1927, p.367).
Kurt Hesse records with dismay how the war had been allowed to turn into a
business from which particular individuals had benefited (Hesse, 1922,
p.163).

Similarly, the idea of a single community of Germans united in war across
class distinctions had to coexist with an awareness of the different experiences
of different classes, even at war. Schauwecker's initial enthusiasm for the
community of Germans is expressed in his portrayal of men donning their
uniforms, a process in which 'all differences fall away' (Schauwecker, 1926,
p.6). Yet in the same work he gives an account of how the socialist workers
regard him as spoilt and privileged, and of how they refuse to treat him as an
equal. He feels isolated within his own company (Schauwecker, 1926, pp.165–
71). Kurt Hesse gives a more overtly political view when he moves from his
first impression of the nation at war as 'all forces pulling together' to the
realization that within the army people are starting to look very closely at the
different rations, pay and promotion opportunities (Hesse, 1922, pp.142 and
160). Such differences were also institutionalized in post-war Germany
where, for example, before the pension system was reformed in 1920, very
different financial treatment — based on rank — was given to wounded
soldiers and to the dependants of the war dead. (For a good account of the
bitterness and resentment caused by this see Whalen, 1984).

In psychological terms and in political terms then the writings of the radical
right on the First World War were shot through with ambiguity. They reveal
minds racked with doubts about whether the vast sacrifices had been in any
way meaningful, and they show an awareness not only of community but also
of division and isolation, not only of comradeship but of class antagonism.

Yet although the sources are complex, they do contain a recurring
structure, and this structure can given considerable guidance when it comes to
understanding the motives behind conservative revolutionary accounts of the
war. There is a clear tendency for the positive elements of the war to come to
the fore. The switch from expectations of the war to disillusionment with its
reality is not the last stage in the development of attitudes. For it is clear that
different sources of meaning and justification emerge, with war being
portrayed as a natural event, as the expression of the fate of the nation.
Moreover, these different sources of meaning emerge in response to the
counter-images of war: Jünger writes of his impressions when he comes under

heavy artillery fire that he had a 'sense of something inescapable and the absolutely inevitable as if it were an eruption of the elements' (Jünger, 1920, pp.51f.). What is natural is inevitable, and against a background of 'futility' and 'chance' — the vocabulary of the counter-image of war in Jünger's work — inevitably lends a kind of meaning.

It is the natural mode of existence which Jünger and his fellow conservative revolutionaries see as the ultimate source of meaning in their accounts of the war. Reflection loses out to instinct, awareness of chance gives way to an insistence on inevitability, the unsettling unique experience of war gives way to a reassuring, stylized, ritualized version of war which can be held up as typical of an entire generation. In Oswald Spengler's massive *Untergang des Abendlandes* (Decline of the West) the task of the historian is defined as perceiving history not merely as the sum total of past events without any essential order or inner necessity, but as an organism with a firm structure and a meaningful form. Seen in this light, all events are determined, indeed predetermined, by the organic structure of a culture, and within this structure Spengler insists that the First World War was inevitable (Spengler, 1920, p.67).

In these accounts of the First World War we see the emergence of two of the key elements of conservative revolutionary thinking — vitalism and activism. As we shall see, they come to dominate many other areas of political debate, but first it is worth asking to what extent these features of the radical right in the Weimar period drew upon any tradition of German thought.

'Mentors'

Many conservative revolutionaries openly acknowledge that they owe a philosophical debt to Friedrich Nietzsche. Their point is made not in a display of modesty but rather in an attempt to add weight and credibility to their arguments. For an examination of the ways in which Nietzsche's ideas were taken up and made to serve the radical right's purpose shows that the inspirational effect of Nietzsche was far less significant than the need for his legitimizing presence. Distortion was essential, however, before Nietzsche could be invoked as the ultimate authority. Thomas Mann showed considerable insight when he wrote as early as 1909 of the 20-year-olds who did not know Nietzsche's work very well, had hardly read him, and yet regarded him as a prophet. Mann also accused Spengler of giving a stupidly unambiguous interpretation of Nietzsche as the philosophical patron of imperialism (Mann, 1967, p.208). The accusation holds good for many conservative revolutionaries. Looking at connections between Nietzsche and the twentieth-century 'Nietzscheans' sheds interesting light on just how much, but often how little, the conservative revolutionaries owe to any German tradition of political culture.

Typically the conservative revolutionaries take up Nietzsche's ideas on vitalism and the 'Will to Power', the inevitability and even desirability of war, the rights of the strong over the weak, the objection to the democratization of Europe, and they see the Germans as the direct descendants of the race for which they assumed Nietzsche had only admiration — the Germanic race.

In *Der Kampf als* inneres *Erlebnis*, for example, Jünger writes that a struggle is certainly sanctified by the cause, yet still more the cause is sanctified by the struggle. This is an unacknowledged borrowing from *Also sprach Zarathustra* (Thus Spake Zarathustra) where Nietzsche had written: 'you say a good cause can even sanctify war. I tell you: it is a good war which sanctifies any cause'. What we know of Jünger's need to find meaning in a chaotic war, a war which had left Germany the loser, partly explains why he should take up Nietzsche's idea on war as a source of meaning. Yet Nietzsche had made his point in the context of a critique of Christianity and he had stressed the need for careful control of man's animal and bellicose instincts. Ultimately, Nietzsche advocated acknowledging such instincts and their potentially beneficial effect on man's culture. For Jünger, however, the idea of acknowledging and sublimating man's base ultimately gives way to the view that this base is in fact divine in its own right and the expression of man's true being (Woods, 1982, pp.59–97).

Encouraged by Elisabeth Förster-Nietzsche's distorted accounts of her brother's thinking (accounts which have since been largely discredited), the conservative revolutionaries also latch on to the idea that life is essentially the 'will to power'. This allows them not only to propagate a vitalist view of the lost war but also to fill the ideological gap created when the contents of traditional nationalism have been discarded. Moreover, the treatment of Germany at the hands of the victorious powers showed to the satisfaction of the conservative revolutionaries that they were living in a world where power had taken over from morality.

Whereas Nietzsche had reservations about unrestricted self-assertion and saw power as a precondition of right and the will to power as a mark of quality, the conservative revolutionaries generally *equated* power with both right and quality. A self-justifying version of the will to power emerged at the heart of numerous political programmes after the lengthy debates over the precise aims of 'new nationalism' produced little of substance and served largely to highlight the ideological dilemma of nationalists who reject the traditional dogma of right and left alike. This 'conservative dilemma' is artificially resolved: the ideological vacuum is filled with vitalist arguments when all other paths are seen to end in political reaction or in a commitment to traditional socialism. Germany had to throw off democracy and become strong again. In order to retain Nietzsche as an authority for such a goal, the conservative revolutionaries needed to come to terms with his rejection of nationalism for his own times. For Nietzsche had mocked 'dull and hesitant' European races which might take half a century to get over their 'atavistic attacks of jingoism and clinging to their native soil' (Nietzsche, 1973, p.706). Indeed, for Nietzsche, German cultural and political ambitions were necessarily alternatives, the one thriving at the expense of the other. Thus the Franco-Prussian war which brought Germany political success also rendered it 'stupid' (Nietzsche, 1973, pp.983–6).

Here the conservative revolutionary, Kurt Hildebrandt, came to the rescue with his work on Nietzsche. Just as the conservative revolutionaries rejected the tradition of nationalism in their time and advocated a new nationalism, they suggested that this was also Nietzsche's position. Hildebrandt actually acknowledges Nietzsche's argument that German military victory had posed a threat to its culture, but maintains that what Nietzsche did not accept about nationalism was the accompanying trend towards democracy, liberalism and parliamentarism. Nevertheless, argues Hildebrandt, Nietzsche's concept of the will to power is 'very fruitful' for the nation (Hildebrandt, 1927, p.2f.).

The last phase in the adaptation of Nietzsche for nationalist purposes was to establish a connection between modern-day Germans and the notorious 'blond Germanic beast' who had prowled through Nietzsche's work. Whereas Nietzsche had discussed this figure not as an ideal but as a counterbalance and corrective to European civilization, which sought to suppress all instincts of strength in man, and whereas Nietzsche had expressly stated that there was hardly any connection at all between the blond Germanic beast and the Germans of his day, the conservative revolutionaries elevated the spirit of the all-conquering blond beast who has no conscience to the status of an ideal in its own right. In the process it was a straightforward enough matter to establish the link between Germanic and German that Nietzsche had denied for his own time. Describing a German offensive in the First World War in an account written at the start of his nationalist phase Ernst Jünger (1925, p.127) declares:

> Now we really start to feel our strength and we are on our way! This is where we appear like the war god himself, as the Germans have appeared occasionally in the course of history, with that Germanic rage which nothing can withstand.

If Nietzsche's philosophy was unobtrusively reworked to make it serve the new nationalists' cause, Spengler's was at once loudly praised and condemned by the conservative revolutionaries. His insistence that each nation had its own immutable political character was eagerly echoed by those who rejected Weimar democracy as an alien import. Yet his reservations about the future of the West as a whole met with angry protest. Spengler's interpretation of the growth of cities and the technological spirit that prevailed in them as signs of a decadent culture is dismissed by the conservative revolutionaries as reactionary, and this reflects their interest in winning over the urban proletariat to the new nationalist cause. Yet disagreement within the ranks of the conservative revolution over the precise shape of new nationalism indicates that many a writer's 'break with the past' was far from complete. It also indicates that Spengler's hostility towards the urban environment and his praise for the peasant do not in fact banish him from the ranks of the conservative revolution. Just what was the 'new nationalism' to look like?

'New Nationalism'

The 'new nationalism' of the radical right has been characterized in terms of its 'four supporting pillars' — these were national, soldierly, social and dictatorial in nature (Jünger, 1926, p.1). National and soldierly implied a world in which life is acknowledged as fundamentally unjust and in which the strong create their own right to extend their power. In this scheme of things

wars are the inevitable expression of man's true being. Social is a term which
is paraphrased elsewhere as 'comradeship', and this gives a clue to its meaning.
For it refers back to the sense of community which the conservative
revolutionaries claimed to have found in the First World War. 'Social' also
invokes an image of a society in which class divisions no longer exist, and the
collapse of the socialist principle of internationalism in 1914 is taken as
historical proof of the superiority of community over class. A socialism of the
blood is offered in conscious opposition to the 'rational socialism based on
concepts'. In *Preussentum und Sozialismus* (Prussianism and Socialism)
Oswald Spengler had written that true socialism was the will to power and
that the socialist values were service, subordination and freedom in obedience.
Edgar Jung quotes Spengler's thesis that socialism is not a 'type of economy
but rather a social ethos' (Jung, 1933, p.17). Jünger saw the task of modern
nationalism as the creation of a classless society, a goal which could be
achieved not by radical social and economic reform but rather by bringing
together the forces of nationalism and socialism within a political order based
on authority. That this German socialism was not such a revolutionary break
with the past as is sometimes supposed by modern commentators is suggested
by research which has revealed details of the financial backing given to the
new nationalists by those often publicly criticized as reactionary. In particular
the financial links between Alfred Hugenberg's publishing empire and
conservative revolutionary organizations, such as Moeller van den Bruck's
Juni-Klub in Berlin, serve to underline the dilemma conservatives found
themselves facing in their attempts to produce a new form of conservatism.

A separate strand of conservative revolutionary thought embraced many of
the elements of traditional socialism, adopting its vocabulary and, more
importantly, its class analysis of society. Karl Paetel, of the Group of Social
Revolutionary Nationalists, and the National Bolshevist Ernst Niekisch are
the main exponents of this line, the one favouring cooperation with the
German Communist party, the other an alliance with Russia against the West.
Within these circles it was not uncommon for Spengler's 'decline of the West'
to be interpreted as the decline of capitalism. Such attitudes did not go
unnoticed by the communists who offered Paetel a seat in the Reichstag in
return for collaboration.

The fourth pillar of the new nationalism — dictatorship — points to the
demand for a great leader. Jünger declared that the new state would be
founded by revolutionary groups committed to a single leader, and that he
would welcome any move by this new state to abolish the freedom of the press
since this freedom 'allowed any scribbler to denigrate his own nation'. Such a
state would of course be the mortal enemy of parliamentarianism.

It has been pointed out that there is a distinct shift in the run-up to the Nazi
takeover of power towards more abstract, metaphysical politics
(Schüddekopf, 1972, p.233f.). This trend towards abstraction and vagueness
of aims is particularly apparent in the ranks of the radical right. The new
nationalism outlined above is vague enough, and by the end of the 1920s it
becomes vaguer still. Moreover, negation is central to its outlook: old-style
nationalism and patriotism, restoration, the West and the Weimar Republic,
communism and social democracy all come in for sharp criticism at one time

or another, and it is hard to resist the conclusion that conservative revolutionary thought consisted exclusively of a series of negations.

There is in fact a link between this negation and the gradual shift towards abstract politics. New nationalists often state that they have no political programme, and this has been emphasized by modern observers as one of the key features of the conservative revolution. Here, the snapshot approach of the observers — an approach which assumes an unchanging body of beliefs — has produced a clear image of the conservative revolution, but an image which is in fact only correct for one particular period in the history of the movement. The snapshot approach has actually hindered an understanding of historical processes which are in turn crucial to an understanding of how abstract politics came to be regarded as necessary.

In late 1925 and early 1926 Ernst Jünger repeatedly calls upon nationalists to work out a programme, insisting that they must take leave of the past and establish a new state which will be fundamentally different from Weimar and from the old *Kaiserreich*. Individual nationalist movements are too small to operate independently, and they must form a nationalist front around a clear programme. A social programme has to be worked out since its absence is causing concern to nationalist workers' leaders, and a central council of leaders needs to be formed to maintain the purity and clarity of the movement (Jünger, 1926b, pp.222–6).

The replies to this and other calls for unity and a statement of aims within the nationalist camp are revealing. Despite general agreement on the need for unity, few positive ideals emerge to sustain it. What definite political stances are proposed are far from being a new or 'revolutionary' departure for the nationalist camp. The deputy leader of Stahlhelm, Theodor Duesterberg sees opposition to the 'red terror' as the great impulse which can ensure unity among nationalists (Duesterberg, 1926, pp.318f.). For the Ludendorff–Kreis and Tannenberg–Bund Constantin Hierl, a retired colonel, asserts that young nationalism should struggle to protect the German people from further 'bastardization through inferior alien races, particularly the Jews' (Hierl, 1926, p.249). Contributors' claims to have abandoned traditional nationalism and reaction are frequently undermined by the form of new nationalism they advocate: while calling for the established political divisions to be overcome, Gustav Sondermann, editor of the Bund Oberland's journal *Das Dritte Reich*, criticizes Jünger's declared enthusiasm for the 'vital energy of the cities' (Sondermann, 1926, pp.296f.). Sondermann thus indulges in the anti-urbanism which Jünger saw as a feature of traditional conservatism which needed to be put aside if the nationalist camp was to draw closer to the worker and his environment.

Other contributors to this debate about the aims of nationalism merely lament the lack of unity and a unifying ideal or programme among nationalists while reaffirming the need to avoid mere reaction. This and other similar debates drive home to the proponents of new nationalism that their position is in fact untenable, and it is in this education process that one of the roots of their abstract politics is to be found.

Jünger wrote two commentaries on the responses to his call for unity, the first in July 1926. Here he asserts that the interest which his call met with shows that one can speak of a single movement, even if it is progressing along different routes. The movement also has a common goal, even if it is not one which can be laid down in the form of a programme. He goes on to argue that nationalist groups are essentially soldierly, and elections and compromises are irrelevant to them. Beneath the cracked crust of the existing state these soldierly nationalists are the dynamite which will clear the way for a new state. All words fade into insignificance when blood starts to flow: the nationalists' path is revolutionary and does not lead through debates and German soirées. Whereas he had originally seen it as essential that nationalists unite around a political programme, he now argues that the suggested creation of a hard core of nationalists on the basis of a special programme is tantamount to removing the yeast from one's daily bread. Here Jünger is taking a step away from rational debate, a consequence of his realization that the nationalist debate has largely failed. Indeed, he reaches the point where debate and action are practically alternatives: words and blood, programmes and fighting units are set against each other and the former lose out to the latter. The attempt to work out a revolutionary programme gives way to a revolutionary stance whose aims cannot be articulated. He moves towards a more abstract and irrational form of nationalism based on the 'heart's commitment' and towards activism as an alternative to fruitless debate.

A further consequence of the problems of nationalism is Jünger's change of attitude towards the idea of a single great personality to lead the nationalist movement. Before the debate, Jünger had argued that a plan was necessary, and only a 'great personality' could draw it up and execute it. But he also says that the 'strong man' cannot be summoned and will only emerge when his time has come. Until then the nationalists must work upon themselves so that they become 'hard material for hard policies'. He suggests a dual task for the nationalist movement in preparation for the great leader: firstly, disputes must be settled and ideas clarified, and secondly the movement must be made into a resolute instrument of power (Jünger, 1925b, p.2).

By the time he returns to the point some eighteen months later, i.e. after his abortive call for unity, he has rather different ideas about the leader principle. He looks back to the call for unity and says that it was both right and wrong to assume that there was basic agreement about the aims of the nationalist movement. In domestic politics there was certainly no agreement, yet Jünger does see unanimity about the aims of foreign policy: a strong, independent Reich secure against the outside world. If the threat of an attack from outside Germany's borders will always be the greatest force for unity within Germany the second greatest force is an outstanding personality. Here Jünger looks approvingly to fascist Italy where a great individual is seen as an object of commitment which is both more acceptable than and an alternative to a political programme. Jünger returns to the German scene and states that the nationalists have programmes enough and that the arguments these provoke are a waste of time. What is needed is not a new organization but a man who can reduce the available forces to a common denominator. The disputes within the movement will not prevent his appearance, indeed he will transcend them and 'create a higher unity' from them. Thus whereas Jünger had originally seen it as a task of the nationalist movement itself to eliminate its internal disagreements, this task is now redefined as finding a higher unity and is left to the future leader. The original task of clarifying the ideas of nationalism seems now to be dismissed by Jünger with his comments on the relative unimportance of programmes, and he favours instead enthusiastic devotion to a leader who will turn the nationalist ranks into an instrument of power. The dual task becomes a single task (Jünger, 1927, p.3f.).

It is against this background of failed attempts to work out a genuinely new series of goals that we must understand any statements on the nature of the 'new nationalism' proposed by the conservative revolutionaries. The failed attempts encourage an ever more abstract, activist attitude by the end of the 1920s, with Jünger coming to believe that the times demand one virtue above all others — decisiveness. One must possess a strong will and belief, regardless of their contents (Jünger, 1929, pp.180f.). Nationalism must survive without dogma and its task is anarchic, lying outside the realms of political debate. Nationalist organizations are rejected as part of the bourgeois world in decline, a fact which is vividly illustrated by their eternal disputes and 'political barrenness'. The nationalist youth of Germany must learn that it can 'march without flags' (Jünger, 1929b, pp.1552–8).

Weimar Democracy under Fire

Conservative revolutionaries are at least clear when it comes to the Weimar Republic and the democratic system it embodies. This they regard as a foreign system of government imposed upon Germany by the victorious West. Here the conservative revolutionaries are able to latch on to a tradition of political thought in Germany stretching back to the start of the nineteenth century, a tradition which sees a profound difference in the political culture of the West and that of Germany. Democracy is an alien import to be resisted at all costs, since to accept it is to accept a subtle form of domination by foreign powers.

The political representatives of the republic are accused of adopting Western standards to the extent of accepting Germany's weakened status and failing to challenge the right of other nations to exact reparations. The republic also comes under fire for its 'ingratitude' towards the German soldiers who fought in the war. Rathenau is accused of viewing the war as a senseless loss of life, and other representatives of the republic are accused of holding Germany responsible for the slaughter. This relentless attack undoubtedly helped to destabilize the republic.

To the extent that the features of the republic under attack were also associated expressly with Jews, the conservative revolution also helped foster anti-Semitism. The supposed absence of anti-Semitism among conservative revolutionaries is generally seen as the main reason for distinguishing between it and National Socialism. Yet it is not difficult to find examples of anti-Semitism among the conservative revolutionaries (see for example, Oldenburg, 1932).

There is also a psychological aspect to the conservative revolutionary scorn for democracy. Observers have often pointed out that the republic did not satisfy the need for authority and order fostered by centuries of authoritarian rule in Germany. This idea is in fact common among conservative revolutionaries, and it provides an insight into one further source of their nationalism. The democratic order is rejected partly because it demands that the individual take responsibility for himself.

Conservative Revolution and National Socialism

Within the conservative revolutionary movement Edgar Jung expressed the sentiments of some, though certainly not all, when he declared in 1932 (see Sontheimer, 1968, p.283):

> Through our untold efforts, particularly among the educated, we prepared for the day when the German people voted for the National Socialist candidates. Our work was heroic, for it renounced all thought of success and public acclaim.

There is at any rate no doubt that many conservative revolutionaries were highly enthusiastic about the NSDAP in the early years of the republic. Hitler is praised as a skilful orator, and the Nazis in general are regarded as comrades in the nationalist struggle against Weimar and the West. This enthusiasm is, if anything, heightened by the abortive beer-hall *putsch* of November 1923, with Oswald Spengler and Ernst Jünger rejoicing and praising the party's 'revolutionary fire', which was an inspiration to all those nationalists who had turned their back on traditional nationalism (see Rhodes, 1969; Jünger, 1925c, p.62). The party's later electoral successes are similarly greeted as a sign that Germany is ready to cast aside the democratic order in favour of a dictatorship (Jünger, 1930, pp.11f.).

For their part the Nazis were certainly eager to win over new nationalists, for many of them were nationally known and respected figures. Ernst Jünger was repeatedly offered (and he repeatedly refused) a Nazi seat in the Reichstag. Other, less well known figures were absorbed into the party: Wilhelm Weiss moved from co-editing *Arminius* to become editor-in-chief of *Völkischer Beobachter* and a Nazi member of the Reichstag in 1927. Werner Best, who had written on legal aspects of the First World War in a new nationalist collection of essays, was able to put his ideas of natural justice and the 'absolute state' into practice when he became an SS Oberfuhrer (documents of Preussische Geheime Staatspolizei, R58/243).

The early enthusiasm for National Socialism is somewhat dampened, however, when the party's revolutionary fire gives way to a policy of legal opposition: 'Hot-blooded Adolf declares himself in favour of the legal revolution', mocks one *Standarte* writer (*Standarte*, no. 2, 1926, p.45). Yet it is not merely Hitler's involvement in the democratic process that alienates many conservative revolutionaries. In 1929 Hitler cooperated with Stahlhelm leaders and Alfred Hugenberg (by that time chairman of the Deutschnationale Volkspartei) in forming the so-called National Opposition to the Young Plan on German reparations. For many this undermined the image of the NSDAP as distinct from the nationalists who could not let go of the past. Ernst Jünger expresses 'comradely concern' for the National Socialists and declares that if one is genuinely possessed by the image of a new world this must be clear even in the weapons one uses, and if one really wants to drive out 'the bourgeois' one should not use bourgeois methods.

Among the left-wing conservative revolutionaries there was a steadily escalating attack on the Nazis for their 'pseudo-socialism', and this meant that there was room for some close collaboration between these conservative revolutionaries and the left wing of the NSDAP under Otto Strasser. At about the time when Karl Paetel was asking what forms of cooperation there might be between anti-capitalist forces on the radical right and groups of the revolutionary proletariat, and concluding that there was no chance of entering into any kind of pact with such men as Goebbels (Paetel, 1931, pp.60–3), the group around Otto Strasser and Ulrich Oldenburg which had broken away from the Nazi Party in July 1930 under the slogan 'The Socialists Quit the Party' was demanding that Hitler should drop the word socialist from the name of the party now that it had come out in favour of the private ownership of the means of production ('Ultimatum an Hitler', *Die deutsche Revolution*, 20 March 1932, p.1). In this matter there was a clear division between the two major strands of the conservative revolution, with those advocates of a 'socialism of the blood' relatively unconcerned at the Nazis' ever clearer anti-socialist stance.

Just what ideas did the conservative revolution and National Socialism have in common? Clearly they shared a scorn for liberalism and an insistence on the superiority of a dictatorial order. This was backed up by the elevation of militarism to the status of an ideology. The self-denial and total commitment to a cause which supposedly distinguished the Germans during the First World War were to resurface as the basis for a nationalist community, with the army providing the model for the new state. Both conservative revolutionaries and Nazis knew disputes over the meaning of socialism, and for both the 'socialism' that prevailed was dictatorial, not emancipatory. In this they both claimed to have transcended reaction and traditional nationalism, yet their socialism is ultimately an alternative socialism, formed to a great extent as a reaction against Marxism. Both movements argue Germany's case in vitalist terms. For both, struggle is the law of life, and there is no such thing as the right of the weak. Both lay particular emphasis on the Will, in the case of the conservative revolutionaries largely because of the failure to create a new ideal.

There is evidence, however, of a trend within the conservative revolution running counter to the general drift towards abstract and activist politics. This trend developed because of the rising fortunes of the Nazis. Although conservative revolutionary thought was not free from anti-Semitism, it did not home in on the Jews as the root cause of Germany's problems. In the case of Ernst Jünger his ever growing indifference to political programmes was accompanied by an ever clearer rejection of National Socialism, a rejection which occasionally even prompted him to insist that ideas must be clarified before any action is taken. Here anti-Semitism is the main stumbling block for Jünger: social democracy, internationalism, pacifism, rationalism and Marxism, which Jünger attacks as such, are all primarily attacked by the Nazis as Jewish.

If one is looking for the differences between the conservative revolutionaries and the National Socialists one can point to the refusal of the former to have anything to do with parliament and a 'legal revolution'. As for the often heard argument that the conservative revolutionaries were the 'genuine' national socialists, this view is hard to maintain in view of the inability of the conservative revolutionaries to produce a clear programme which united the forces of nationalism and socialism.

When the Nazis came to power, party ideologues paid homage to figures such as Oswald Spengler, suggesting that the NSDAP was realizing his vision of Prussian Socialism, and explaining that his apparent coolness towards the regime was a romantic's inevitable disappointment with the real-life version of a theory (Eschmann, 1933, pp.673–81). In subsequent references, however, Spengler is taken to task for not appreciating the benefits of racial purity (see documents of the Preussische Geheime Staatspolizei, Bundesarchiv Koblenz, R58/968).

Moeller van den Bruck had gone so far as to threaten suicide if Hitler misused his concept of the Third Reich, but this did not stop Goebbels lavishing praise on him, greeting a new edition of Moeller's *The Third Reich* as 'significant for the intellectual history of the NSDAP'.

Edgar Jung, who in 1932 had claimed to have helped the Nazis to power, was murdered in the course of the Roehm purge in 1934 for writing a speech (delivered by the then Vice-Chancellor, Papen) in which the Nazi claim to exclusive leadership of the 'German Revolution' was questioned.

While the left wing of the conservative revolution had labelled the Nazis pseudo-socialists, the Nazis were not slow to object to the movement's willingness to contemplate communist ideas and cooperation with Russia (see letter of 25 February 1937 from the head of the Sicherheitshauptamt in Berlin to the press section of the Berlin Gestapo, recommending that F. W. Heinz's book *Die Nation greift an!* be banned for its sympathy with Bolshevism; Bundesarchiv Koblenz, R58/908).

Much of the post-1945 thinking of conservative revolutionaries was taken up with showing just how little they had in common with the National Socialists, and there is little to be gleaned from a survey of this thought for an understanding of the connection between the conservative revolution and National Socialism. A more fruitful way of looking at the connection is to consider how the problems of the radical right which found expression in the conservative revolution could be turned to the advantage of the Nazis. For the desperate need to find meaning in the First World War had fostered a view of that experience as self-justifying: the message which went forth from a flood of conservative revolutionary works was that the aims of the war had not been crucial. What mattered was that the war had been fought with a fanatical conviction and commitment. That this image of the war had only emerged after a counter-image of the war as an experience which brought futile suffering had been suppressed was forgotten, and what was preserved as the basis for an upsurge of militarism was the idea of fighting for its own sake. That this activist nationalism could only be tied to the authority of Nietzsche by overlooking Nietzsche's contempt for nationalism was also forgotten. This activism had been reinforced by the failure of the conservative revolutionaries to generate a clear-cut programme and by the subsequent emergence of the notion that political programmes were of no great significance. What the young generation of Germans had to learn was how to march without flags. Here too the willingness to shape a fighting force and foster aggression which would be given direction by a future leader was a crucial development. More important then for the rise of National Socialism than the similarities of outlook between conservative revolution and NSDAP was the encouragement of conflict for its own sake and of commitment to an unspecified cause (see O'Sullivan, 1983, in which the direct ideological precursors of National Socialism are seen as of far less significance than those developments in European political history which gave rise to activism).

Looking back, the conservative revolutionaries themselves hinted that they had gained this much insight into their own contribution to the rise of the Nazis. What starts to emerge in response to the period of Nazi rule is a hesitant acknowledgement of the need for a moral dimension to any commitment. Man is no longer simply part of a Social Darwinist order in which unbridled self-assertion brings its own rights. Any interpretation of man's place in the world needs to be based upon a set of declared values. Thus Ernst Jünger comes to reject Spengler's self-contained, natural interpretation of world history and demands the additional dimension of a universal plan such as is found in religion and morality (Woods, 1982, pp.279–93). This criticism (which is ultimately a subtle form of self-criticism) is both more revealing and more accurate than the widespread habit among radical right-wing intellectuals in the post-1945 period of describing themselves as the seismograph which merely registered the upheavals of the twentieth century without sharing any responsibility for the form they took.

References

The author would thank to thank the British Academy for a grant in order to help research this chapter.

Best, W., 1930. Der Krieg und das Recht, in E. Jünger (ed.), *Krieg und Krieger*, Junker und Dünnhaupt Berlin.

Bracher, K.D., 1973. *The German Dictatorship*, Penguin, Harmondsworth.

Broszat, M., 1966, *German National Socialism 1919–1945*, Clio Press, California.

Bussmann, W., 1960. Politische Ideologien zwischen Monarchie und Weimarer Republik, *Historische Zeitschrift*, Vol. 190, No. 1.

Darnton, R., 1980. Intellectual and cultural history, in M. Kammen (ed.), *The Past before Us: Contemporary Historical Writing in the United States*, Cornell University Press, Ithaca.

Diehl, J., 1977. *Paramilitary Politics in Weimar Germany*, Indiana University Press, Bloomington.

Duesterberg, T., 1926. Schliesst Euch zusammen! Antworten 1V, *Standarte*, No. 14, 1 July.

Eschmann, E.W., 1933. Spengler und die Wirklichkeit, *Die Tat*, No. 9, December.

Grebing, H., 1964. *Der Nationalsozialismus. Ursprung und Wesen*, eighteenth edition, Günter Olzog Verlag, Munich.

Greiffenhagen, M., 1971. *Das Dilemma des Konservatismus in Deutschland*, R. Piper and Co. Verlag, Munich.

Herf, J., 1984. *Reactionary Modernism: Technology, Culture and Politics in Weimar and the Third Reich*, Cambridge University Press, Cambridge.

Hesse, K., 1922. *Der Feldherr Psychologos*, Mittler Verlag, Berlin.

Hierl, C., 1926. Schliesst Euch zusammen! Antworten 1, *Standarte*, No. 11, 10 June.

Hildebrandt, K., 1927. Wagners und Nietzsches Bedeutung für die Nation, *Gewissen*, No. 50, 12 December.

Huch, R., 1928. Im Westen nichts Neues, *Deutsches Volkstum*, No. 8, August.

Jung, E., 1933. *Sinndeutung der deutschen Revolution*, Stalling, Oldenburg.

Jünger, E., 1920, *In Stahlgewittern*, Published Privately, Hanover.

_____ 1925. *Feuer und Blut*, Stalhelm Verlag, Magdeburg.

_____ 1925b. Wesen des Frontsoldatentums, *Die Standarte*, No. 1, 6 September.

_____ 1925c. Der neue Typ des deutschen Menschen, in W. Kleinan (ed.), *Stalhelm – Jahrbuch 1926*, Stalhelm Verlag, Magdeburg.

_____ 1926. Zum Jahre, *Die Standarte*, No. 1, 3 January.

_____ 1926b. Schliesst Euch zusammen!, *Standarte*, No. 10, 3 June.

_____ 1927. Die zwei Tyrannen, *Arminius*, No. 11, 13 March.

_____ 1929. *Das abenteuerliche Herz*, Frundsberg Verlag, Berlin.

_____ 1929b. 'Nationalismus' und Nationalismus, *Das Tagebuch*, No. 38, 21 September.

Jünger, F. G., 1926. *Aufmarsch des Nationalismus*, Der Aufmarsch Leipzig.

_____ 1930. Revolution und Diktatur, *Das Reich*, No. 1.

LaCapra, D., 1983. *Rethinking Intellectual History*, Cornell University Press, Ithaca.

Mann, T., 1967. Geist und Kunst, in Wysling, H. (ed.), 1967. *Thomas-Mann-Studien*, Vol. l, Francke Verlag, Berne.

Mohler, A., 1972. *Die Konservative Revolution in Deutschland 1918-1932*, Wissenschaftliche Buchgesellschaft, Darmstadt.

Muller, J., 1987. *The Other God that Failed*, Princeton University Press, Princeton, New Jersey.

Nietzsche, F., 1973. In Schlechta, K. (ed.), *Werke in drei Bänden*, Vol. 2, Carl Hanser, Munich.

Oldenburg, U., 1932. Der deutsche Sozialismus, *Die deutsche Revolution*, No. 2, 20 March.

O'Sullivan, N., 1983. *Fascism*, Dent, London.

Paetel, K. 1931, Zwischenbilanz, *Die sozialistische Nation*, No. 5, May.

Petzold, J., 1978. *Konservative Theoretiker des deutschen Faschismus*, VEB Deutscher Verlag der Wissenschaften, East Berlin.

Pocock, J.G.A., 1971. *Politics, Language and Time: Essays on Political Thought and History*, Atheneum, New York.

Rhodes, J., 1969. The Conservative Revolution in Germany, doctoral dissertation, Indiana.

Schauwecker, F., 1926. *Der feurige Weg*, Der Aufmarsch Leipzig.

_____ 1927. Auseinandersetzung des Nationalismus, *Standarte*, No. 13, 28 August.

Schüddekopf, O.-E., 1960. *Linke Leute von rechts*, Kohlhammer Verlag, Stuttgart.

_____ 1972. *Nationalbolschewismus in Deutschland, 1918–1933*, Ullstein Verlag, Frankfurtam Main.

Sondermann, G., 1926. Schliesst Euch zusammen! Antworten 111, *Standarte*, No. 13, 24 June.

Sontheimer, K., 1968. *Antidemokratisches Denken in der Weimarer Republik*, Nymphenburger Verlag, Munich.

Spengler, O., 1920. *Der Untergang des Abendlandes*, Vol. 1, Beck, Munich.

Struve, W., 1973. *Elites against Democracy: Leadership Ideals in Bourgeois Political Thought in Germany, 1890–1933*, Princeton University Press, Princeton.

Wette, W., 1979. Ideologien, Propaganda und Innenpolitik als Voraussetzungen der Kriegspolitik des Dritten Reiches, in W. Deist *et al.* (eds), *Das Deutsche Reich under der Zweite Weltkrieg*, Vol. 1, Deutsche Verlagsanstalt, Stuttgart.

Whalen, R., 1984. *Bitter Wounds: German Victims of the Great War 1914–39*, Cornell University Press, Ithaca.

Woods, R., 1982. *Ernst Jünger and the Nature of Political Commitment*, Akcademischer Verlag, Stuttgart.

9 The Extreme Right: Continuities in Anti-Semitic Conspiracy Theory in Post-War Europe

Michael Billig, Loughborough University

Approaching the Extreme Right

The term 'extreme right' is a particularly troubling one to use in political analysis. In ordinary speech and in journalistic writing one could use the term without being misunderstood, and intuitively there seems to be a set of political parties, movements and tendencies which 'go together', for example all outwardly Nazi parties. However, in an academic context this is not sufficient: one would have to justify why such parties are being called both extreme and right-wing. And it is here that the problems start.

Fascist regimes can be seen as the paradigmatic instances of extreme-right politics, but this should not be taken as implying that all extreme right-wing movements are necessarily fascist. The Poujadist movement in post-war France might be such an example, but it is a matter of controversy whether it should be properly classed as fascist. For the sake of convenience, and to avoid interminable wranglings about the classification of difficult cases, in this chapter the emphasis will be upon those fascist parties and movements, which in conventional terms are accepted to be unambiguously extreme right-wing.

One difficulty with the label 'extreme right' is that it seems to imply that such movements are rather like the non-extreme right, but just a bit more so. By the same token, the label can be interpreted to mean that the extreme right bears little similarity to the extreme left. The problem is that the sort of criteria that enable us to stretch the rest of the political spectrum out from left to right do not seem to justify placing the fascists at the far right end of the spectrum. This can be illustrated by considering three different criteria, which can be, and indeed have been, used, to justify arranging the political universe on a simple left-right plane, but which seem unable to cope with the awkward bundle of fascist parties — namely economic policy, social support and modernization (see Chapters 3 and 4).

An alternative strategy for defining the characteristics of the extreme right would be to start with the movements which one wishes to categorize as facist and then to attempt to extract their common distinguishing characteristics. It would not matter if the resulting characteristics led to some difficult, or borderline, cases, which might be hard to categorize, for every political category has its 'fuzzy edges': what matters is to identify major characteristics of the prototypical instances.

The definition of fascism is a much debated question, about which scholars continue to disagree, but three broad characteristics will here be offered as a guide: (a) nationalism/racism, (b) anti-Marxism and anti-communism, and (c) anti-democracy.

Nationalism/racism. The extreme right expresses an ideology, which sees the nation or the race as being the prime political unit and it seeks to mobilize the mass support of the whole race or nation. This ideology can be distinguished from Marxism, which sees the class as the basic unit of political mobilization. Moreover, it can be distinguished from liberalism, which stresses the interconnectedness of the whole world. This mobilization of the nation/race frequently has a negative element, in that support is mobilized *against* those who are believed not to belong to the race or nation. Nazi anti-Semitism provides a case in point, as does the 'anti-immigration' policies of parties like the National Front in Britain, Front National in France, or Republikaner Party in West Germany, which aim to preserve the whiteness of the race/nation by expelling those whose skins are judged too dark.

Anti-Marxism and anti-communism. The extreme right is specifically anti-communist, and it often attacks nationalist conservatives for being 'soft' on Marxism. The anti-Marxism is related to a strong rejection of the notion of equality. If communists seek an ultimate social equality, so the extreme right celebrates a doctrine of inequality, whether it be an inequality between races/nations (i.e., master races and under-races) or within the race/nation (heroic leaders and disciplined followers). In this way the ideology of the extreme right is avowedly elitist.

Anti-democratic. The principles of elitism and nationalism will be formulated in such a way that democratic rights and liberties will be threatened. In some movements the threat will be overt. Thus, Hitlerian National Socialism outwardly attacked liberal democracy as a system which failed to provide necessarily strong leaders, because, as Nazi ideologists claimed, in a democracy elite individuals have the same voting rights as racially inferior individuals. Some extreme right-wing parties, particularly in post-war years, claim to be democratic. However, opponents of these parties will dispute these claims, claiming that beneath the democratic pretensions lies a tendency for anti-democratic practice. The critics will point not only to the implications of the anti-egalitarian doctrines, but also to the style of such political parties. A number of analysts have claimed that the political style of fascism is an important defining characteristic (e.g., O'Sullivan, 1983; Linz, 1976). O'Sullivan has characterized this style as being an 'activist' one, which encourages impatience with constitutional forms and puts the party above the constraints of the law. The preservation of the race/nation is seen as so important that democratic rights have to be sacrificed, particularly the rights of those who might legally have citizenship, but who the party sees as not 'properly' belonging to the race/nation.

The three defining characteristics do not distinguish between fascist and Nazi movements. Whereas all Nazi movements are fascist, and are extreme right-wing, not all fascist, or extreme right-wing, movements are Nazi. 'Nazism' refers to the specific variant of fascism associated with the Hitlerian movement. Partly this is a matter of style — the uniforms, the heel-clicking salutes, etc.; and partly it is a matter of specific ideological features, such as the leader-worship, or *Führer Prinzip*, of Nazism and its obsessive ideology of anti-Semitism. What this means is that the Nazi-style uniforms, the leader-worship and the anti-Semitism are not in themselves necessary defining characteristics of fascism. Similarly, fascist groups are not necessarily anti-Semitic. In the early days of Italian Fascism, there was little overt anti-Semitism.

In analysing political traditions, one obvious method is to look at the major theorists who have formulated the theories embodied by the traditions. As regards liberalism and Marxism, this would mean considering the ideas of major philosophers and social theorists. The intellectual pedigree of liberalism would be distinguished by ideas from Locke, Voltaire, Mill, etc. Similarly, even such philosophical critics of Marxism as Isaiah Berlin and Karl Popper stress that Marx himself was an original thinker of genius, and that his ideas have continued to affect the thinking of both Marxist and non-Marxist social theorists to this day. However, the intellectual traditions of fascism are impoverished when put alongside Marxism and liberalism. When Mussolini swept to power in 1923 he could not present himself as the living realization of an intellectual tradition of political theory, as could the French revolutionaries of 1789, or the Bolsheviks of 1917. To put it crudely, he had no great books to cite. The problem is illustrated by the way he tried to recruit the economist and sociologist, Vilfredo Pareto, as the great theorist of the fascist revolution. In return, Pareto, in the last year of his life, heralded Mussolini's regime with optimism (Bucolo, 1980). However, it would be a mistake to analyse the ideology of fascism in terms of the ideas of Pareto. Although Pareto's social philosophy was based upon anti-democratic premises, which stipulated the necessity and social desirability of elite rule, his great work *Mind and Society* contained other themes, which would have clashed dramatically with Fascism: in particular, Pareto debunked the pretensions of nationalist and racist mythology. German Nazism, of course, had its 'great book'. However, *Mein Kampf*, a mish-mash of self-serving autobiography, psychopathic hatred and prejudice, should not be considered as an intellectual work of political theory. The mystery is how such nonsense became to be taken seriously by so many people.

Fascist writers have tended to draw their themes from various sources. One particularly important source has been from those biological and pseudo-biological writings that argued for the existence of genetic differences between peoples and within races. Thus, Hitler's ramblings about the purity of Aryan blood and the biological superiority of the Leader draw upon the pseudo-scientific writings of eugenicists (Poliakov, 1974). In post-war years there has been at attempt to create an 'intellectual culture' of the extreme right. For instance in France the Groupement de Recherche et d'Etudes pour la Civilisation Européenne (GRECE), under the leadership of Alain de Benoist, has been attempting to reformulate a philosophy of state and nation around biological and anti-egalitarian notions. It would be possible to analyse the ideas and mythology of the extreme right in terms of its biological characterizations of race and nation, and to show how scientific, and more especially bogus scientific, ideas have been incorporated. However, there is also another theme in the ideological mythology of the extreme right. This is the theme of conspiracy. This theme does not draw its intellectual nourishment from the 'great books' of Western political theory. Nor is it derived from nineteenth-century theories of blood and race. Instead, the themes are to be found in what could be called a 'counter-culture' of political books and pamphlets, whose very lack of intellectual prominence in Western philosophy has contributed to the continuing appeal of fascism. Therefore, to examine this appeal, one needs to look, not for the 'great books' of fascism, but at bizarre books, which in the main possess little intrinsic merit but which continue to hold a fascination over the fascist imagination.

Post-War Fascism in Europe

The era of the extreme right was the inter-war period. Not only was there a fascist regime in Italy for most of this period, and one in Germany from 1933, but there were large fascist parties in many European countries. Anti-democratic and anti-Semitic parties could believe that their time had come: their ideas would be the dominant ideas of the twentieth century, replacing the liberalism of the nineteenth century. Of course, it was not to be. Fascism did not merely suffer a massive military defeat in 1945. In addition, the ideas of fascism were discredited as the pictures of the Nazi concentration camps were flashed across the world. After Auschwitz the ideas of the great racial state could no longer be innocently championed.

However, the extreme right wing did not suddenly disappear without trace. There are those theorists who claim that the main focus of the extreme right has shifted from Europe and that nationalist dictatorships in the Third World represent the true heirs of Mussolini. It is, of course, arguable whether the present regimes in Iran, Chile and Uganda, for example, should be classed as fascist in the classic sense. However, the focus of this chapter is not upon the Third World and possible parallels between dictatorships there and those existing in Europe between the wars. Instead, the focus is to remain on Europe, in order to discuss the nature of extreme right-wing parties since 1945. This is not because such parties have been politically important in themselves. In fact, they are, in the main, to be distinguished only by their lack of political distinction. However, the analysis of small parties on the political fringe, beyond the bounds of conventional political respectability, can illustrate more important issues about the nature of political beliefs, and in particular, about the nature of irrational racial prejudices.

No extreme right party in Europe has come anywhere close to attaining power since the war. The most consistently successful party in electoral terms has been the Movimento Sociale Italiano, which has continued to average about 6 per cent of the national vote, with particular pockets of support in urban centres in the south and in Sicily (Caciagli, 1988). The party has managed to maintain its representation in the Italian parliament since 1953. It has always stressed its Fascist heritage and Georgio Almirante, who led the party until early 1988, was a former minister in Mussolini's last government. The new leader Giafranco Fini, however, is reportedly keen to play down the continuity with pre-war Fascism and, instead, to present the party as a new force in politics.

If Italian fascists have managed to maintain a continuous parliamentary presence, this is not true of German fascism. Immediately the Nazi regime was replaced, fascism became politically a fringe movement. The official annual report on the extreme right, issued by the German government, claimed in 1987 that there were sixty-nine fascist organizations, most of which were miniscule. The best-known party is the National Democratic Party, which was founded in 1964 and which briefly in the 1960s awakened fears that West Germany was about to undergo a serious resurgence of fascism. However, it was unable to sustain its electoral support, and soon was beset by internal squabbles between those who wanted to present the party as a 'respectable' democratic party and those who wanted a more activist movement engaging in direct or violent activities (Stoss, 1988). Indeed, in 1989 it was the new anti-immigrant party, the Republikaner, which made notable gains in the Berlin and European Parliament elections (7.3 per cent of the vote in the latter), though the NPD vote also rose notably in the Hesse elections.

This German pattern seems more typical of post-war fascist politics than does the Italian one. Fascist groups tend to inhabit a part of the political spectrum which is shunned by respectable parties and which attracts limited support. However, at particular moments, such parties seem capable of attracting much wider support. Yet initial successes are not followed; internal recrimination follows; and the party slips back to its former fringe status.

This pattern was seen in Great Britain in the 1970s with the rise and fall of the National Front. The party was formed in 1967, drawing together a motley collection of old-style Nazis, anti-Semites and white supremacists (Billig, 1978; Thurlow, 1987). The new party aimed to present itself as a democratic force, contesting local and parliamentary elections. It switched its campaign target from Jews to the growing population of non-whites. For a time in the mid-1970s it emerged briefly from the shadowy fringes of politics, gaining more votes than Oswald Mosley's British Union of Fascists had managed to attract before the war, and so briefly Britain had the dubious distinction of being the only western European country in which post-war fascism was more successful than pre-war fascism. However, the electoral 'successes' were not maintained in the 1979 general election. In the 1980s the party has more or less retired from electoral activity, whilst its various factions debate whether street violence or more clandestine 'revolutionary' activity represent the best hope for advance (for details of the factions see Maolain, 1987).

The same pattern, but on a much more serious and larger scale, may be currently occurring in France. The Front National was founded in 1972 ostensibly on the model of the British National Front. The new leader was Le Pen, who had briefly been a member of parliament for the Poujadist movement, which had a moment of success in 1956 before fading almost without a trace. Initially the party attracted little support, but capitalizing on Le Pen's undoubted oratorical qualities and mounting crude campaigns against foreign immigrants, the party first succeeded in obtaining high voting figures in a number of local council elections after the socialist victories of 1981. In the 1984 European Parliamentary elections, the party achieved almost 11 per cent of the votes cast, sufficient for the party to form a caucus of ten representatives in the European Parliament (Lorien, Criton and Dumont, 1985). Success continued in the elections to the National Assembly in March 1986, which brought over 2.5 million votes and thirty-five seats (Cole, 1986). Nor was this the peak. In the April 1988 Presidential election, Le Pen obtained nearly 4.5 million votes, approximately 14 per cent of the votes cast. A few weeks later in elections to the National Assembly, the party slipped back to its 1986 standing in terms of votes, but because the electoral procedure was no longer based upon proportional representation, the party lost all but one of its seats (Eatwell, 1988; Hainsworth, 1988). Nevertheless, in the 1989 European Parliament elections the Front National went on to win 11.6 per cent of the vote.

The Substitutability of Prejudices

From looking at the rises and falls of these fascist groups, it would be easy to formulate a theory about the substitutability of political prejudices. The theory would go something like this. Extreme right groups attempt to play upon fears which indigenous members of the population might have about foreigners and immigrants. They do this in basically similar ways, and there is a familiarity in the language, which fascists use to depict the 'foreigner'. However, the target of these prejudices changes, for it is not always the same 'foreigner' who is being denigrated: fascist groups, depending where and when they arise, select different objects for hatreds. Thus, the form of their beliefs and of their appeals may be similar. Yet the content differs, because there is a substitutability of targets.

Le Pen, in his various electoral campaigns, has played upon French fears and dislikes of North African immigrants. Not only does he evoke stereotyped images of foreign immigrants, but he appeals to economic insecurities in the indigenous population: the Front National used the slogan that 'two million immigrants are the cause of two million French people out of work' (Mitra, 1988; for other discussions of the party's support see Lorien, Criton and Dumont, 1985; Plenel and Rollat, 1984; Schain, 1987). Le Pen's complaints against Arabs living in France have evoked in many observers memories of pre-war political campaigns against Jews living in France. At first sight one might be tempted to say that the Front National had gone further than merely to substitute new hatreds for old hatreds: it had reversed some of its old hatreds. Using an anti-Arab rhetoric, Le Pen had been seeking Jewish votes. Moreover, some Jews had been attracted by his message. For example, the information officer of the Marseilles Jewish community's main religious organization claimed that Le Pen was the 'most pro-Israel of France's political leaders' (*Jewish Chronicle*, 11 September 1987). Earlier in 1987, Jacques Torczyner a prominent figure in the World Union of General Zionists had arranged a luncheon in New York to be given in Le Pen's honour, in order to forge links with right-wing American Zionists. It should be added that the World Zionist Organization, which is the main Zionist organization, was not so sanguine that old hatreds had been reversed, nor in any case that it was desirable to consort with politicians of hatred, regardless of their target. The general council of the organization therefore passed a strongly worded motion on 15 June 1987, stating that the values of Le Pen were 'in total contradiction to the values of Judaism and Zionism and that a dialogue with such a person is undesirable'.

A substitutability of overt targets can be observed in the history of British fascist and anti-immigrant movements. At the turn of the century there were concerted attacks against Jewish immigrants, especially those living in the East End of London. Later the British Union of Fascists campaigned against the Jewish immigrants. The propaganda of these groups depicted the Jewish immigrants as being dirty, criminal, hostile to British society, disease-ridden and so on (Holmes, 1979; Thurlow, 1987). In fact, the complaints are virtually identical to those which today's fascists in the National Front direct against immigrants from the Indian sub-continent (Billig, 1978; Husbands, 1983). And, indeed, the complaints are similar to those voiced against Irish immigrants in the generations before the Jews started arriving in Britain in any sizable numbers (Holmes, 1978). The history of immigration into the United States also suggests that the movements of populations can sometimes produce a reaction, especially in times of economic shortage. Lipset and Raab describe how nativist anti-immigrant movements have followed most large-scale migrations into the United States (Lipset and Raab, 1970). Again, the pattern of reaction suggests that the target is substitutable, but the form of the complaints is constant; whether the accusations are directed against Irish, Jewish, Italian immigrants, they bear an all too familiar ring.

One might, therefore, predict that the movements of population in western Europe since the last war would be accompanied by the development of political groupings, who would attempt to exploit insecurities and fears of host populations. In France, the target would be North Africans, in Germany the 'guest workers' from Turkey and Yugoslavia, in Holland the Surinamese and the Moluccans, in Britain the West Indians and Asians, etc. Certainly there is evidence of prejudice against these different target populations and the growth of fascist groups attempting to exploit such prejudices. Again, this suggests that the former target, the Jews, should have drifted out of the picture, there not having been a comparable recent movement of Jewish populations, which might have left Jews being perceived as a highly visible and recently arrived group. The studies of national prejudices, and in particular of those who might be attracted to the politics of right-wing extremism, show little evidence of widespread anti-Semitism. For instance, in Britain a high proportion of white working-class youths expressed racist views and there was a growth in expressed support for the National Front in the years 1979 to 1982, corresponding to the rise of unemployment in the area (Billig, 1982; Billig and Cochrane, 1987). The National Front supporters, most of whom expressed support in an abstract way, showed strong ethnocentric prejudices against West Indians and Asians. By contrast, Jews seemed totally irrelevant to their concerns. A similar position has been found in studies of Dutch and West German young people (Hagendoorn and Janssen, 1986; Hagendoorn and Hraba, 1987; Hraba, Hagendoorn and Hagendoorn, 1988).

However, the surprising thing about the contemporary fascist scene is that the Jews have often not drifted out of the picture. In the natural recruiting ground of the fascist parties —often the younger, white males living in inner city areas — one might observe the prejudices of one generation being substituted by the prejudices of a new generation. On the other hand, it will be suggested that the leaders of the fascist parties have not kept pace with this process of substitution. Instead these parties have clung to the traditions of anti-Semitism, so beneath the outward substitutability of these groups' targets has continued something else, whose dynamics and psychology are of a different order.

A Detail of Le Pen

On 13 September 1987, Jean-Marie Le Pen made a strange outburst during a radio programme. At the time he seemed to be riding upon a tide of popularity. He was boasting that he would attract at least 20 per cent of the votes in the presidential contest. He, of course, had no chance of winning the presidential election, but he was seeking to establish himself as a serious politician, and his party as a fixture on the political scene (Schain, 1987). In short, Le Pen had achieved a measure of success, aspired to more, and therefore had much to lose, when he made his radio broadcast in September 1987.

Le Pen was asked about the mass gassing of Jews by Germans in the last war, and, in particular, whether he accepted that those events took place. He did not answer as any other major politician would have done: namely, that it was absurd and malevolent to deny such historical facts. Le Pen's reply was of a different order (quoted in *Observer*, 20 September 1987):

> I ask myself a certain number of questions. I'm not saying that gas chambers did not exist. I have not been able to see any myself. I have not specially studied the question. But I consider it a matter of detail in the history of the Second World War...I say that some historians are debating these questions.

The result was an immediate outcry. Leading figures rushed to condemn Le Pen for his anti-Semitism. There were resignations from his party. More importantly, public opinion polls registered a sharp decline in his popularity. (In the event, his support recovered for the actual election.)

The radio broadcast is of great interest if one seeks to understand the beliefs and motivations of those on the very far right of political life. Le Pen was saying something outrageous, from which no political advantage could accrue. In fact, only political damage could be caused. Perhaps it had been tiredness in the course of an arduous campaign, or perhaps it was a flash of temper, but it was as if the public were suddenly allowed access to some of the inner thoughts of Le Pen — thoughts which, for sound political reasons, were not normally on public display.

If Le Pen's outburst reflected merely an individual preoccupation, it would be of scant interest, except to those interested in his personal psychology. However, it will be suggested that the anti-Semitism expressed in Le Pen's outburst is not a personal eccentricity, but is something which is common on the extreme right. The generality of such anti-Semitism prompts the following question: why do extreme right-wing parties continue to adhere to a position from which no immediate political advantage can be gained? Because the question cannot be answered in terms of political strategy or advantage, the very question raises important issues about the social psychology and cultural heritage of anti-Semitism.

Anti-Semitism and the Conspiracy Theory

Le Pen's outburst about the possible non-existence of the Holocaust must be understood in terms of the ideological background of the extreme right. The natural supporters of fascist groups may no longer be preoccupied by the Jews as a target, but anti-Semitism has continued to circulate at the highest levels of fascist groups (Billig, 1978). The Front National has contained a number of senior members who have been quite open in their anti-Semitic beliefs. Le Pen has a history of anti-Semitic connections. In the 1960s he wrote the sleeve notes for a record of Nazi songs, praising the Nazi movements for its democratic character (Plenel and Rollat, 1984). In March 1986 he was convicted of making statements which contained anti-Semitic threats (*Le Monde*, 13 March 1986).

The National Front in Britain provides a classic example of a fascist group seeking to build a mass support on the basis of racism, whilst its leaders preserved an anti-Semitic ideology. It was formed precisely because there was a diminishing market for overtly Hitlerian or anti-Semitic politics. However, the leadership, keeping tight control upon the publications of the party, ensured that the National Front did not lose its ideological origins. Instead, there were two tiers in the party's propaganda. Messages designed for mass appeal concentrated upon West Indian and Asian targets, whilst the 'serious' party magazines, to be read by the inner core of members, were fundamentally anti-Semitic (Billig, 1978; see also Fielding, 1981; Taylor, 1982; Thurlow, 1987). The political disreputability of leaders hampered the growth of the National Front, and its public protestations of being neither fascist nor anti-Semitic were easily refuted by anti-fascists. However, in the 1980s a new generation of leaders ousted the old Nazis. These are young, often educated men, who have no record of having taken part in overtly Hitlerian activities. Getting rid of the old Nazis has not entailed disposing of the anti-Semitism, for the new leaders do not quarrel with Nazism because it was anti-Semitic. For instance, the June 1987 issue of *Vanguard*, published in support of the National Front, criticizes the philosophy of Nazism. Neither Jews nor anti-Semitism is mentioned. Instead, Hitler is accused of not being racist enough. According to the author, the German Führer took his theory of race from Houston Stewart Chamberlain, who 'had no belief in any biological basis for racialism, and certainly had no faith in racial purity or racial preservation'.

Currently there is a split in the National Front, between those who wish the party to concentrate upon becoming an elite fighting force of 'political soldiers', and those who want to see the party recruit widely from the white working class (Billig, 1988b). The former group seek to maintain links with European fascist groups promoting the 'Third Way', which embraces both the terrorist strategy of Destra Radicale and the cultural strategy that has been most notably pursued in France by Alain de Benoist and GRECE (for discussions of GRECE and the strategy of reformulating a fascist intellectual culture see Brunn, 1979; Billig, 1981; Lesselier, 1988; Seidel, 1981 and 1986). In proposing its 'Third Way' this section of the National Front seeks to preserve and promote anti-Semitic ideology and this desire overrides any wish for mass support. In fact, this anti-Semitism allows the sort of strange ideological alliances that would alienate working-class racists. This faction, through its magazine *Nationalism Today*, has been praising the anti-Semitic American black leader, Louis Farrakhan. Even more surprising has been the championing of Colonel Gadaffi, whose Green Book is frequently recommended. The magazine regularly prints articles attacking Israel and advocating the Palestinian cause (e.g., *Nationalism Today*, 1988, p.42). This sort of rhetoric has not been favoured by all within the National Front. It is criticized in *Vanguard*, produced by the rival clique, who have specifically attacked Islam as a deadly enemy of the 'White Race'. This faction scathingly dismisses their rivals as the 'Colonel Gadaffi Admiration Society' (*The Flag*, January 1988).

Despite the differences between the two factions of the National Front, and despite the differences between both of these factions and the Nazi old guard who formerly ran the party, all three elements draw upon a common ideological tradition. Similar books and pamphlets are to be found on the booklists issued by all groupings. And these publications outline the ideology of the conspiracy tradition (for an analysis of the published ideology of the National Front, see Billig, 1978; more generally on the conspiracy theory of politics, see, for instance Lipset and Raab, 1970; Groh, 1987). The conspiracy theorist has a particular view of political life: all events are seen in terms of an evil conspiracy to take over the world. The conspirators are said to work insidiously to subvert independent nations and races. They do their evil damage by poisoning the minds of ordinary people, who are innocently unaware of the conspiracy. Moreover, there is an apocalyptic tone to such publications, for it is asserted that the conspiracy is nearing success. The conspirators have already succeeded in controlling most of the powerful organizations of the world. Communism and capitalism are seen as being controlled by the conspirators and their apparent opposition is yet another dastardly trick to confuse the unsuspecting public. So powerful is the conspiracy that the manipulators are on the threshold of attaining their goal of complete world domination.

In National Front publications, the conspiracy is usually described as being Zionist. *National Front News* (April 1987) makes the claim that Zionism is more than Jewish nationalism. It stated that Zionism was a huge empire which 'menaces the entire world': Zionism was an 'iceberg of hidden power of which the bandit state of Israel is only the cruel tip...The tentacles of Zionist power grip the mass media, economies and political life of the Western world'. It is the basic ideological assumption of a world Jewish conspiracy, which enables this section of the National Front to seek common cause with like-minded sections in Arab and black nationalist politics. The same assumption of a Jewish-dominated conspiracy underwrites the ideology of the rival faction (e.g., see *Vanguard*, August and October 1987).

The theme of a Jewish/Zionist conspiracy has not been invented by the British fascists. Nor is it, of course, peculiar to post-war fascism. Instead it represents a common theme linking extreme right-wing groups from different countries and linking them to pre-war fascism. The theme of an evil conspiracy, lying behind the outward form of political life, is an old one. Norman Cohn in his book *Warrant for Genocide* traces the conspiratorial interpretation of politics back to Auguste de Barruel, who having lived through the French Revolution, then wrote at length that the revolutionary turmoil was the product of a conspiracy of Freemasons. The conspirators had succeeded in poisoning the minds of the masses so that they turned from their natural allegiances to the monarchy to espouse the alien and internationalist ideas of republicanism. Katz has suggested that these Masonic themes became united with anti-Semitic themes in the writings of des Mousseaux in the mid-nineteenth century (Katz, 1980). From then on, the traditions of anti-Semitic conspiracy ideology have continued unbroken. It can be shown that not only do present-day fascists draw upon the notions of older conspiracy theorists, but they are aware of their ideological heritage and read and republish the older late eighteenth- and nineteenth-century texts (Billig, 1978).

Not all conspiracy theorists express their ideas in the same way, and on occasions they criticize each other. Sometimes the basic assumption of a world conspiracy is expressed with a crudity which embarrasses some of the more sophisticated theorists. One of the cruder versions of the theory was studied by Norman Cohn (Cohn, 1967). *The Protocols of the Learned Elders of Zion*, a text forged by the Russian secret police at the turn of the century, had a great impact upon Nazi thinking. The text purported to be the instructions written by the king of the Jews and distributed to his underlings, explaining how to take control of the whole world. The king was telling his followers the stages by which independent nations could be destroyed, and how the minds of their populations could be confused by deception. Some conspiracy theorists deny that the conspiracy is directed by a single Jewish king, who has issued instructions. *Vanguard*, for example, poured scorn on the simplicities of the mentality of those who believe in the *Protocols* (January 1988). Yet, as has been seen, this rejection of the conspiracy theory in its simplest form, does not entail a rejection of the whole ideological tradition: it means that the theorist believes that the networks of the Jewish/Zionist movement for world domination are much more complex, and, indeed, thereby that much more insidiously dangerous.

The Denial of the Holocaust and the Conspiracy Theory

Le Pen's remarks in his radio outburst have been assumed to be anti-Semitic. However, we have not yet analysed the nature of this anti-Semitism, nor yet suggested how the outburst might be the product of the wider ideological tradition of the conspiracy theory of politics. Le Pen, as he later said in his defence, was not actually denying the actuality of the Holocaust: he was merely keeping an open mind on a matter of debate. Le Pen's statement must be seen in the context of the publications which have denied the existence of the Holocaust. Seidel, in her analysis of the myth of the non-existence of the Holocaust, shows that as soon as the Second World War finished, a number of anti-Semites and ex-Nazis were denying that there had been a mass gassing of Jews (Seidel, 1986). However, in the immediate post-war years the pamphlets denying the existence of the Holocaust had a limited circulation, even in fascist circles. This was to change in the 1970s, with the publication of Richard Harwood's pamphlet *Did Six Million Really Die?*, and A. R. Butz's book *The Hoax of the Twentieth Century* (see also Vidal-Naquet, 1987; Eatwell, 1990). These publications immediately found themselves on the sales lists of Nazi and fascist groups throughout the world, and they were followed by others written on the same theme. These texts had an important propaganda function, for it was as if they had suddenly lifted an immense burden from the shoulders of Nazi propagandists. New recruits could be reassured that fascism was not an evil creed, as they might have assumed, for the well-known atrocities simply did not exist: credulous recruits could then be directed to the relevant pamphlets and books. In France a university teacher, Robert Faurisson, gained notoriety with his articles and books denying the existence of the Holocaust and his claim that the Diary of Anne Frank was a fake (Seidel, 1986; Vidal-Naquet, 1981). It was against the background of Faurisson's notoriety that Le Pen had been asked about his views on the Holocaust. Significantly, by his 'open-minded' response Le Pen did not distance himself from the anti-Semites seeking to deny the Holocaust.

The denial of the Holocaust should not be seen merely as an attempt to reinterpret one aspect of history, for it is part of the conspiratorial interpretation of politics. The writers of the denial texts are not merely suggesting that a historical detail needs to be corrected, although they do pose as reputable historians seeking the details of the past. However, the authors of the denials, or 'revisionists' as they like to call themselves, are offering a theory about politics, for they are suggesting that the world has been subject to a myth. Thus these texts are not mere 'revisions' of history, they are also 'explanations' how the world at large has been deliberately duped. As such, these texts provide a modern twist to the much older tale of conspiracy. The title of Butz's tract is significant: it refers to a 'hoax'. In the opening pages he talks of the 'monstrous lie' that 6 million Jews had been murdered by the

Nazis (Butz, 1976, p.8). Similarly Harwood asks on the first page of his booklet 'Why the Big Lie?' Having claimed that the Holocaust was a lie, authors like Butz and Harwood then feel the need to explain the why and wherefore of the big lie. The answer given by both Butz and Harwood is predictable. Powerful Zionists were the liars, for the whole notion of the Holocaust was nothing but a 'Zionist hoax' to justify driving the Palestinians from their own land (Butz, 1976, p.250). Of course, for Zionists to be able to manufacture and to spread a lie of these proportions, they must have immense power over the populations of the whole world. Thus, Israel or Palestine is just the tip of the iceberg.

Vidal-Naquet has shown that the denial of the Holocaust is not confined to the extreme right-wing but it is 'situated at the crossroads of very different, and sometimes contradictory, ideologies: Nazi anti-Semitism, anti-communism of the extreme right, anti-Zionism, German nationalism, diverse nationalisms of Eastern Europe, libertarian pacifism and Marxism of the extreme left' (Vidal-Naquet, 1987, p.118). Even if the denial has wider circulation than the world of fascism, then it and the general tale of Jewish/Zionist conspiracy are common ideological currency in extreme right-wing groups like the Front National. A fascist group seeking mass support and political respectability might like to play down these themes in its overt propaganda. Certainly the Front National, during its successful years in the 1980s, distanced itself publicly from such themes, just as the National Front in Britain had attempted to conceal the anti-Semitic themes of conspiracy from the mass gaze (Billig, 1978). Yet the themes are very much part of the continuing ideological heritage of such groups. In 1978 the *National*, a Front National magazine, published a tribute to the murdered fascist François Duprat. The tribute praised Duprat for understanding who were the real enemies of the French nation, and for piercing the prejudices and taboos against unmasking these enemies. The tribute went on to cite specifically 'historians' such as Richard Harwood (text quoted in Lorien, Criton and Dumont, 1985, p.150).

One should not be surprised that a political figure, who emerges from an extremist background, should preserve elements of these ideological traditions. Le Pen, in his outburst referred to the reality of the Holocaust as an issue about which 'historians' are debating. It is, of course, nothing of the sort. No serious historian has denied its reality. Butz and Faurisson are not historians; 'Harwood' is the pseudonym of Richard Verrall, who in the 1970s was a leading figure in the National Front. Thus, Le Pen, by his choice of words to describe these propagandists, revealed his own ideological heritage, and thereby was perpetuating some of the assumptions of this heritage.

Le Pen's outburst is interesting for the question it raises. Despite the political inconvenience of the anti-Semitic heritage, the ideology has not been discarded, as extreme groups substitute other targets for their overt hostility. There may be attempts to remove the anti-Semitic tales of conspiracy from sight but, as the case of Le Pen illustrates, old assumptions and habits are liable to assert themselves at inconvenient moments. Therefore one can ask why the heritage should be continued. Political strategy or expediency cannot be the reasons, because the heritage is a pronounced disadvantage. Nor can economic factors satisfactorily explain the continuation of the anti-Semitism. There is evidence that one, at least, of the Holocaust denial publications was subsidized by certain elements in the Arab world (Seidel, 1986). The pro-Gadaffi and pro-Palestinian stance of the National Front (or to be more precise, of one of its factions) appears to be designed to seek finance, as is the party's adoption of phrases that are more usually found in the propaganda of the anti-Zionist far left, rather than the far right (i.e. phrases like 'Israel, the bandit state'; for an analysis of far left anti-Zionist rhetoric, see Billig, 1987). However, such funding is a possibility *because* the group possesses an ideology of conspiracy, and it has not adopted the ideology (as opposed to the style of phrasing the ideology) *in order to* attract funding. If economic and political answers are ruled out, then the possibility of psychological explanations is raised. Are there psychological factors which draw those on the extreme right towards such a bizarre explanation of politics as the conspiracy theory? If so, do these psychological factors ensure that believers hang on to this particular explanation of politics, despite the obvious political disadvantages of doing so?

Psychological Approaches to Conspiracy Theory

The psychological approaches to the study of conspiracy theory can basically be grouped around two themes: the study of cognitive and of motivational factors. The former approach concentrates upon the conceptual patterns and strategies of the conspiracy theory, whilst the latter looks at the emotional forces that might be expressed in the theory or that might make the conspiracy theory attractive to potential believers. It will be suggested that both sorts of factors, although important, do not explain the non-substitutability of the conspiracy theory.

Cognitive Factors in Conspiracy Theory

There has been a considerable amount of social psychological research investigating the ways that people explain social events. Much of this research has gone under the heading of 'attribution theory', which assumes that people have a basic need to understand why social events occur. Attribution theorists have suggested that people generally offer two different sorts of explanation: sometimes events are explained in terms of the actions of the actors involved, and sometimes they are explained in terms of the situations in which actors find themselves (for summaries of attribution research, see, for example, Antaki, 1985; Eiser, 1987; Fiske and Taylor, 1984). For instance, it has been claimed that explanations of poverty can be phrased in personal terms (i.e., the poor are poor because they are lazy), or in situational terms (the poor are poor because society is unfair). Findings suggest that political beliefs can affect the sorts of causal attributions which are made (Furnham and Lewis, 1986).

It has been claimed that attribution theory is relevant to understanding conspiracy theory, because, above all, the conspiracy theory offers an explanation of political events (Kruglanski, 1987). The conspiracy theorist can explain whatever happens in the world: everything is said to occur because the conspirators are manipulating events secretly. If, as attribution theorists suggest, the desire for explanation is natural, then conspiracy theorists, far from being abnormal, have an abundance of this 'natural' tendency. And the more implausible the explanation, the more the theorists will take this as proof of the cunning nature of the conspirators. Consequently, lack of evidence about the conspiracy is turned around and cited as evidence that the conspirators are so powerful and devious that they do not even leave obvious signs behind them. An example of this style of thinking can be cited. *Candour* is a magazine which was founded by the first chairman of the National Front, but which today publishes its anti-Semitic conspiracy theories independently of any particular party. In its July/August 1987 issue it explained the 'immutable principle' for understanding world events: 'the masters of international policy — and let it be said without hesitation that whoever denies the reality of that masterdom is blind — have so well organized the world that their stakes in any given programme are equalled only by their stakes in the alternative programme, whatever the alternative might be'. In other words, whatever a government might do, or not do, is taken as further evidence that the 'masters' are still in control.

There is a further feature of the conspiracy theory of politics, to which attribution theorists have drawn attention (Kruglanski, 1987; Zukier, 1987). The conspiracy theory continually makes personal attributions. Whatever happens is said to be the result of deliberate planning by the conspirators. Having denied the existence of the Holocaust, these anti-Semitic theorists do not assume that the belief in the Holocaust arose out of a series of accidents: they claim that the Holocaust was a deliberately manufactured lie, designed to achieve certain ends. The conspiracy theorist extends such personal explanations to practically everything which occurs in politics. However, the overabundance of personal attributions is not, of itself, psychologically remarkable. In fact, some attribution theorists have claimed that many, if not most, people show evidence of the 'fundamental attribution error' or preferring situational explanations to personal ones (Nisbet and Ross, 1980). Although attribution theorists often talk as if the propensity to make situational rather than personal attributions is somehow part of human nature, some critics have suggested that the so-called 'fundamental attribution error', if it exists, reflects the style of thinking prevalent in contemporary society, rather than a universal style (Billig, 1982; Sampson, 1981).

The attribution research does not deny that conspiracy theorists possess a distinctive cognitive style, which differs from that of non-conspiracy theorists. However, the difference does not lie in the fact that personal attributions are made, nor in that explanations of social events are sought. The cognitive peculiarity of the conspiracy theory is that it is always the same personal attribution which is made. Monomanically the conspiracy theory comes back time and again to the same simple explanation (Lipset and Raab, 1970). Because not every aspect of the conspiracy theorists' cognitive style is distinctive, it is possible for the conspiracy theorist to appear quite reasonable, at least for a while. Sometimes governments are not quite honest and sometimes things are not quite as they appear; but then, there is what

Hofstadter called a sudden leap of the imagination (Hofstadter, 1966). The implausibility arises because it is always the same explanation that is offered; events are said to fit into an overall pattern.

Motivational Factors in the Conspiracy Theory

A description of the possible cognitive factors involved in the conspiracy theory of politics is not on its own sufficient to explain the possible attractions of this style of belief. One must also ask about emotional aspects. If the conspiracy theory pushes personal attributions to the point of absurdity, one can ask what motivational forces might lead the conspiracy theorist to this bizarrely one-tracked view of the world.

Kruglanski points to the importance of 'defensive attribution', which occurs when people make attributions to protect their own sense of self-esteem and to justify their own apparent failings. Thus, instead of blaming themselves, people seek explanations which blame others for anything that has gone wrong. Firmly believing in the superiority of their own race or nation, conspiracy theorists are explaining why that nation or race is not behaving in a superior way. Auguste de Barruel was explaining why the masses were no longer enchanted with the aristocracy. His account suggested that it was nothing to do with the actions of the aristocracy; the minds of the masses had been duped by the freemasons. Similarly, in the post-war years fascist ideologists explain away the minority status of their beliefs by claiming that people have turned against fascism because their minds have been subverted: they have been blinded by the 'myth' of the Holocaust and by other cunning devices.

There are psychological compensations to be gained by a belief in the conspiracy theory. Most obviously there is a sense of superiority. The conspiracy theorist claims to know a hidden truth, of which ordinary people are ignorantly unaware. There is some evidence that the conspiracy theory may appeal to those who have educational pretensions but themselves lack educational attainments (Rohter, 1969). Billig describes how the publishers of conspiracy theory like to present their authors as 'proper' intellectuals: their educational qualifications are prominently listed and, as has been seen, propagandists can be portrayed as if they were professional historians (Billig, 1987). Those reading such material can therefore pride themselves upon familiarity with 'intellectual' issues and a knowledge of what educated people are reading. Ray Hill, a former hard-line Nazi has described how this occurred in his own case (Hill and Bell, 1988).

In addition, there may be much deeper motivational themes expressed in some of the conspiracy theories. Repressed emotions may well be projected upon the shadowy figures in the conspiracy mythology. Thus Nazi theorists, who in fact planned a racial domination of the world, people their imaginations with Jewish plotters. The shadowy conspirators are often imagined to be engaged upon all sorts of immoral acts. Commenting upon this aspect of the conspiratorial tradition, Davis wrote: 'Freemasons, it was said, could commit any crime and indulge any passion when "upon the square" and

Catholics and Mormons were even less inhibited by internal moral standards' (Davis, 1971, p.336). It is not difficult to find modern examples, in which sexual fantasies appear to have been projected on to the image of the conspirators. David McCalden for a while ran the so-called Institute for Historical Research in America, which devoted itself to promoting the denial of the Holocaust. He wrote a pamphlet entitled *Exiles from History* which claimed to be an examination of the 'Jewish psyche'. This deeply anti-Semitic tract repeated old themes of Jewish conspiracy, which were mixed with allegations about Jewish sexual perversions. For example, McCalden claimed that Jews were obsessed by sex and that the Talmud permitted Jews to engage in sodomy with 3-year-old girls and with corpses; he went on: 'Jews are still practising weird sex cults...We have found that rabbis will masturbate, then mutilate and then fellate a baby's penis' (McCalden, 1982, p.25). It is difficult to say what motivates a writer to make such assertions, but it is hard to escape the impression that certain hidden emotions are being expressed in the imagination of the writer.

The Traditions of Anti-Semitism

The social psychological accounts of the mentality of the conspiracy theorist point to a number of cognitive and motivational factors that may be involved in this strange set of beliefs. From the psychological accounts one might hypothesize that individuals who wish to search for complete and surprising explanations of the social world and who wish for such explanations to express certain fantasies may be drawn to the world of the conspiracy theorist. One might also hypothesize that the world of extremist politics will contain more than its average share of such individuals. Disillusioned by conventional politics and embittered in various ways, such people may be attracted by the glamour of the important truths that the conspiracy theory offers (Billig, 1987). However, it should be emphasized that any such psychological explanation does not solve the questions of why the anti-Semitic conspiracy theory should be continued in extreme right-wing circles. The psychological theories suggest that one might expect to find a conspiratorial account of politics, but not why that account should be anti-Semitic.

What one finds on the extreme right is the non-substitutability of the anti-Semitic conspiracy theory. The fascist groups may have found new targets for their anti-immigrant rhetoric, but they have not adjusted correspondingly the targets of their conspiracy theories. The National Front magazine *Vanguard* illustrates the issue. In order to distance itself from the pro-Islamic faction of the National Front, *Vanguard* attacks Islam directly as the 'third deadly enemy of the white race, apart from communism and capitalism' (November/ December 1987). It should be noted that the magazine identified Islam as a third enemy, existing independently of the other two. There was no hint of a conspiratorial theme: Islam was not seen as manipulating the other two, nor were they in turn seen as controlling the third enemy. The ideology of the National Front, expressed clearly in its publications, is that the first two enemies, communism and capitalism, are really the outward form of a single enemy — Zionism. The anti-Islamic theme was not supplanting the themes of the conspiracy theory, but was being added as a complicating factor upon the simple cognitive structure of the conspiratorial ideology. As a result, the article, by the way it introduced its anti-Islamic themes, was illustrating the non-substitutability of the anti-Semitic conspiracy theory.

In order to understand why an anti-Islamic conspiracy theory has not been slotted conveniently into an ideological space previously occupied by an anti-Semitic conspiracy theory, one needs to consider a further aspect in the social psychology of the conspiracy theory. The conspiracy theory is more than a cognitive structure which gives a simple ordering to the believer's perceptions of the social world. It is more than an expression of certain unfulfilled wishes or fantasies. It is also, like other attitudinal positions, a stance in an argument (Billig, 1987b and 1988). The conspiracy theorist is arguing against conventional explanations of politics. The accusations of 'hoax' and 'lie' are not so much arguments directed against the hoaxers and the liars, who in any case are presumed to be beyond the reach of ordinary discussion. The arguments are directed against those who might believe in conventional explanations of politics. Thus the denial of the Holocaust is directed against those who accept the Holocaust as fact: primarily, of course, it is directed against the beliefs of those who have entered fascist political circles with ethnocentric hatreds and fears of 'immigrants' but without any familiarity with the conspiratorial interpretation of politics. Consequently, the conspiratorial tracts are arguments against those who fail to see the conspiratorial forces at work in the world.

That being so, an obvious factor is at work in aiding the continuation of the anti-Semitic conspiracy theory: it is easier to adapt old arguments than to invent new ones. A certain originality would be required in order to construct afresh another conspiratorial interpretation of politics; and this would require more intellectual and argumentative effort than the repetition and development of existing explanations. The ideologists of fascist groups have a vast library of books and pamphlets to draw upon and which can be cited as 'proofs' of the Jewish conspiracy. If the authors of *Vanguard* wished to substitute a tale of Islamic conspiracy for the tales of Jewish conspiracy, they would have to do something more difficult than quote from already well-thumbed, favourite texts, and something more intellectually demanding than substituting one set of 'foreigners' for another set in the old complaint that 'foreigners' are spoiling 'our' way of life. To substitute one theme of conspiracy for another would entail arguing with one's own ideological heritage. The ideologist would have to say that the books on the booklists, and the previous issues of the magazines, were all in error with their tales of Jewish conspiracy. The ease with which the denial of the Holocaust has made its way into the mythology of anti-Semitism shows how much simpler it would be to add to that cognitive structure which is ideological currency in extreme right-wing circles.

An ideological tradition can, therefore, have a momentum of its own. Because it exists and because it possesses its own cultural traditions, the chances of its perpetuation are increased, for it does not have to be invented anew. Moreover, its ideas can spread to new circles. It is no surprise if, in the course of the Arab–Israeli struggle, some Arab ideologists draw upon the images and mythology of traditional anti-Semitic traditions, as old themes are inserted into a new context. Nor is it a surprise that some Arab ideologists might be directly aiding the continuation of this tradition. After all, in these cases there is a real political conflict with an actual Jewish dimension on which the old mythology can be imposed. More surprising, at first glance, is the fact that the traditions can assert themselves where there is no political conflict with a Jewish dimension. This can be seen in the case of Le Pen and the Front National. Moreover, it is shown in the reports that the mythology has found a presence in Japan, virtually a country without Jews. Masami Uno's book *If You Understand the Jews, You Understand the World*, which is a repetition of old conspiratorial themes, has reputedly sold nearly half a million copies.

Léon Poliakov, in his discussion of the mythology that the Russian revolution was a Jewish conspiracy, asks why there was no corresponding mythology about a Lett conspiracy (Poliakov, 1987). After all, the Letts were just as powerful as the Jews and just as prominent in Russian revolutionary circles. The answer must be, at least in part, that there is something culturally specific about the traditions of anti-Semitism and that cultural, or ideological, traditions are not easily subsituted one for another. Just as older themes about the Jews could be more easily incorporated into far-right mythology of the Russian Revolution than new notions about Letts could be formulated, so too Le Pen, on the verge of a political breakthrough, shows the persistence of his ideological traditions. Le Pen's radio outburst might have put an end to his own political future, as it revealed his ideological roots. However, the outburst revealed something more disturbing about the non-substitutability and perpetuation of anti-semitic mythology. Because this mythology has a past and is part of a continuing ideological tradition, it has that much more of a chance for a future. In this way, the future of anti-Semitism is strengthened, not in spite of its history, but because of it.

References

Antaki, C., 1985. Core concepts in attribution theory, in J. Nicholson and H. Beloff (eds), *Psychological Survey, Vol. 5*, British Psychological Society, Leicester.

Billig, M., 1978. *Fascists: a Social Psychological View of the National Front*, Academic Press, London.

_____ , 1981. *L'internationale raciste: de la psychologie à la 'science' des races*, Maspero, Paris.

_____ , 1982. *Ideology and Social Psychology*, Blackwell, Oxford.

_____ , 1987. Anti-semitic themes and the British far left: some psychological observations on the indirect aspects of the conspiracy tradition, in C.F. Graumann and S. Moscovici (eds), *Changing Conceptions of Conspiracy*, Springer Verlag, New York.

_____ , 1987b. *Arguing and Thinking: a Rhetorical Approach to Social Psychology*, Cambridge University Press, Cambridge.

_____ , 1988. Rhetorical and historical aspects of attitudes: the case of the British monarchy, *Philosophical Psychology*, Vol. 1, 83–104.

_____ , 1988b. Rhetoric of the Conspiracy theory *Patterns of Prejudice*, Vol. 22, No. 2.

_____ and Cochrane, R., 1987. Adolescents and politics, in H. McGurk (ed.), *What Next?*, ESRC, London.

Brunn, J., 1979. *La nouvelle droite*, Nouvelles Editions Oswald, Paris.

Bucolo, P., 1980. *The Other Pareto*, Scolar Press, London.

Butz, A. R., 1976. *The Hoax of the Twentieth Century*, Historical Review Press, Richmond.

Caciagli, M., 1988. The Movimento Sociale Italiano — Destra Nationale and neo-fascism in Italy, *Western European Politics*, Vol. 11, No. 2.

Cohn, N., 1967. *Warrant for Genocide*, Chatto Heinemann, London.

Cole, A. M., 1986. The return of the right: the French election of March 1986, *Western European Politics*, Vol. 9, No. 4.

Davis, D. B., 1971. Some theories of countersubverion: an analysis of anti-Masonic, anti-Catholic and anti-Mormon literature, in D.B. Davis (ed.), *Fear of Conspiracy*, Cornell University Press, Ithaca.

Eatwell, R., 1988. The French Presidential and National Assembly elections, April–June 1988, *Political Quarterly*, Vol. 59, No. 4.

_____ , 1990. The Holocaust denial in L. Cheles *et al.* (eds), *Neo-Fascism in Europe*, Longman, London.

Eiser, J. R., 1987. *Social Psychology*, Cambridge University Press, Cambridge.

Fielding, N., 1981. *The National Front*, Routledge and Kegan Paul, London.

Fiske, S. T. and Taylor, S. E., 1984. *Social Cognition*, Random House, New York.

Furnham, A. and Lewis, A. 1986. *The Economic Mind*, Wheatsheaf, Sussex.

Groh, D., 1987. The temptation of conspiracy theory, or: why do bad things happen to good people?, in C. F. Graumann and S. Moscovici (eds), *Changing Conceptions of Conspiracy*, Springer Verlag, New York.

Hagendoorn, L. and Janssen, J., 1986. Right wing beliefs among Dutch secondary school pupils, *Netherlands Journal of Sociology*, Vol. 22, No. 1.

Hagendoorn, L. and Hraba, J., 1987. Social distance towards Holland's minorities: discrimination amongst ethnic outgroups, *Ethnic and Racial Studies*, Vol. 10, No. 3.

Hainsworth, P., 1988. The 1988 French Presidential Election, *Parliamentary Affairs*, Vol. 44, No. 4.

Hill, R. and Bell, A., 1988. *The Other Face of Terror: Inside Europe's Neo-Nazi Network*, Grafton, London.

Hofstadter, R., 1966. *The Paranoid Style in American Politics and Other Essays*, Jonathan Cape, London.

Holmes, C., 1978. *Immigrants and Minorities in British Society*, Allen and Unwin, London.

_____ , 1979. *Anti-Semitism in British Society, 1876–1939*, Edward Arnold, London.

Hraba, J., Hagendoorn, L. and Hagendoorn, R., 1988. Social distance in the Netherlands: the ethnic hierarchy as a social representation, unpublished ms. University of Nijmegen.

Husbands, C. T., 1983. *Racial Exclusionism and the City*, Allen and Unwin, London.

_____ , 1988. Extreme right-wing politics in Great Britain: the recent marginalisation of the National Front, *Western European Politics*, Vol. 11, No. 2.

Katz, J., 1980. *From Prejudice to Destruction*, Harvard University Press, Mass.

Kruglanski, A., 1987. Blame placing schemata and attributional research, in C. F. Graumann and S. Moscovici (eds), *Changing Conceptions of Conspiracy*, Springer Verlag, New York.

Lesselier, C., (1988). The women's movement and the extreme right in France, in *The Nature of the Right: a Feminist Analysis of Order Patterns*, Benjamins, Amsterdam.

Linz, J. J., 1976. Some notes toward a comparative study of fascism in sociological historical perspective, in W. Laqueur (ed.), *Fascism: a Reader's Guide*, Wildwood House, London.

Lipset, S. M. and Raab, E., 1970, *The Politics of Unreason*, Heinemann, London.

Lorien, J., Criton, K. and Dumont, S., 1985. *Le système le Pen*, EPO, Anvers.

Maolain, C. O., 1987. *The Radical Right: a World Directory*, Longman, Harlow.

McCalden, D., 1982. *Exiles from History*, Londinium Press, London.

Mitra, S., 1988. The National Front in France: a single issue movement?, *Western European Politics*, Vol. 11, No. 2.

Nisbet, R. E. and Ross, C. 1980. *Human Inference*, Prentice Hall, New Jersey.

O'Sullivan, N., 1983. *Fascism*, Dent, London.

Plenel, E. and Rollat, A., 1984. *L'effet le Pen*, La Découverte, Paris.

Poliakov, L., 1974. *The Aryan Myth*, New American Library, New York.

_____ , 1987. The topic of Jewish conspiracy in Russia (1905–1920) and the international consequences, in C. F. Graumann and S. Moscovici (eds), *Changing Conceptions of Conspiracy*, Springer Verlag, New York.

Rohter, I. S., 1969. Social and psychological determinants of radical rightism, in R. A. Schoenberger (ed.), *The American Right Wing*, Holt Rinehart and Winston, New York.

Sampson, E. E., 1981. Cognitive psychology as ideology, *American Psychologist*, Vol. 56, July.

Schain, M., 1987. The National Front in France and the construction of political legitimacy, *Western European Politics*, Vol. 10, No. 2.

Seidel, G., 1981. Le fascisme dans les textes de la Nouvelle Droite, *MOTS*, Vol. 3, March.

_____ , 1986. *The Holocaust Denial*, Beyond the Pale, Leeds.

Stoss, R., 1988. The problem of right-wing extremism in West Germany, *Western European Politics*, Vol. 11, No. 2.

Taylor, S., 1982. *The National Front in English Politics*, Macmillan, London.

Thurlow, R.C., 1987. *Fascism in Britain, 1918–1985*, Blackwell, Oxford.

Vidal-Naquet, P., 1981. *Les juifs, la mémoire et le présent*, Maspero, Paris.

_____ , 1987. *Les assassins de la mémoire*, Editions de la Découverte, Paris.

Zukier, H., 1987. The conspiratorial imperative: medieval Jewry in western Europe, in C.F. Graumann and S. Moscovici (eds), *Changing Conceptions of Conspiracy*, Springer Verlag, New York.

10 The New Right: The Quest for a Civil Philosophy in Europe and America

Noël O'Sullivan, University of Hull

Approaching the New Right

Although this chapter is primarily concerned with the political theory of the new right, the theme which it explores can be traced back to the French Revolution. The significance of the revolution for the subsequent course of Western political thought is not hard to identify. What the revolution did was to highlight the tension between two rival modes of integration which had already been discernible in the early modern period, but now emerged as the principle theme of modern Western politics.

The tension in question consists of a conflict between the ideal of civil association, on the one hand, and of what may be termed social politics, on the other. The essence of civil association is limited politics, based on hostility to arbitrary power and the rule of law. The greatest statement of this ideal in the pre-revolutionary era is to be found in Montesquieu's *Spirit of the Laws*. During the revolutionary and immediate post-revolutionary era, the thought of Burke and Constant provided the most impressive restatement of the meaning and implications of civil association. The essence of social politics, by contrast, is integration through the adoption of a shared purpose to which everyone and everything within the state is subordinated. The state, in this case, has no intrinsic value, but is merely an instrument for implementing their social purpose, whatever it may be. The greatest statement of this ideal of integration in the pre-revolutionary era was provided by Rousseau. During the revolutionary and post-revolutionary decades, the most impressive formulations were provided by Saint-Simon, Comte and then Marx.

The detailed story of the tension between the civil and the social conceptions of politics is not relevant in this chapter, however, since attention will be concentrated upon the most recent episode of the story. I refer to the period since 1945, a period during which the social mode of integration made rapid advances over the civil, under the guise of a middle way which was widely thought to offer the best of every world. In fact, the middle way of social democratic ideology merely concealed the tension between civil and social politics, without eliminating it. Whether the advent of the new right heralds an incipient revival of civil association, or merely means a further (albeit unwitting) extension of social politics, is the question with which I am chiefly concerned in what follows. The chapter may help, at any rate, to illuminate the character of our period, in which we face for perhaps the last time any real possibility of choosing between the freedom offered by civil politics, and the arbitary power inherent in social politics.

With this general background in mind, we may turn immediately to the contemporary literature on the new right. What is mainly lacking in this literature is a clear perspective from which to evaluate it. What we find amongst the critics are vague and emotional charges of obscurantism, fascism, racism, nationalism and totalitarianism; and what we find amongst defenders are equally vague and emotional references to the need for rolling back the frontiers of the state, reinvigorating capitalism and ending a culture of moral dependency. The main aim of this chapter is to make good the lack of an adequate perspective which is reflected in phrases of this kind. But where are we to look for such a perspective? The answer cannot be found in relatively narrow and short-term considerations relating to such things as the emergence of the new left, the growth of inflation, disillusion with the welfare state, and various local issues peculiar to each country. We must begin, instead, by considering more carefully the relation between the civil and the social in the Western political tradition at large during the past half century.

The Eclipse of the Civil

With the distinction between civil and social philosophy in mind, it may be suggested that the main task of contemporary conservative political thought is once more to take up and restate the classical tradition of civil philosophy which has almost entirely disappeared during the past half century. It is, in particular, from this perspective that I want to assess the contribution of the new right to the restatement of the requirements of limited politics in the modern world. Before proceeding further, however, it is necessary to formalize the contrast between civil and social philosophy, in order to dispel any possible ambiguity. This can best be done by identifying four main features which distinguish them:

1. The first feature of civil philosophy is that the bond which holds a state together is defined in terms of law. What must be stressed is that law is a *formal*, non-instrumental bond, which therefore does not impose any aim or purpose on citizens. That is why the members of a civil association enjoy freedom.

A social philosophy, by contrast, identifies the bond of the state, not in terms of law, but in terms of a shared vision of happiness or welfare, usually described as an ideology. Because the rule of law can do nothing to promote these ends, social philosophy ignores it and concentrates instead on the apparatus of managerial or bureaucratic government — it works, that is, through plans, policies, decrees, orders, inspectors, coordination measures, bargaining procedures, and so on.

2. Secondly, civil philosophy is concerned above all with legitimacy.

Unfortunately, the concept of legitimacy is now widely misunderstood, mainly because it is confused with efficacy. Thus Habermas, for example, uses the term in connection with the success or failure which governments have in implementing policies: if governments do not meet expectations of success, what results is the prospect of a legitimation crisis. This, however, is sheer confusion. Legitimacy has nothing to do with the success or failure of policies. What it refers to is compliance with constitutional forms, by which alone we are able to distinguish authority from power.

In social philosophy, by contrast, the problem of legitimacy has no place, since social philosophy is concerned only with the *most desirable and most effective ways of using power*. Social philosophy, in a word, is mainly concerned with efficacy.

3. Thirdly, civil philosophy entails a distinction between state and society, or between private and public life. It entails this vital feature of limited politics because the essence of civil philosophy is a *legal* conception of citizenship; a conception, that is, which distinguishes between man in his private capacity and man in his public (or legal) capacity.

In social philosophy, by contrast, there is in principle no distinction between state and society. This does not mean that social philosophy creates the so-called 'totalitarian' state; what it means is that social philosophy aims to create a particular kind of society, and therefore tends to replace the ideal of equality before the law by a simple division of the community into those who support the desirable society, and those who oppose it. This is why the greatest twentieth-century theorist of social philosophy is Carl Schmitt, who recognized clearly that social philosophy reduces politics to a relationship between friend and foe, or between an in-group and an out-group.

4. Fourthly, civil philosophy is directed, as I said at the start, to promoting human freedom and dignity by eliminating arbitrary power from the political order. To this end, it incorporates a suspicion of power as such, regardless of who exercises it, or for what ends, or with what motives.

Social philosophy, by contrast, is *not* suspicious of power in principle; what matters is only that power should be used in approved ways, by approved groups or individuals.

These, then, are the main features of civil and social philosophy. Before going further, I want to dramatize the issue which confronts us in the West today by briefly recalling the most profound meditation we possess on the different attitudes of civil and social philosophy to the nature and purpose of politics. This is Dostoevsky's story of the encounter between the Grand Inquisitor and Christ, in the *Brothers Karamazov*. In this story, the Grand Inquisitor presents the case for social philosophy, which he defends as being the politics of compassion. Christ stands for the freedom defended by civil philosophy. The politics of freedom, the Inquisitor argues, are only for the elite: the mass of mankind finds freedom too harsh and demanding. In return for security and comfort, the Inquisitor continues, most men are prepared to abandon their freedom, on three conditions: (1) they must get uninterrupted prosperity; (2) they must be provided with an authority before which they can bow down and worship — the cult of the sovereign people presumably being excellent for this purpose; and (3) this authority must speak to them, not in harsh accents but in an idealistic language that prevents them feeling any loss of self-respect in their comfortable but servile condition. In this story, Christ's silence finally provokes the Grand Inquisitor so much that he flings open the door of the cell in which he has imprisoned Christ and tells him to get out and never again appear on earth. It is well worth pondering on why Christ never replies to the politics of compassion.

Let us now turn to the new right, then, with a view to deciding whether it has made any contribution to the theory of civil association. Two general points must be noticed straight away. The first concerns the word 'new'. In fact, none of the ideas associated with the new right is novel; what is new is rather the *situation* of the new right. In this situation, characterized as it is by the eclipse of the civil, what has happened is that old and once familiar ideas have acquired a new significance. The second point is that it is not, of course, suggested that the new right constitutes a homogeneous movement with a homogeneous doctrine. On the contrary, within the new right three different and ultimately incompatible schools of thought must be distinguished.

The first school is usually referred to as the school of economic liberalism. In this school, primary stress is laid upon the intimate connection between the civil ideal and the preservation of a free market. Civil association, in other words, tends to be confused with the defence of capitalism. This school is best represented by the so-called Austrian and Chicago political economists; by the public choice school of Virginia; and by the Ordo group in West Germany.

The second school may be referred to as the conservative school, which for present purposes includes liberal and neo-conservative thinkers. In England, the most controversial members of this school are those associated with the *Salisbury Review*. In the United States, a parallel new right movement revolves around the *National Review* and *New Republic*, but also includes an influential group of scholars who contribute to a journal called *The Public Interest*, founded by Irving Kristol and Daniel Bell.

Finally, there is a third school, which may be called the radical new right. This is mainly confined to the continent. From the present point of view, the most relevant groups within this school are the latter-day defenders of the so-called 'Conservative Revolution' in West Germany, and the Euro-Nationalist advocates of a 'new paganism' in France. What links these schools is their demand for nothing less than the complete spiritual renewal of modern civilization. In France, to which I shall restrict myself here, the principal organs of the school are the journals *Eléments* and *Nouvelle Ecole*.

There are of course many other groups in the new right, but an exhaustive analysis is not my concern; my interest is in those thinkers who shed most light on the problems which are involved in a reformulation of civil philosophy today.

Self, Society and State in Post-War Social Philosophy

In spite of the major differences between the three schools of new right thought, there is nevertheless a certain degree of common ground amongst them. They all have a common enemy, which is the liberal collectivist consensus that has dominated Western culture since the 1960s, and dominated British politics for much longer. What needs to be brought into focus here, however, is not so much the surface compromises made by political parties in the name of the middle way, as the underlying beliefs about the nature of man, society and the state which were implicit in this consensus. Together, these beliefs comprise the foundations upon which all post-war versions of social philosophy have been built. Since some of the best new right theorizing has been devoted to identifying and criticizing these beliefs, it is necessary to indicate briefly what they are, and why the new right dislikes them.

1. Self

Consider first the main feature of the concept of self which has prevailed in most post-war social philosophy, which is that man is thought of as a self-contained or autonomous being whose main task is to pursue his various interests, needs and wants. What the new right objects to are four crucial assumptions about the self which lie hidden beneath this simple and familiar picture. These assumptions are that:

(a) The self is 'given' or pre-formed, owing nothing of significance to the civilization which surrounds it, which is fundamentally thought of as merely an external adornment.

(b) The self is ahistorical, which means that the whole of the established order must be viewed as a potential threat to its freedom. The implication is that any destructive measures may be seen as a positive contribution to human liberation.

(c) The self is asocial, in a sense which implies that all social relationships are external to it, and are therefore only acceptable in so far as they are self-chosen. This self, in other words, can only understand contractual and utilitarian relationships. It is impossible on this view, the new right holds, to understand the nature of such fundamental human institutions as the family, the state or friendship.

(d) The self is predisposed towards value-relativism, since its absolute autonomy leaves it free to find value anywhere, or nowhere, entirely as fancy dictates. And since the only acceptable limits on autonomy are self-chosen ones, there is no independent standard by which any value may be criticized.

The principal objection made by the new right to the concept of the autonomous self is that it amounts essentially to a philosophy of the drop-out, and must end by reducing civilization to rubble. The villains ultimately responsible for foisting this concept of the self on the world are usually held to be thinkers like Descartes and Rousseau; and the heroes, who reject this view of the self, are thinkers like Hegel and Burke.

The great difficulty with all this, however, is to know whether it is all merely speculative, or whether the concept of the autonomous self described by the new right does in fact have the destructive consequences with which it is credited. It is obvious, of course, that the philosophy of the new left, and that of the counterculture even more so, relied upon this concept of the self; but is there any concrete evidence that it has affected the mainstream life of the Western world in the ruinous ways envisaged by the new right?

On this, the new right is divided. The most interesting work available is that done in recent years by members of the new right in the United States, where the cult of the autonomous self is now credited with responsibility for inner-city problems brought about by the creation of a new under-class that is entirely beyond any prospect of social integration. Consider, for example, Andrew Sullivan, the Associate Editor of *The New Republic*. According to Sullivan, the concept of the autonomous self need not be self-destructive for the prosperous, but is ruinous when the cultural values associated with it spread through society and are adopted by the poor. As Sullivan himself puts it, 'the cultural signals given by elites since the 1960s — the downgrading of fidelity, the rejection of marital self-discipline, the rise of female independence — have coincided with the collapse of the poor black family. While perfectly sustainable among the prosperous, such permissive forms have proved disastrous in the ghetto'. Unfortunately, Sullivan observes, the measures proposed by George Bush and Michael Dukakis — measures such as day-care subsidies and tax credits for anyone earning less than $45,000 a year — were likely to make matters worse: 'As elite culture undermines social stability, among the poor, elite welfare in an era of tight budgets would divert resources away as well' (*Daily Telegraph*, 23 May 1988). So far as any constructive measures are envisaged, attention is focused at present on the replacement of welfare by 'workfare', which is not intended to be a training scheme, but requires real work in return for welfare benefits. Although such ideas have aroused great interest, both in the United States and in Britain, contributors to *The Public Interest* have expressed misgivings (Gilder, 1987), partly on the ground that workfare would only intensify the culture of dependency by creating a sense of job entitlement instead of a spirit of self-help.

There is, however, a second school of thought critical of the autonomous self to be found in the United States. This second school, is far less empirical than the former one. One of its most recent recruits, Allan Bloom, has imported the spirit of Nietzsche into the land of Clint Eastwood, maintaining that the relativism fostered by the autonomous self has produced *The Closing of the American Mind* (Bloom, 1987). Already, however, thinkers like Irving Kristol had found sources of nihilism in the free-market ideal of Milton Friedman and Hayek (Kristol, 1970). In West Germany, Wilhelm Röpke and the Ordo group have spread a similar message (see Röpke, 1960). This side of new right thought, however, is constantly vulnerable to the charge of failing to distinguish between facts, on the one hand, and the prejudices of the publicists concerned, on the other. I shall therefore move on.

2. Society

I now turn to the view of society which has dominated post-war intellectual orthodoxy. What has attracted new right attention is, above all, the belief that society is in some sense a system, whole or stucture by which men can be said to be 'conditioned', and of which they can in therefore some sense be regarded as victims.

In Britain and Europe, of course, the idea that 'the system is to blame' has been a commonplace of radical thought for over a century. In America, however, this way of thinking was largely alien to the individualist tradition, and its emergence in recent decades has therefore provoked an especially powerful attack from the American new right. It was the concept of society as a system, in fact, that was the central target of Charles Murray's recent work, *Losing Ground* (Murray, 1984). This is an absorbing study of the reasons for failure of much post-war social policy. Like many other moderate members of the American new right, Murray is prepared to accept much of the pre-war Roosevelt New Deal; but disaster struck in 1962, Murray believes, when Americans almost overnight abandoned their belief in the American Way, according to which anyone with enough gumption could make a good living. By the mid-1960s, they had all uncritically adopted the new belief that poverty was not the fault of the individual but of the system. Why this change occurred need not detain us here; what matters are the three reasons which Murray gives for believing that it guaranteed from the very outset that the welfare programme of the 1960s and 1970s would be self-defeating.

In the first place, the concept of system meant that those at whom the programme was aimed were treated as wholly passive, and therefore completely dependent upon government action for any remedy. The very notion of system, that is, discouraged self-help of any kind.

Secondly, Murray maintains the concept of system has 'Balkanized' the American population by fermenting a universal sense of grievance which leads to demands that threaten the rule of law itself. Before 1964, Murray wrote, 'blacks were unique'. They constituted the only group suffering discrimination so pervasive and so persistent that social laws *for that group* were broadly accepted as necessary. By 1965, blacks were just one of many minorities, each seeking equal protection as a group. Every group, in short, now wants its own personal rule of law, so to speak, since each believes that only special legislation spelling out and protecting its own peculiar rights will secure fair treatment of individual members of the group. This development is not confined to the United States, of course; there is a parallel story in the British case (Mishan, 1988).

The American side of the new right, it will be obvious, has mainly attacked the concept of system at the empirical level. Elsewhere, however, the 1980s have witnessed a powerful philosophic attack on the idea. This attack concentrates upon deconstructing the idea of system or structure itself. In Britain, the most brilliant example of this philosophical attack is Kenneth Minogue's recent study of ideology, *Alien Powers* (Minogue, 1985). For Minogue, the concept of system belongs to the world of Kafkaesque fantasies conjured up by ideologists who cannot manage in life without what he aptly terms a 'do-it-yourself resentment kit'. Logically, Minogue rightly maintains, the notion that men are conditioned by a social system is literally absurd, since creatures who are 'conditioned' do not possess free will, and therefore cease to be human beings at all. In the same connection, there is an admirable study by Harro Höpfl of how the idea of system has developed in the West since the seventeenth century, tracing the various insidious ways in which it has found a place in current academic orthodoxy in particular. The essay has the splendid title, 'Isms' (Höpfl, 1983).

It must be added, finally, that the concept of system is not universally rejected by the new right. The economic liberal school, in particular, has a vested interest in retaining it, as part of the strategy for defending the free market. Thus Hayek, for example, takes over the concept of system in its entirety, but tries to make it respectable in conservative quarters by showing that, far from oppressing men, the spontaneous or unplanned working of the system is the principal source of human well-being.

3. State

What, finally, is the place of the state in post-war social philosophy? The short answer is that, strictly speaking, social philosophy cannot provide a theory of the state at all; and that, indeed, is the most remarkable feature of Western political thought today — it has no coherent theory of the state. Social philosophy creates this problem because, by thinking of the state solely in terms of the ends or purposes it can be made to serve, it converts the state into an enterprise organization whose logical structure is formally indistinguishable from any other enterprise association. What social philosophy offers, instead of a theory of the state, is a variety of visions of the good society. During the past half century, three in particular have dominated Western thought. Since they are all familiar, I will merely list them. The first is the social democratic model of a third (or middle) way, based on a quasi-Platonic theory of government which attributes omniscience and impartiality to rulers who are thought of as expert guardians of the national interest. What characterizes this is the assumption that a planned social order is always intrinsically superior to an unplanned one. The second is the liberal-democratic model of pluralism. The third is the neo-corporatist model. Much criticism of various kinds has been levelled at all these models, as pluralists have vied with planners, and neo-corporatists have in turn heaped obloquy on pluralists. From the new right standpoint, however, the decisive nail has now been put into the whole lot of them by the public choice school. For this school, political rationality is no different to economic rationality: politicians, like businessmen, are guided solely by self-interest. The work of this school — of scholars, that is, like Downs (1957), Buchanan (1962) and, most recently, Mancur Olson (1982) — has dispelled the last vestiges of the idealistic optimism about man and the state which have infused the liberal consensus. Nevertheless, this school of new right thought will not be pursued here because it seems, more than on any other side, to lead straight to unadulterated political despair, in so far as it reduces the ideal of an impartial or disinterested state to an absurdity. If it seems at times to stop short of that, this is only because it falls back on the vice of its great predecessor, Jeremy Bentham. Like Bentham, the school equates political reform with political gadgeteering (see Letwin, 1965), of which the best instance is Buchanan's ingenious attempt to impose constitutional restrictions on government deficit financing.

Such, then, are the basic assumptions about man and society that have prevailed in the post-war period. Some of the more plausible new right criticisms of the social philosophy which has been based upon them have been considered; but what must now be asked is whether the new right has anything better to offer. Bearing in mind the perspective established at the outset — the need, that is, for a civil philosophy which provides a coherent theory of the limited state — I will consider briefly four thinkers who illustrate clearly the strengths and weaknesses of the new right in this respect.

Hayek, Scruton, John Gray and de Benoist

The radical school of the new right can quickly be dismissed as the least constructive, from the present standpoint. Discussions of the radical new right frequently dismiss it on the ground that it is neo-Nazi. In fact, this kind of emotional response not only obscures the real objections to the radical new right, but also the fact that the logical structure of the radical left is identical.

What then is the real objection to the radical new right? The sense of its doctrine can be summarized in a single sentence from de Benoist: 'All dictatorship is bad, but all decadence is worse' (cited in Taguieff, 1984). It is this concept — namely decadence — which provides the key to the ideas of the radical new right, and explains why it wins scarcely any support in Britain and America. The British had Oscar Wilde; but we locked him up very quickly. For most British people, decadence has always meant little more than not brushing your teeth at night. The Americans, likewise, have no significant place for the concept; they would think it meant *Dallas* or *Dynasty*, or — if they admire Allan Bloom — too much pop music. Decadence, in short, is a continental rather than an Anglo-Saxon concern; and even on the continent, the Germans and French have always made more of it than the Italians, for whom the antics of d'Annunzio were always somewhat untypical.

In de Benoist's case, however, the term decadence is used in a very unFrench way. Until not so long ago, decadence was a very demanding and highly elitist phenomenon, of which Huysman's *A Rebours*, de l'Isle-Adam's *Axel's Castle*, and Lautramont's *Maldoror* were the finest specimens. More recently, works like Montherlant's novel *The Bullfighters* helped to keep the tradition alive. The fact that something remarkable has happened to the concept in the meantime is indicated, however, by the fact that de Benoist thinks of the Americans as examplars of decadence, in spite of their seemingly harmless ways.

What exactly has happened to the concept? The answer — of course — is that the French new right has discovered Nietzsche, partly as a result of Gilles Deleuze's splendid work (Deleuze, 1962). The upshot is that, whereas the old right wanted to be good Christians, the radical new right want to be good pagans. This has opened up a transnational, European identity for the new right, by enabling it to look sympathetically on anyone with Indo-European roots.

It would not be profitable, however, to explore the supposed attractions of paganism, beyond noting that it is meant to ensure the end of the divided self, of democracy, equality, capitalism, of mediocrity and everything spiritually slavish. It would not be profitable because what de Benoist seems to forget is that there is, on the French new right, something worse than decadence. This is political nympholepsy: the desire, that it, for the unattainable. It is here that the new and the old French right join hands: both have as their ultimate goal an impossible ideal of moral purity and political unity.

Consider first the quest for moral purity, in the form of a heroic ethic inspired by a tragic vision of life. The trouble with heroic ethics was made clear by the fate of Don Quixote long ago: the quest for heroic purity in a post-heroic world is prone to make a man somewhat ludicrous. If it does not — and it need not — then it tends to mean a Nietzschean cult of extremist pastimes which is splendid, so long as it is kept entirely out of politics: Julius Evola's quest for the existential moment in mountain climbing is one illustration, and Montherlant's love of bullfighting another. The difficulty, for the radical new right, is that it insists on finding political significance in these fundamentally apolitical individualists. If a theory of tragedy applicable to the modern world is sought in France, then Nietzsche is a bad bet; a native, and far more viable, theory of tragedy was offered by Benjamin Constant, who wisely insisted that it must seek to build on, and not to reject, the prosaic complexities of our post-heroic world.

So far as the quest for spiritual renewal through politics is concerned, the result is inevitably not merely total politics, as Rousseau saw so clearly, but also an opening for extra-constitutional action, since constitutions belong to the world of civil philosophy which the radical new right rejects. It is true that de Benoist subscribes to monarchism, but monarchy does not refer in his usage to a type of constitution; it refers, rather, to the general principle that power comes 'from above' and is sacred (de Herté, a de Benoist pseudonym, 1987).

The irony in all this is that the radical new right completely fails to break out of the conceptual framework of the social philosophy which it despises. This is especially obvious in its exact replication of Marxist categories. Thus, the Marxist concept of alienation is replaced by a cult of Indo-European pagan races; the Marxist vision of history as an economic struggle between classes is replaced by the Nietzschean vision of history as a cultural struggle between 'master' and 'slave' races; Marxist internationalism is replaced by stress on the right of every nation to preserve its own way of life; and the Marxist egalitarian Utopia is replaced by an aristocratic and hierarchical one. The same replication is obvious in the case of de Benoist's critique of Christianity: the triple historical schema of Golden Age, Fall and Salvation is replicated in a parallel myth of an original pagan Golden Age, followed by the Fall occasioned by the intrusion of Christianity, with a pagan Euro-national restoration yet to come.

Why is the radical new right unable to get beyond this replication of the dualist categories which are its main target of attack? Because it lives in a world of absolutes which always engenders dualist polarities. Thus in moral life, for example, its cult of heroism and purity entails the rejection of compromise and conciliation; while in political life it rejects out of hand the only non-coercive, non-arbitrary bond there can be, which is the rule of law. This offers, indeed, only a limited transcendence; but that is preferable to the impossible quest for absolute transcendence.

Consider now Hayek, the great spokesman for the school of economic liberalism. The central doctrine of this school is that 'liberty is indivisible', by which is meant that a free society is impossible without a free market; in other words, a civil society must be a capitalist society. This, it may be said immediately, is the problem with Hayek's own attempt to situate civil philosophy within the context of economic theory: the defence of civil association, that is to say, is never disengaged from the defence of capitalism. The difficulty, to be more specific, is that Hayek never establishes any clear connection between the two positions which are fundamental to his thought. On the one hand, he is deeply committed to maintaining the intrinsic value of the rule of law; on the other hand, he is equally committed to maintaining the unrivalled merits of the free market as a means of achieving human progress and prosperity.

In the latter case Hayek relies on two well-known arguments. One is epistemological, and presents the free market not so much as a mere economic system for exchange as a delicate information storage system. The other relies on analogies between organic adaption to their environment by lower creatures, and the kind of natural and spontaneous adaptation which Hayek believes is brought about by the free market. I will not pursue either, for a reason which immediately points to the central weakness of both arguments. This is that neither contains an ethical element; both, indeed, are intended to be 'scientific', in a sense which precludes any ethical content. Yet, without an ethical basis for his thought, how is it possible for Hayek to assert the intrinsic value of the rule of law, without which his defence of what he calls 'the Great Society' cannot even begin to constitute an adequate civil philosophy? The answer is that it is impossible for him to do so. He maintains that legal rules, which he rightly identifies — as civil philosophy must — with formal rules, are the only satisfactory kind of rules because they alone permit individuals to adapt to their environment in a wholly spontaneous way; but that, of course, is not an ethical argument. Conscious of this deficiency at the heart of his political philosophy, Hayek can only fall back on the demand that we should act 'as if' laws are categorically binding (Hayek, 1973; Forsyth, 1988). Hayek's thought, then, presents the supreme paradox of a thinker attempting to restate civil philosophy, even though there is no place in his thought for the problem of arbitrary power, which is the centre of civil philosophy. Hayek ignores arbitrary power, because he is concerned only with man's rational adaptation to his environment — and this, logically at least, might well be facilitated, rather than impeded, by arbitrary power.

We may now turn to Roger Scruton, the most controversial representative of the British conservative school of the new right, and to John Gray, who has done most to link the new right with the civil ideal of early modern political theory. The starting point for Scruton's thought is that the modern world has turned man into a monster by destroying the objective or public status of all moral, political and cultural values. Here we return, in other words, to the new right attack upon the concept of the autonomous self. Earlier, in his *Short History of Modern Philosophy* (Scruton, 1981), he had turned to the phenomenological theory of 'intentionality', in order to reconstitute the public world by transcending the concept of the autonomous self to which he ascribed the destruction of the public world. It is this theme — the need to transcend the autonomous concept of the self and the destructive egoism which it entails — that was the starting point for his most important political work, *The Meaning of Conservatism* (Scruton, 1980). In that work, he sought to do this by developing a theory of civil association. How far, one must ask, did that theory carry him?

In terms of civil philosophy, the strongest part of the book consists of four related themes which may be summarized as follows:

1. The self is a civilized achievement, and not a natural endowment. This was a healthy return, in part at least, to the Aristotelean and Hegelian position.

2. The basic bond of society is 'transcendent', in the sense that it cannot be derived from individual consent, or a social contract. This transcendent bond may best be described as 'piety', the essence of which is that it is founded not on the will, but on man's capacity for respect and allegiance.

3. The book was also strong in its analysis of the need for autonomous institutions as the substance of civil society. The 'internal' or intrinsic meaning of these institutions, Scruton maintains, is almost inevitably destroyed by state-imposed external purposes. Particularly notable in this context was Scruton's willingness to accept the TUC as an integral part of the British constitution.

4. Lastly, Scruton strongly emphasized the non-instrumental or non-purposive nature of the state, to the extent that it approximates to the ideal of civil association.

Now these themes provided Scruton with an excellent foundation upon which to develop a civil philosophy. Unfortunately, what spoilt things was the fact that Scruton's book also contained three theses which were wholly incompatible with the civil ideal, and therefore created a tension within his work which has still not been fully removed. The first of these theses was his claim that civil society possesses an organic, pre-political unity. The second was his contention that the central task of modern politics is to overcome alienation. The third was his claim that state and society must no longer be separate, but must be reintegrated in a single whole. Here I shall confine myself to considering the first two claims, since the third is so obviously incompatible with civil philosophy that there is little to be said: to pursue it would immediately lead into the arms of Rousseau and the conversion, more generally, of civil into social philosophy.

The difficulty with Scruton's first claim — namely, the claim that civil society rests on a pre-political unity — begins with his assertion (1980, p.25) that:

> Conservatism presupposes the existence of a social organism...There are people who, in their vociferous part, reject the politics of a 'Conservative Party'. But this does not imply that there is not some deeper part of themselves that lies embedded in the social order, motivated and consoled by the forces to which the conservative instinct is attuned. Somewhere beneath the fluster of 'opinion' lies an unspoken unity.

The problem, of course, is to know how conservatives are to locate the 'deeper part' of the social self or organism. More precisely, the introduction of this pre-political unity creates a strong current of anti-constitutional thought in Scruton's work, since he is convinced that not all the organs of the established constitution articulate the real social self properly. Thus Scruton seems, for example, to deny 'the opinion-ridden turmoil of the Commons' (Scruton, 1980, p.69) any significance in this connection. The radical tone becomes even more evident when Scruton maintains that 'for a conservative the movement of the constitution must express the movement of social feeling, and not the opportunistic aims of that small professional class — the class of politicians' (Scruton, 1980, pp.69–70). The way is then open for anyone (including Scruton) to set himself up as the authentic voice of the 'underlying social unity' which lies hidden beneath 'the opinionated crust which smothers it' (Scruton, 1980, p.25). It is this manner of thought which opened the way, for example, to Carlyle's outright rejection of parliamentary government, in favour of a cult of hero-worship.

The tension created within Scruton's civil philosophy by the idea of underlying organic unity was further intensified by the fact that Scruton seemed to derive from it a sort of cultural nationalism, which was interpreted by some as a form of cultural racialism, even though Scruton himself properly disclaimed any kind of genetic racialism, or any desire to foment racial unrest. It should be stressed at once that any such ideas are wholly alien to him. Nevertheless, it was somewhat ambiguous to claim that organic unity derives from cultural ties which, it would seem, cannot be shared by what he referred to as the 'alien wedge'. Hostility to members of another race, he writes, does not necessarily imply racialism, since it arises inevitably from 'natural prejudice and a desire for the company of one's kind' (Scruton, 1980, p.68). There is much truth in the distinction, but Scruton's error was to confuse considerations which might provide reasons for restricting immigration with the basis for a plausible theory of the civil bond. If a 'desire for the company of one's kind' were in fact the basis of civil association, there could have been no Roman Empire, no United States, and no Britain, since all the disparate peoples that have constituted each of these would have remained forever frozen within their own circle.

Equally problematic is his belief that the central problem of politics today is to alleviate the 'alienation' which he considers is endemic in the modern world. This side of Scruton's thought is of course quite foreign to the British tradition of civil philosophy, linking him rather — as he acknowledges — with the tradition of the German Romantics, to whom, he writes, 'we owe the concepts with which modern humanity can be represented...concepts [that] reflect a philosophy which I have intuitively tried to follow' (Scruton, 1980, p.120). More immediately relevant, however, is Scruton's endeavour 'to borrow (largely from the Hegelian side of Marxism) the concepts with which to refine our political vision' (Scruton, 1980, p.121), in ways which will enable him to deal with alienation. This side of Scruton's thought is profoundly sympathetic to the new left. It is impossible, however, to reconcile this sympathy for radical philosophy with the requirements of civil philosophy. The tension between the two is nowhere more apparent than in a sentence which stretches his interpretation of civil philosophy to breaking point. This is his contention that 'The conservative, like the radical, recognizes the civil order reflects not the desires of man, but the self of man' (Scruton, 1980, p.120). The problem, to be precise, is that the civil order does not, and cannot, reflect the 'self of man', in the sense in which Scruton uses that term here. The essence of the civil order is that it is constituted by the impersonal, abstract bond of law; and for this reason, it *cannot* satisfy the quest for 'roots', or self-fulfilment, which engages the radical, and to which Scruton refers sympathetically in the sentence quoted. As all radical literature, from Marx to Marcuse and Habermas, indicates, the attempt to realize a 'deeper' self by ending alienation leads to an immediate repudiation of the civil bond, as itself merely a means of perpetuating alienation.

Scruton, it must be concluded, has in fact committed the greatest of political errors and the one to which the British conservative tradition stands most deeply opposed — and nowhere more so than in the case of Lord Salisbury, the spiritual patron of the *Salisbury Review*. Scruton has asked too much of politics. Ironically, the result is that he threatens to submerge civil in social philosophy.

The new right quest for a civil philosophy might seem at this point to have finally run into sands. Such an interpretation would, however, be superficial, as the recent work of John Gray bears witness. In the course of a study of *Liberalism*, Gray defended the thesis that classical liberal thought is not merely one ideology amongst others but is 'the political theory of modernity' (Gray, 1986, p.82). By this, Gray means that liberalism alone addresses the main problem presented by the 'post-traditional' order of Europe, which is extreme cultural diversity. At the present day, Gray believes, the predicament posed by cultural diversity is more acute than ever before, since the historical evidence suggests that the types of political order best able to cope with it are no longer possible at the present day. These have been either empires, religious institutions, or else monarchies, 'as in the splendidly anachronistic case of the United Kingdom' (Gray, 1986, pp.43–44). The problem today is that the tolerance of diversity which such regimes displayed had its roots within religious faith, or else in secular myths (such as those of natural rights and global progress) which few any longer take seriously. We are, in short, 'heirs to all the achievements of modernity, but not to its seminal myths' (Gray, 1986, p.x). The result is that the contemporary world confronts a situation which Gray portrays with almost Nietzschean pessimism. Since conservatives of any complexion will do well to weigh Gray's analysis, his words (1988, p.258) may be quoted at some length:

> the modern development of age-old European moral and intellectual traditions has produced an outlook that is deeply destructive of civilised institutions. The peculiarly modern outlook — a combination, I should say, of homeless moral passion with rationalist fantasy — is now so pervasive as to have acquired deep roots in popular sentiment and a secure place in virtually all the disciplines of thought. It results in what Hayek calls 'unviable moralities' — systems of moral thought and sentiment incapable of sustaining any stable social order; in the bizarre intellectual constructs of contemporary sociology; and even, as in architecture, in a corruption of the practical arts. Taken together, these developments create a climate of culture which is profoundly hostile, not only to its traditional inheritance, but even to its own continued existence. We confront the phenomenon of a culture permeated throughout by a hatred of its own identity, and by a sense of its purely provisional character.

Confronted by a culture possessed in effect by a death-wish Gray concludes that a modern conservative 'must also be a moral and intellectual radical'. This mixture of pessimism and radicalism might seem to point towards the alienated and extremist conservatism of de Benoist, but what is unusual about Gray's position is the entirely different direction in which his pessimism impels his quest for a viable ideal of civil association.

Gray finds little in the political thought of the West during the past century upon which to construct a theory of civil association. This is not merely because the world of empires, religion and monarchy mentioned above has disappeared. To an even greater extent, Gray maintains, it is because all the characteristic ideologies of our age are fatally flawed by an untenable assumption. This assumption is that the task of politics is to provide a solution to the problem of personal identity created by the collapse of cultural homogeneity in modern Europe. As Gray himself puts it, what the dominant forms of liberalism, socialism and conservative ideology have in common is the assumption that 'the varieties of human identity, if they are not altogether constructions of political practice, ought nevertheless to be mirrored or imprinted in the central institutions of political order' (Gray, 1988b, p.38). Why, one must ask, does Gray regard this assumption as disastrous? It is because it is radically incompatible with the cultural pluralism of modern societies. Instead of facilitating the accommodation of cultural pluralism by a mutual acknowledgement of the rule of law, the search for human identity within the political arena requires that everything in society should be subordinated to the creation or maintenance of a single moral community, since that is deemed to be the only adequate way of situating the self. In its simplest form, Gray maintains, this belief originally characterized nationalist doctrine, but today it is almost universally held, being shared by 'leftist communitarian theorists such as Sandel and by Hegelian conservatives such as Scruton'. However, the belief in a pre-existent moral solidarity entailed by this view is untenable, being no more — in Gray's words — than a 'chimera produced by a mistaken theory which understands political order in a quasi-naturalistic fashion, when it is properly understood as a matter of shifting political allegiance to the artefact of sovereign authority' (Gray, 1988b, pp.40–1).

Where then does Gray believe we must turn in order to discover a model of civil association relevant to present-day needs? His answer is that such a model can only be found by stepping back over the last two centuries of Western thought, past the Enlightenment, to the early modern period. Our main task is to re-establish contact with the classical thought of the early modern era, because it was a time 'when many of our current dilemmas were perceived with a drastic clarity which we have lost'. We must turn, more especially, to Hobbes, who offers 'the outlines of a form of government suited to our lives', and an ideal of civil association conceived 'for an age of religious wars and barbarous movements much like ours'. In precisely what sense, though, is Hobbes's pre-modern ideal of civil association relevant today? What Hobbes's civil ideal suggests, Gray replies (1988b, p.44):

> is the salience to our condition of a state that is strong but small, in which the little that is not privatised is centralised, and in which practitioners of diverse traditions are left at liberty, so long as they do not disturb the common peace, to refine and develop their forms of life. This is a form of government devoted not to truth, or to abstract rights, and still less to any conception of progress or general welfare, but instead one which by securing a non-instrumental peace creates the possibility of civil association.

Gray's attempt to re-establish contact with the classical analysis of civil association is one of the most suggestive pieces of theorizing to emerge from the new right. Whilst his earlier work on liberalism had disengaged the civil ideal from the rationalist universalism and mythology of progress which have for so long flawed the liberal vision of civil association, his more recent work has extended the analysis by disengaging it from the distractions of both socialist and conservative communitarianism. There is a problematic side, however, to Gray's quest for 'a form of political solidarity that does not depend on a shared moral community, but only on the mutual recognition of civilized men and women' (Gray, 1988b, p.44). This is his readiness to follow Hobbes in jettisoning the parliamentary system, along with all other methods of securing political accountability. It is not easy, for example, to share the equanimity with which he contemplates the disappearance of any semblance of the separation of powers, on the ground that in the United States the massive apparatus of federalism, separation of powers and judicial review 'has not prevented (and may well have facilitated) the extensive politicisation of social life with the exploitation of litigation and the invocation of constitutional rights' (Gray, 1988b, p.44). That may be so, but to conclude that the whole idea of restraints on arbitrary power should therefore be abandoned seems not only overly hasty, but also incompatible with Gray's own desire to resuscitate the Western tradition of limited politics.

Bearing these misgivings in mind, it will be instructive to consider the two main proposals for restoring substance to the civil ideal that have come to the fore during the decade of Thatcherism. One is the increasingly vocal demand for a written constitution provoked by a regime whose individualist ideology is notably at odds with its constant engrossment of executive powers; the other is the demand for 'active citizenship' which has become part of the current rhetoric of Thatcherism. Neither of these topics can be properly considered, however, without first considering the meaning of Thatcherism.

Thatcherism

The essence of Thatcherism, Minogue has claimed, 'was always a form of realism based on economics'. This realism means, more precisely, the rejection of the naïve conviction that lay at the heart of the social-democratic consensus, which was the belief that there is a political remedy for any social misfortune, together with almost unbounded economic resources from which to fund it. But Thatcherite realism, Minogue continues, also has a vital moral dimension: 'After too much sickly compassion, there is something umistakeably refreshing, even bracing, about a realistic call to the sterner forms of duty, and no one who ignores this transformation of the moral and rhetorical atmosphere of British politics in the late 1970s will have understood Thatcherism' (Minogue and Biddiss, 1987, p.xvi).

To its radical critics, by contrast, Thatcherism is a ruthless attempt to arrest industrial decline by using the techniques (in Stuart Hall's view) of 'authoritarian populism' (Hall, 1988; see also Gamble, 1988). More generally, it is presented as a new 'hegemonic project', intended to create the basis for a new consensus in the novel international and domestic context of contemporary problems. The Gramscian concept of a 'hegemonic project', however, suggests more coherence and unity than actually exists. Even sympathetic critics have sensed this. As Bhiku Parekh remarked (*New Statesman and Society*, 16 December 1988):

> Even her parliamentary colleagues remain agnostic about her economic and social policies. Her ideas have not taken root in universities and do not command the allegiance of those in the business of shaping public culture. Not surprisingly, there has so far been no Thatcherite art, literature, films or architecture. Apart from a small coterie of prize-fighters she has no 'organic intellectuals' essential for a hegemonic project.

It may be replied, however, that the hegemonic interpretation of Thatcherism is only prone to such criticism when the kind of hegemony in question is restricted to the ideological sphere. It is with this objection in mind that Andrew Gamble, for example, has insisted that the concept is applicable, provided that it is extended to embrace 'political calculation aimed at winning and maintaining support', on the one hand, and 'a programme of policies for managing the state, improving economic performance and reversing British decline' (Gamble, 1988, p.24), on the other. The price of extending the concept in this way, however, is increased incoherence rather than any gain in analytic precision. Gamble himself seems to acknowledge this when he admits that the extended concept of hegemony 'makes Thatcherism, like every other complex political phenomenon, highly contradictory', but nevertheless persists in making the concept the foundation of his recent work. The justification for doing so is presumably that the contradictions belong to reality. Unfortunately, since our only access to reality is through concepts, such a view would make it possible to say anything.

In the present context, however, details of the skirmishing between friends and foes of Thatcherism may be set aside, in order to focus attention upon the emergence in recent years of a certain amount of common ground between them. This consists of a concern for the future of the constitution under a regime which appears hostile to constitutional values of any kind.

Concern for subversion of the traditional constitution is of course not new. In the early 1970s, Hayek began his *magnum opus* by asking 'What function is served by a constitution which makes omnipotent government possible?', and devoted three volumes to a reply (Hayek, 1973, p.1). In the middle of the decade, Lord Hailsham attracted extensive publicity by taking the prospect of elective dictatorship as the theme of his Dimbleby lecture. Subsequently, other works, such as William Waldegrave's *The Binding of Leviathan* (Waldegrave, 1978) and Nevil Johnson's *In Search of the Constitution* (Johnson, 1977), explored various aspects of the constitutional question. Until the advent of Thatcherism, however, the constitution was primarily the object of conservative and liberal concern, whereas what is new about the present situation is the fact that a concern for constitutional forms has belatedly emerged on the left, as many of the signatories of Charter 88 recently bore witness.

Shortly after the appearance of the Charter, the *New Statesman and Society* gave a prominent position to an analysis of the dangers facing parliamentary democracy by John Keane, a Charter 88 signatory with impeccable radical credentials (*New Statesman and Society*, 16 December 1988). In an essay much of which would have been approved by Lord Salisbury himself, Keane identified five key areas in which constitutional reform is necessary in order to restore the sovereignty of parliament. The first concerns the stranglehold over parliamentary proceedings exercised by the executive, partly as a result of the system of party government, and partly because of the prime minister's widespread powers of patronage. The second threat to the constitution consists of parliamentary procedures which reinforce the grip of party discipline and executive domination. Keane singled out in particular procedures which place heavy restrictions on backbenchers' rights to speak, extensive use of the closure, and the privileges of the executive in order to restrict debate. The third great threat consists of the reduced significance of parliaments in Western political life brought about by the growth of the mass media. The fourth threat is the expansion of bureaucratic state power, especially in the form of 'unaccountable and invisible government', and the constant invocation of state secrets as a means of enhancing state power.

Finally, Keane observes, 'the postwar growth of a supra-national policy-making and administrative bodies, like NATO, the EC, IMF, the European Councils, etc., limits or forecloses a wide range of parliamentary choices, particularly on investment, foreign and defence policy'.

Many members of the new right would sympathize, not only with the analysis, but also with the more or less familiar proposals for reform which Keane puts forward. These include proposals for weakening the grip of the party system by electoral reform, the limitation of prime-ministerial powers and patronage resources, transformation of the House of Lords into a 'social parliament' based on functional representation, and the introduction of a written constitution, as advocated by Charter 88. But what prospects of restoring civil association do reforms like these offer in practice?

The principal weakness of Keane's proposals, as of all others like them, is that they occur in isolation from the cultural milieu at large. In its left-wing form, this is the central criticism which would be made by those (like Jürgen Habermas) who seize upon 'instrumental rationality' as the ubiquitous vice of our culture. In its conservative form, the parallel criticism was made by Peregrine Worsthorne when he wrote that the real danger facing the country is moral rather than political, and that 'far from modern intellectuals wanting to rescue us from this danger, they either ignore it or glory in it' (*Sunday Telegraph*, 1 January 1989). What is therefore needed in Britain today, Worsthorne maintained, is a new morality or a new religion. Similar scepticism about the efficacy of constitutional reform would seem to be the logical implication of Nicholas Boyle's recent sustained attack upon Thatcherism, despite the fact that he himself ended up by pinning his hopes on a written constitution (Boyle, 1988). Since Boyle's essay is the most powerful critique to have emerged thus far, it is worth considering it in some detail.

For Boyle, the significance of Thatcherism lies in what it lacks. Its most remarkable lack is any theory 'of the public, social world as a medium in which people exist and which shapes their lives'. It has, in a word, 'no theory of the constitution, of institutions, or of social, as distinct from economic, behaviour'. What then gives Thatcherism its identity? Its essence is to be found, not in any theory, but in its instrumental attitude to everything whatsoever. The organs of central government, for example, are simply instruments for putting into practice 'our ideas', ideas for which there exist only consumers, 'the meeting of whose quantifiable desires is the one task government should set itself.' The ultimate tendency of this purely instrumental outlook is to create the 'totally mobilized state', in which 'the labour of the entire population, regarded as an undifferentiated mass of individual workers, is directed to meet the desires of the same population, regarded as an undifferentiated mass of individual consumers.' Thatcherism thus converges with the Marxist vision of society in eliminating the civil ideal, since neither permits the existence of a plurality of functions, groups or interests with an autonomous ideology, or the existence of a public, political realm in which non-instrumental rules facilitate the harmonious co-existence of free citizens. To that extent, Boyle asserts, Thatcherism has 'Europeanized' Britain well ahead of 1992, by introducing the kind of rationalization originally undertaken on the continent by Enlightened Despots in the eighteenth century, then by Napoleon in France, and finally by 'their twentieth-century socialist and national-socialist successors [in] Germany and Russia.' In even more sweeping terms, Thatcherism is ultimately located by Boyle in a global process of the 'flexibilisation of human nature'. By this Boyle means that the Thatcher government is 'simply the local political solvent applied to British society not just by multinational companies but by the entire multinational currency and capital markets whose degree of political integration could briefly and embarrassingly be glimpsed on Black Monday in 1987.'

This powerful critique suffers from at least four major defects. In the first place, Boyle attempts to explain Thatcherism as the outcome of three decades of imperial decline which followed 1947. Those decades, he observes, were years of illusion, in which Britain still tried to live as an imperial society, even though the cushion of Empire had gone. By 1979, however, the facts of life made themselves felt in Britain, and Thatcherism was what happened when Britain tried to adapt to them. Although Boyle is in fact right to seize upon British post-imperial illusions as the background to Thatcherism, he runs the risk of exaggerating this aspect of British post-war history in a way which distracts attention from the deeper roots of Thatcherism in recent history. The weakness of Boyle's argument is an underlying, almost neo-Marxist assumption that the British ideal of civil association only flourished so long as Britain enjoyed the prosperity brought by imperial ascendancy. This view, however, makes it impossible to explain the fact that the ideal of civil association characterized British politics prior to empire and quite independently of it. Indeed, far from the civil tradition being dependent upon the possession of Empire, the relationship might plausibly be reversed, since the British theory and practice of imperial politics were themselves shaped by that civil tradition. But in that case the illusion which accompanied post-imperial decline is in itself insufficient to explain the roots of Thatcherite instrumentalism. The main source of those roots is not to be found in external factors relating to Britain's changed position in the world order; it is to be found, rather, in a native British intellectual tradition which has nothing at all to do with world politics. This is the great instrumental tradition begun by Francis Bacon in *The New Atlantis* (1627).

Secondly, Boyle's attack on Thatcherism consistently assumes that the task of 'true' politics is to give expression to a British national identity which he seems to interpret in the same nationalistic fashion adopted by Scruton, but rightly rejected by Gray. As Gray makes clear, the essence of the British tradition of civil association is the belief that no government, Thatcherite or otherwise, has as its task the expression or preservation of anything as vague and comprehensive as 'the national identity'. Yet an important part of opposition to Thatcherism, Boyle insists, must be concern for our national identity. The nature of this identity is a topic upon which historical precision is impossible, since academic inquiry is inevitably replaced by nostalgia and personal idiosyncrasy. Thus Boyle writes, for example, that 'there was a time when to be British was to belong to a nation characterised by certain institutions...the bobby, the BBC, the British Museum, bowler hats and rolled umbrellas, and so on ad lib.' Well yes; not to mention Dinky toys, the 'William' books, and red telephone boxes.

Thirdly, Boyle's insistence on the need for a written constitution is odd, as has already been noticed, because it is a prescription that appears to offer no remedy for the disease which he diagnoses at the heart of Thatcherism. Boyle's diagnosis seems to point towards Worsthorne's moral and spiritual interpretation of the contemporary situation, rather than to any specifically political and constitutional one. To be precise, Thatcherite society is one in which 'we each become a Faust, whose endless and innumerable desires can all be satisfied, provided only that he gives up his identity, his soul'. The result, Boyle says, is nihilism — the destruction, that is, of all intrinsic values, and their replacement by functional ones. Unfortunately, nihilism is not the kind of thing that can be remedied by constitutional reform.

Finally, it has already been indicated that Boyle's whole analysis of Thatcherism is constantly in danger of obscuring its deeper roots. The long-established instrumentalist side of British culture stemming from Francis Bacon was mentioned in this connection. There is, however, a more general feature of modern societies which encourages the instrumental tendency in terms of which Boyle defines Thatcherism. As de Tocqueville noted long ago, instrumentalism is an almost inescapable feature of all mass democratic culture, tending as it does to elevate security and equality above civil and political liberty. This feature is so familiar that it would hardly be worth mentioning, were it not for the fact that Boyle's mistaken stress on global capitalism, the loss of national identity, and nihilism, all lead him to ignore it. It is this taste for security and equality which in particular encourages the universal vice of modern democracy, which is the indifference to the forms and formalities of liberty upon which Thatcherism thrives.

It is the somewhat belated spread of the democratic mentality in the post-war era, one may suggest, rather than the illusion of imperial grandeur and the loss of national identity, which has done most to pave the way for Thatcherism by producing the backdrop of constitutional indifference which nurtures it. In de Tocqueville's view, the only remedy for such indifference was the promotion of an active form of citizenship which would remove the dangers that would otherwise be created by apathy in an age of mass politics. Since the theme of active citizenship has recently been revived by supporters of Thatcherism, it is worth considering what implications, if any, it has for the ideal of civil politics.

For the new right, the concept of active citizenship offers three advantages. Firstly, it is a handy tool for branding Labour as the party of passive dependency. Secondly, it seems to add a political dimension to an ideology which otherwise remains vulnerable to being dismissed as a purely economic creed. And thirdly, it seems to provide a moral underpinning for private property, since ownership of property is a necessary condition for the independence which active citizenship requires. The question to be asked is whether a credible account of citizenship emerges from all this, or whether the concept is entirely comprised of rhetoric.

The most penetrating critique of the concept of the active citizen has come from Michael Ignatieff, who rejects the conservative version as a mere sham, while simultaneously endeavouring to retain the ideal for the left. In its conservative form, Ignatieff maintains, talk of active citizenship is an essentially futile attempt to give a communitarian gloss to an ideology of radical individualism with which it is wholly incompatible. The contradictions in the conservative version of the ideal become evident, he believes, when it is recalled that 'the core of the electoral case made for the free market by the British Conservatives in 1979 was not just that it would enrich the British people, but that it would also enfranchise them'. This is where the Conservative conception of citizenship is incoherent, flying as it does in face of the principal feature of twentieth-century political life, which is 'the indissoluble interdependence of the private and the public' (*New Statesman and Society*, 3 February 1989). It does not follow that there is anything wrong with Mrs Thatcher's values, Ignatieff adds: enterprise, initiative, personal responsibility, and even the lawful pursuit of private profit, are all morally respectable phenomena. What is incoherent about her Conservatism is her belief that these goals can be achieved 'without a citizenship of entitlement, without the shared foundation that alone makes freedom possible'. Acceptance of the necessity for a 'citizenship of entitlement' must not, however, be confused with sentimental left-wing rhetoric about a 'caring' or 'compassionate' society of the type made familiar by attempts to present Labour as the party of altruism. Properly understood, Ignatieff insists, 'welfare is about rights, not caring, and the history of citizenship has been the struggle to make freedom real, not to tie us all in the leading strings of therapeutic good intentions'. It is also no less important to avoid confusing a citizenship of entitlement with the purely passive kind of citizenship encouraged by the welfare state during the post-war decades. What is mainly required, Ignatieff believes, is that we should rethink the whole role of the welfare state in a way which acknowledges that its ultimate concern is not simply to provide private benefits, but to generate civic solidarity. In this sense, Ignatieff suggests, the 'civic contract' embodied in the post-war welfare state is the only viable answer to the problem of citizenship as it was classically formulated by Rousseau, in his critique of the lack of public spiritedness of the modern market man (in the *Discourse on the Origin of Inequality*, 1755). What is to be said about this ingenious attempt to link the concept of active citizenship with the welfare state, on the one hand, and the old republican ideal of citizenship advocated by Rousseau, on the other?

In the first place, Ignatieff's civil ideal perpetuates the tension, long ago made familiar by Rousseau, between the requirements of active citizenship, and those of individual liberty. The requirements of active citizenship are those which the General Will sought to promote, namely, consensus, solidarity and community; whereas the requirements of individual liberty are essentially formal, being confined to mutual recognition by citizens of a sovereign authority and acceptance of the rule of law. Being purely formal, these latter requirements are compatible with maximum diversity, whereas the requirements of active citizenship are substantive and therefore create pressure for uniformity. The precise way in which Ignatieff's argument obscures the tension between these two ultimately incompatible concepts of citizenship is evident, for instance, in his assertion that 'The history of the welfare state in the twentieth century can be understood as a struggle to transform the liberty conferred by formal legal rights into the freedom guaranteed by shared social entitlement'. This is a very imprecise way of thinking. Shared social entitlement does not, strictly speaking, confer freedom: what it provides is welfare. To identify freedom with welfare, as Ignatieff does here, is to ignore the fact that liberty means the restriction of arbitrary power, whereas the provision of welfare under the banner of social entitlement is perfectly compatible with techniques of administration that flout the rule of law. While Ignatieff strongly rejects the nanny state, it is not at all clear that he is sufficiently on guard against the arbitrary state. In other words, his ideal of 'social citizenship' (or the citizenship of social entitlement) is in principle indifferent to the problem of legitimacy, and has no necessary connection with the rule of law.

In the second place, it is not at all clear that Ignatieff is correct to maintain that civic consciousness is now inseparably connected with welfare provision. Even if it is true - which is highly questionable - that private satisfactions depend in the modern world on shared entitlements, that does not mean that public provision of those satisfactions creates civic consciousness. As Ignatieff acknowledges, the state provision of private benefits may create a dependency culture, rather than civic sentiment. It would seem, then, that the concept of 'active' citizenship does not rise beyond a vague communitarian sentiment, of the kind already rejected as unsatisfactory earlier in this chapter, and that the concept of social citizenship begs too many questions for it to be capable of lending much substance to that idea.

Conclusion

Reviewing the changes which have occurred during the past twenty years from the standpoint of the new right, Daniel P. Moynihan laconically remarked: 'We know more and expect less' (Moynihan, 1985, p.108). The conclusion of the present chapter perhaps suggests that a little more can be said. On the critical side, the new right has helped to lend theoretical precision to the general disillusion with which the optimism of the post-war decades is viewed. On the positive side, what it has opposed to optimism is not mere pessimism about human nature, but something far more constructive: the quest for a civil philosophy. This is true, at least, outside the ranks of the radical school of new right thought, for which civil philosophy is merely an obstacle to the dream of wholesale moral and cultural regeneration.

Needless to say, this quest has encountered major difficulties. In the case of the economic liberal school, it has constantly tended to be subordinated to an ideology of capitalism which has often threatened to acquire the character of a new religion in which sin is redefined as intervention, and mortal sin as systematic state planning. In the case of the conservative school, the confusion of the civil with the economic has been avoided, but only for civil philosophy to be burdened by other extraneous and incompatible concerns, such as communitarian and nationalist zeal. Nevertheless, the conservative school has identified the creation of a civil philosophy as the principal concern of our time, and this alone must be hailed as a major intellectual advance beyond the

dirigiste, contractarian and instrumental theorizing which still surrounds us
on every side.

However, if it is asked how much of the civil concern has penetrated
through into the politics of governments loosely associated with the new
right, then a fairly unqualified answer is possible: not much. In the case of the
Thatcher government, for example, constitutional questions have mistakenly
been identified with 'law and order' themes that serve only to extend still
further the power of the executive and to destroy the conditions of limited
politics; while the much vaunted privatization programme has not only
increased state intervention, through the creation of special bodies to
supervise the privatized industries, but has also assisted the growth of arbitary
power through the spread of invisible government. In the United States,
similar developments have been referred to by Thomas Soewell as creating
'hybrid agencies combining the very powers which the constitution had so
carefully separated' (Sowell, 1980, p.382).

None of this is encouraging, and it may well be that the new right quest for
a civil philosophy will fail to stem the powerful currents which have impelled
Western societies towards the adoption of an unqualified social philosophy,
expressed in a form of social integration to which limited politics will have no
relevance. In so far as it is possible to find a more positive development on
which to end, we may note that the quest for a civil philosophy is not
restricted to the new right. The most interesting contemporary theorizing to
be found on the left is currently devoted to precisely this theme. In fact, an
appropriate ending is provided by the concluding sentences written by one of
the contemporary left's leading members in his introduction to a volume of
essays on *Civil Society and the State*. 'The contemporary viability of a
forward-looking normative theory of civil society and the state', John Keane
observed, 'arguably depends in part upon its ability to look backward, so as
to build upon and imaginatively transform a heritage which becomes more
precious the more it is half-forgotten, or abolished outright' (Keane, 1988,
pp.28–9). One can only agree wholeheartedly.

References

Bloom, A., 1987. *The Closing of the American Mind*, Penguin Books, London.
Boyle, N., 1988. Understanding Thatcherism, *New Blackfriars*, July/August.
Buchanan, J., 1962. *The Calculus of Consent*, Ann Arbor, Michigan.
Deleuze, G., 1962. *Nietzsche and Philosophy*, Athlone Press, London.
Downs, A., 1957. *An Economic Theory of Democracy*, Harper and Row, New York.
Forsyth, M., 1988. hayek's bizarre Liberalism, *Political Studies*, Vol. 36, No. 2.
Gamble, A., 1988. *The Free Economy and the Strong State*, Macmillan, London.
Gilder, G., 1987. Welfare's new consensus: the collapse of the American family, *The
    Public Interest*, No.89.
Gray, J., 1986. *Liberalism*, Open University Press, Milton Keynes.
_____ , 1988. Hayek, in R. Scruton (ed.), *Conservative Thinkers*, Claridge Press,
    London.
_____ , 1988b. The politics of cultural diversity, *Salisbury Review*, Vol.7, No.1.
Hall, S., 1988. *The Hard Road to Renewal*, Verso, London.

Hayek, F.A., 1973. *Law, Legislation and Liberty*, Routledge and Kegan Paul, London.

Herté, R. de, 1987. Editorial, *Elements*, Vol. 62, Spring.

Höpfl, H., 1983. Isms, *British Journal of Political Science*, Vol.13, No. 1.

Johnson, N., 1977. *In Search of the Constitution*, Pergamon, Oxford.

Keane, J., 1988. *Civil Society and the State*, Verso, London.

Kristol, I., 1970. When virtue loses all her loveliness: reflections on capitalism, socialism and nihilism, *The Public Interest*, No. 21.

Letwin, S., 1965. *The Pursuit of Certainty*, Cambridge University Press, Cambridge.

Minogue, K., 1985. *Alien Powers*, Weidenfeld and Nicolson, London.

_____ and Biddiss, M. (eds.), 1987. *Thatcherism: Personality and Politics*, Macmillan, London.

Mishan, E. J., 1988. What future for a multi-racial Britain? Part 1, *Salisbury Review*, Vol. 6, No. 4.

Moynihan, D.P., 1985. The paranoid style in American politics revisited, *The Public Interest*, No. 81.

Murray, C., 1984. *Losing Ground*, Basic Books, New York.

Olson, M., 1982. *The Rise and Decline of Nations*, Yale University Press, New Haven.

Röpke, W., 1960. *A Humane Economy*, English translation, Oswald Wolff London.

Scruton, R., 1980. *The Meaning of Conservatism*, Penguin Books, Harmondsworth.

_____ , 1981. *Short History of Modern Philosophy*, Ark Paperbacks, Routledge and Kegan Paul, London.

Sowell, T., 1980. *Knowledge and Decisions*, Basic Books, New York.

Taguieff, P-A., 1984. Alain de Benoist, philosophe, *Les Temps Modernes*, No. 451, February.

Waldegrave, W., 1978. *The Binding of Leviathan*, Hamish Hamilton, London.

Note on the Contributors

Dr Arthur Aughey is Lecturer in Politics at the University of Ulster at Jordanstown. His main fields of research interest are conservatism, terrorism and Northern Ireland. Among his publications on conservatism is (with P. Norton) *Conservatives and Conservatism* (1981). Among his most recent publications is *Under Seige: The Unionist Response to the Anglo-Irish Agreement* (1989).

Professor Michael Billig is Professor of Social Sciences at Loughborough University. His particular fields of interest are political pyschology and social psychology. His prolific publications specifically on the extreme right include *Fascists* (1978). Among his more recent publications are: *Arguing and Thinking* (1987), and (joint author) *Ideological Dilemmas* (1988).

Dr Roger Eatwell is Lecturer in Politics at the University of Bath. His main fields of interest are the ideology and sociology of the right. He is Editor of the series Themes in Right-Wing Ideology and Politics. His publications on the right include articles in the *Political Quarterly*, and chapters in K. Lunn and T. Kushner (eds), *Traditions of Intolerance* (1989), L. Cheles *et al*. (eds), *Neo-Fascism in Europe* (forthcoming), P. Hainsworth (ed.), *The Extreme Right in Europe and America since 1945* (forthcoming in this series) and S. Larsen *et al*. (eds), *Modern Europe after Fascism* (forthcoming).

Dr J. S. McClelland is Lecturer in Politics at the University of Nottingham. His main interests are right-wing politics, especially in France, and political radicalism. His publications on the reactionary right include (as editor) *The French Right (from de Maistre to Maurras)* (1970). Among his most recent publications is *The Crowd and the Mob* (1988).

Dr Noël O'Sullivan is Reader in Politics at the University of Hull. His main field of interest is political theory, especially conservatism. Among his publications relevant to the right are: *Conservatism* (1976), and *Fascism* (1983). His recent publications include (as editor): *Terrorism, Ideology and Revolution* (1986), (joint editor) *The Corporate State* (1988), (as editor) *The Structure of Modern Ideology* (1989) and (as editor) *The New Right* (forthcoming).

Dr Roger Woods is Lecturer in German at Aston University. His main field of interest is German politics, especially the radical right. His publications on the radical right include *Ernst Jünger and the Nature of Political Commitment* (1982). Recent publications include *Opposition in the GDR under Honecker* (1986), and *The Conservative Revolution in Weimar Germany* (forthcoming).

Subject Index

Index of Names